FRIDAY IS TOMORROW *OR* THE *DAYENU* YEAR

Chronicles from the NYC Covid-19 Oral History, Narrative and Memory Archive

BARRY JOSEPH

June, 2021

Denise,

So after all of this time, what do you think?

You and your colleagues spent over a year gathering the daily "chronicles", interviews, images and more from nearly 200 New Yorkers during the first year of the COVID-19 global pandemic. Collected into your archives at Columbia University, do they now tell a unified story of a city under siege? Have you found ways to weave together our individual voices into one choir? Is the total greater than the sum of its parts?

This book is a collection of the parts I submitted to you over the year, within my own feeble effort to exert some control over how they are interpreted. Initially I offered you an article I had written about losing my father. I wanted the act of capturing that moment to live on in a memory greater than my own. You and Columbia accepted that. But like a drug dealer in reverse, you roped me in, the addiction coming from my love of writing, and of sharing my experiences with others. That one article grew into a series of interviews, then online entries chronicling my days, all supplemented with digital ephemera I collected over the year.

Your Archives will soon open. Anyone will be able to dive into my folder and check out any of these submissions. But here is my attempt—with my own imposed structure, and only slight edits—to seek some greater meaning. And with that explanation I add this book, itself, into the folder, as my final contribution, a whole alongside its parts.

It will start with a note to the reader and then, from there, it will begin.

With more thanks than words can express,
Barry Joseph

CONTENTS

"Obsessing over what it did to *me specifically* almost inexcusably leaves out my constant awareness of the damage to my community,... to say nothing of the half a million dead Americans."

—Nico Muhly, composer, when asked to reflect on one year of COVID.[1]

1 "75 Artists, 7 Questions, One Very Bad Year". The New York Times, March 10, 2021, Page 4, Art section.

NOTE TO THE READER

Every child who grew up in the *School House Rock*-era of Greater Metropolitan New York was bitten by this particular earworm inserted into the pro-bono advertising space between Saturday Morning Cartoons: "The most important person in the whole wide world is you, and you hardly even know you. The most important person!"

In this book, the most important person is you, and I don't even know you. So welcome! And nice to meet you.

We already have something in common. I survived the COVID pandemic. If you are reading this, so did you.

In other ways our stories will be vastly different.

This book is less about me than it is about us, about the similarities and differences you experience as you explore my personal story. Did you also lose someone you loved to COVID? Did you also lose your job? Did you also discover things about yourself—some you wish you'd known earlier, some you wish you'd never known?

I give my story to you as an offering. You may receive it as an opportunity to reflect. Perhaps to mourn. During the pandemic we were afforded precious little space to do either. As with any traumatic experience it is going to be our responsibility—to ourselves, to our loved ones—to (as Peter Gabriel sings) "dig into the dirt".

Where our stories are similar, accept my words as my hand as we revisit it together.

Where our stories are different, accept the safety provided by our anonymous conversation. Use it like a confessional.

So come dig into the dirt with me. Then narrate your own story, if at least to yourself.

At the start of the pandemic, I read stories of people turning lemons into lemonade by committing themselves to new projects to make the most of being self-quarantined: learning how to make sourdough bread, or how to play a new musical instrument. I tried the latter but failed. Our apartment overlooks a park; when it was padlocked by New York City officials I took a photo from our apartment balcony, capturing how empty it was. The next day I did the same. Then again, day after day as spring returned and nature took over. I'd found a daily project!

A few weeks later the park re-opened. That ended that.

Meanwhile, I read an article about projects being set up to document how we experienced the social disruptions wrought by COVID-19. One was at Columbia University. I sent them an article I had recently written, about losing my dad the previous month. The story, I felt, should have a good home, and a university archive seemed as good a place as any.

Within minutes I received a response from the COVID-19 Oral History Project:

> **Subject: Re: Any interest in this COVID-related article from me?**
> Date: May 7, 2020 at 10:16:57 AM EDT
>
> Dear Barry,
>
> Thanks so much for sharing this wonderful and heartbreaking article. I'm so sorry that you lost your father, especially in this difficult time.
>
> Would you be interested in participating in our archive? You can choose to write chronicles if you'd like, or to participate in interviews, or just to fill out our survey. If you'd like to do any of this, here is a link to our intake questionnaire. I think your perspective would be important to have.
>
> If you decide to fill out the questionnaire, we'll get back to you about the next steps to participation.
>
> Hoping you stay as well as possible under the circumstances,
>
> Denise

She asked so nicely, how could I say no? I filled out the intake questionnaire with no expectations but, based on whatever criteria they had in place, I was selected as one of two hundred people they would interview over the next year (because, surely, in a year, it would all be over, right?). All I had to agree to was two interviews. Everything else was optional. Talking on the phone twice in the next year sounded easy-peasy.

Every few weeks I would receive the following email prompt:

> What are you thinking about this week? What is going on in your neighborhood? What kinds of conversations are you having? What effect have the events of this week had on your thinking about the COVID-19 pandemic? We want to hear from you. **You can contribute chronicle entries to the archive any time by** clicking here**, or copying and pasting the link below into your browser:**

Rather than click on the archive I trashed the email. Not with malice, mind you. I just did not have the bandwidth to even consider it.

Something changed after our first interview. Maybe things had lightened up, just enough. Maybe I saw the value of a daily place to record my thoughts. In any case, while I had not written a daily diary since college, I thought it seemed like a worthwhile endeavour. Columbia asked us all to share our posts, digitally, in a web-based form, which is fine with me. But I didn't want to write it on the computer. There was something freeing in the constraint of writing it by hand each day. It forced me to be concise, and to create it on the page without belaboring an idea or reworking a sentence. It just was what it was. Then I'd type it up and share with the Columbia team for their archives.

My interviews with Denise and the daily diary make up the bulk of this book, lightly edited (mostly to protect the innocent).

To fill in the gap between the start of the pandemic and my time with Columbia, I included two things. The first are articles I wrote during the spring as a way to process my life and connect with others. The second are the notes I took when my father was in the hospital, its own sort of diary, created less for processing the pandemic life than as a tool for navigating it.

I wanted to prepare this fast, as something that could be available as soon as possible, to enter our lives during the transition out of COVID. So while the contents of the book are a record of one life during COVID, the book itself is an artifact of our transition to what came next.

Finally, I'm writing this book so after a year plus of social distancing I can reconnect with the whole wide world, one person at a time, starting with you: the most important person.

CAST OF CHARACTERS

Akiva: My son.

Andy: A best bud from high school.

Barry: Me!

Becky: Noemi's sister.

(the) Biens: Family friends with children the same age as our own.

Carol: My step-mom.

Dad: My father. Also known as Daddy, or **Paul**.

Debby: My sister (I'm older).

Denise: Director of the MA Program in Sociology at Columbia University and Co-Director of the NYC COVID-19 Oral History, Narrative and Memory Archive.

Lily: My step-sister. Married to Michael. Children are Eva and Delia.

Mira: My youngest child. Often called Miri.

Noemi: My wife.

Oma: My wife's mother (also known as Gaby).

Paul: My father. Also known as **Dad**.

Paul: A best bud from high school. Not my dad.

Steven: A best friend since elementary school.

PART 1

THE SEASON OF FEAR

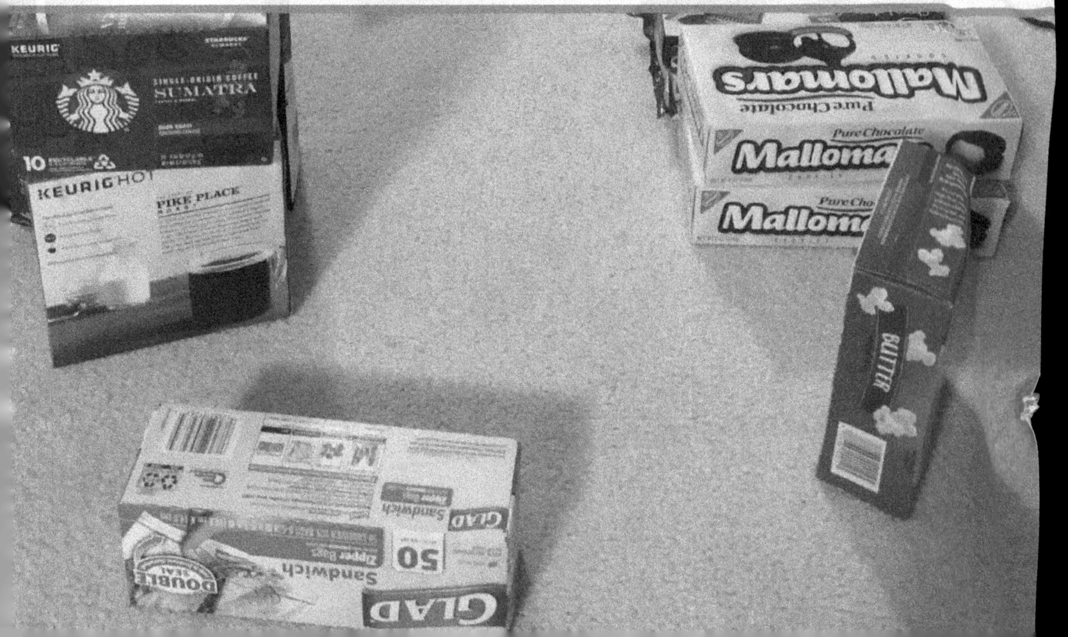

MARCH 2020

In which the author is introduced. As is Denise, from Columbia. The pandemic hits... the Girl Scouts pivot… schools move online… a city closes…

COVID-19 Oral History Project: July 2020

The Reminiscences of
Barry Joseph

Columbia Center for Oral History
Columbia University
2020

The following oral history is the result of a recorded interview with Barry Joseph conducted by Denise Milstein on July 10, 2020. This interview is part of the COVID-19 Oral History Project.

The reader is asked to bear in mind that s/he is reading a verbatim transcript of the spoken word, rather than written prose.

Q: Good morning. I guess I'll just say formally for the people watching this or listening to this or reading it in the future, that I'm talking with Barry Joseph, and this is Denise Milstein. Today is July 10, 2020, Friday afternoon, 3:00 p.m.

Joseph: It's currently raining.

Q: It's also raining here, yeah. Where are you in the city?

Joseph: Forest Hills. Queens.

Q: Okay, so you're a good distance from me. I'm in Harlem right now. I think it would be great if you could start by saying a little bit about yourself. That would be useful for people encountering this interview in the future, just to frame your experiences. Who are you? How did you get to where you are today?

Joseph: I'm fifty-one years old. I grew up on Long Island, which if you aren't from the area is just east of New York City. Went to school outside the city, came back for graduate school to go to New York University in the early '90s and have been here ever since. I've spent the past twenty-five years working in ed-tech in one way or another, starting in the new media industry and then, twenty years ago, going into the after-school education space, and eight years ago, specifically, in the museum education space. For the last two years, I've been working at the headquarters of the Girl Scouts of the USA. I'm the Vice President of Digital Experience.

Q: Interesting. So you came into the pandemic already with a lot of experience with digital communication, it sounds like.

Joseph: Yeah. I've been online before the term "online" even existed, starting when I was using bulletin board systems back in the '80s to use my phone to call into other local computers to chat with other people and play games. My degree was called, in the early '90s, Integrated

Media Arts, which was all about thinking about how to integrate different forms of technology together for artistic or other reasons.

When the web hit big in '95, I was already more than a decade experienced in that space and have been leveraging it ever since, largely for educational purposes and often to create opportunities for young people who didn't have the economic advantages and the resources that came with them that I had growing up. I've helped them be empowered to use technology, in one way or another, to pursue their interests and dreams.

The pandemic forced people to figure out how to communicate online, socialize online, work online, dance online, do performances online, run Passover Seders online. I'd been doing this stuff for decades, and quite specifically working with young people. It's what I do—supporting adults to work with young people.

It's a strange moment for me that the stuff I've been trying to build the capacity for organizations to do for years is now what suddenly everybody needs.

Q: Has your work changed very much as a result of the pandemic, given that you were already doing a lot of work with online communication?

Joseph: My perspective hasn't changed, but the needs I'm filling certainly have. I work at Girl Scouts, as I mentioned. It's about 1.4 million girls around the country in troops that are organized into 111 different Councils. Within a few weeks of the pandemic starting to hit America in March, all Councils were told to stop their troops meeting in person. This was also in the middle of our cookie season, which is where the bulk of the income comes from for all of the Councils. Many people know the cookies. Those cookies aren't sold all year. They're only sold over a few months. So it was right in the middle of it for many folks.

The troops tend to be tied—not always—to the school season. We knew that if schools weren't reopening, then troops weren't going to continue in person. That meant that they all would have been interrupted in the middle. Schools were continuing online, in some capacity, but Girl Scouts had little in place to support troops to be able to run remotely, to support the girls to keep connecting.

So within a very quick period of time, within a period of days, we had to come up with a number of different strategies and approaches to support the girls at home with their families to get content, to keep doing the Girl Scout activities, to support troop leaders with tools and resources they needed to run their troops online, in order to support them to do whatever they were figuring out. And to create new ways for girls to connect with each other and with Girl Scout activities, like through live events, and selling their cookies online.

So what I do hasn't changed. What's changed is that now everybody needs someone like me, and I'm able to contribute to many more areas of our work. Of course, we're going to be back in person someday, and between now and then, there are going to be lots of pivots between in-person, not in-person, things being blended during those same periods, depending on what peoples' needs are and what the communities are doing. So we are in a period of tremendous change for the next year—maybe eighteen months, maybe two years—where we're going to be pivoting back and forth between fully online, fully in-person, and blended. The switches need to happen very fast between the two.

Like every informal learning organization, we are trying to figure out how you build for that in a sustainable way to help girls feel like their troop is not always about meeting in person. Their connections will be with their troop leaders, with the values, with the traditions of being able to pursue their interests and being able to demonstrate what they learned. We think it's better to do it in-person, but that's not what is required. So how do we figure out what that essence is?

And whether they're doing it in-person or virtually, that it's still a constant for them during this time of change.

Q: It's pretty amazing. When did that change first begin for you?

Joseph: I actually wrote about it for the *Forward*, like an online opinion piece. I'll submit it into my file so you can have all the details...

Article: *This is Not About the Bagel, nor the Seltzer Man*

An excerpt. Originally published in the Forward June 3, 2020

For me, it was a bagel—my last taste of normalcy before the "new normal" arrived, eaten mere hours before NYC effectively cancelled the school year for my children. The inevitable was fast approaching—had arrived in fact—and I was just slow to accept it.

My family was in Philly for the weekend, the only guests at my wife's sister's youngest's birthday party, the only ones brave/foolish enough to make that trip. That Friday, Philly had cancelled school. The hotel where we stayed, usually sold out, was at 10% capacity. So when we packed our bags to return home to Queens, to what was beginning to feel like the opening scene of a post-apocalyptic movie, I could not resist popping into the Montreal-style bagel shop just south of Rittenhouse Square.

For over a decade I've started each work day buying one toasted bagel with butter, which I'd devour walking between the cafe and my office, finishing before arriving at my desk. But my bagel place would close down along with other New York City non-essential businesses; as I write this, it has yet to open. So that day in Philly, I bought an everything bagel, still steaming hot, plus a bag of more that could last for days. It was my "what would you bring to a desert island" moment. It was my last grasp at the old normal. It was the last time in now two months I've bought food, let alone anything, from a store.

Back to that hotel in Philly, and how empty it was. I want to explain what I did there, after sending my wife in advance to walk to her sister's place with the kids. I needed some privacy. I needed to speak at a funeral.

That morning, back in Brooklyn, Eli Miller would be laid to rest. It had nothing to do with the pandemic. He was a Brooklyn icon, a recently retired seltzer delivery man whom I featured in my book on seltzer[2]. His family, fans of the book, had reached out to me to provide a eulogy. Sorry, I said with true regret, I would be in Philadelphia.

But just a few days after the call, by the time I was in Philly, Eli's funeral had moved to Zoom so that family from Pennsylvania to Israel could participate. It turned out, I could eulogize the greatest Brooklyn seltzer man. As I sat alone in my hotel room, empty of people — both in my room and throughout the hotel—staring at the panel of close-up videos revealing the exquisite intimacy of faces in mourning, I was not only taking my first steps into the Wide World of Zoom that was poised to transform my life. I was developing new skills that I would need just six weeks later when I delivered a socially-distanced eulogy for my own dad.

2 *Seltzertopia: The Extraordinary Story of an Ordinary Drink. Available where all fine books are sold.*

APRIL 2020

In which Passover goes virtual… hospitals are negotiated… Dad dies... A funeral is held… mourning is re-defined… an iPad is donated….

July Interview Continued: COVID-19 Oral History Project

...Q: I read what you wrote about the experience with your father's death, and then the subsequent experiences doing things online. I want to make some space to talk about that. If you feel comfortable talking about it, it would be really great.

Joseph: This year was the first time I hadn't been to a Passover Seder[3] with my dad. My dad ran them when I was a kid. And when I was an adult—well, when I was away at college, I guess I didn't do it then for a few years—but then eventually, as I became older, we were always together. And eventually I took over from him and led our Seder.

We had set it up for him to join us on Zoom. Forty minutes before it was supposed to start, Carol, my stepmom, contacted me and said that he had fallen and wasn't doing well and maybe had a fever and couldn't join.

The Seder was great and I loved it. It worked really well. We did a lot of innovative stuff that made it really meaningful for me and, I hope, for people in attendance.

3 The Passover Seder is a home-based meal ritualizing the story of Moses leading the Jewish people from slavery to freedom. In the U.S. it is usually repeated two nights in a row.

But the whole time, I was terrified because he wasn't there and I didn't know what was going on.

Over the next three days, it became clear that something was wrong and that he'd have to go to the hospital. Now, the context here is that he went to the hospital a month earlier—this is before the pandemic became a problem—and had other issues. He had fallen actually, clipped a piece of furniture on his way down, and lost a chunk of his ear.

Q: He's 87?

Joseph: 87, yeah. And there was no reason to think it's COVID-related. I mean, it could be COVID, but it was just as likely that it was something else. He wasn't having COVID symptoms. It was other stuff, or so I was told.

He went to the hospital the next day...

Hospital Diaries

Day 1: Friday, April 10[4]

12:00 AM (midnight): I spoke with a nurse who saw Dad. She said he's in a room, comfortable, and is very funny. He is stable and currently being evaluated. They are awaiting results in the next few hours from imaging, and from the lab test (blood work). They'll know that in the next few hours but I might not be up then. They also tested him for COVID but that will take much longer (I don't know how long) to get those results. That's the latest.

1:00 AM: Dad still in emergency room. He just went to X-ray so they can check if he has had a fracture, just because he had been falling. The initial lab blood work looks fine—nothing jumped out to them. They did a CT scan on his head, due to the falls, but those results are not yet back. When he came into the hospital his fever was at 99.1 (last I heard when he was at Atria it was around 102). They do not believe he had a stroke. I don't know when the COVID test comes back, but the earliest they've seen is 4 hours. I'm going to bed and will call them first thing in the morning.

7:47 AM: I spoke with a new nurse. She has had him since last night. She said "he has been a gentleman." He is having a hard time peeing so they gave him an antibiotic for possible urinary tract infection

[4] Dad was transported around 10:30 pm from his place at Atria, the assisted living facility, by ambulance to the emergency room at Long Island Jewish Hospital. He'd been falling repeatedly, was physically weak, had issues urinating, wasn't totally with it, and had a fever. I took notes every time I called the hospital, to help me track my dad's condition and record whom I spoke with (when and why) so I could advocate for him. Sometimes I re-wrote them to share the highlights via text with my wife, sister, step-mom, and step-sister; other times they were my reference guide and to-do list.

(UTI). He has no fever (he's been around 99 degrees) and had no chills since arriving there (she suspects he was given some Tylenol before he arrived at the hospital and that that brought down his fever). His other vitals are good. He is breathing on his own. She suspects the falling is from the UTI, as well as the fogginess. The lab work doesn't look like COVID to her (the usual markers are not there—so it *could* be but it'd be a coincidence with why he needed medical care) but they did the test anyway and they are keeping him in isolation until the results come back; the results are returned to the hospital in batches and can be up to 24 hours. His CT scan came back fine (so with his 5 or so falls this week, it looks like both his brain and his bones are fine). Although he is still in the emergency room, they have admitted him to the hospital, due to the falls. She said the falling and fuzziness is common to UTI and once resolved, with some physical therapy (PT) and antibiotics over the next few days at the hospital, his balance should come back. Since he is still in the emergency room he can't yet use a phone; there are no phones there for patients—to stop the spread of COVID—so we can't reach him until he gets admitted into his own room. The hospital is not full, just busy, and they need to bleach the rooms from head to toe first. Once he's in his own room, in a few hours, he can use the phone there to call us. He has asked to speak with Carol a number of times. They explained staff are not allowed to let patients use their phones, but she will give him a message I gave her from Carol (I made some stuff up but, trust me, it sounded good). I asked about his spirits and she said "He's a sweetheart. We're buddies." So there's not much for us to do other than to wait a few hours and call back to learn if he has his own room and phone.

12:40 PM: I spoke with a new nurse. She said "He's not doing too bad." Vitals are okay. She checks up on him every :30 minutes, to make sure he's okay. No fever at all. COVID test not returned yet. Still in emergency room, just waiting for his bed. He is taking a nap right now. They can FaceTime on someone's iPad now (!!). So I gave them my number. This is something new—someone brought it in to try it out. They did a urine culture for UTI, and currently waiting on the results. She said: "He's great. He was talking with me about his pediatric practice, then talking about the measles vaccines, and some study in Europe…" Then she held the phone while speaking to another nurse while I was listening and I heard her call him "My awesome guy there…" So: he seems in good spirits, waiting for his room and COVID results. The doctor will call me as well, at my request, just to confirm all of this. If you have messages you want me to share with him if we can FaceTime, please let me know (and Carol, what number can I give them so they can try to FaceTime with you as well?)

8:20 PM: Just spoke with a weird doctor. He told me nothing.

10:23 PM: He is in Tower 411, in a private room. The night nurse I spoke with, who has been working with him, will be there until 7a.m. She said he is sleeping now but will wake him soon for his medicine and will tell him we send our love. No COVID results yet. When I asked how he seemed she said he seemed okay, but tired (which made perfect sense). There is a phone in the room, but she didn't know how to direct us to call it; instead she said to call tomorrow and ask for "the secretary," who will be in at 8 a.m., to connect us with room 411. I will call him then. She said physical therapy won't happen on the weekend, so if he'll be receiving it that should happen on Monday. That's all folks for today. Good night!

Day 2: Saturday, April 11

6:30 AM: Dad just called with the help of the night nurse. She left the room so we could speak. The volume was not loud enough so I could hear him but he could not hear me. It was very frustrating for him and he called for the nurses. We agreed to hang up and that I would call the nurses.

I called the nurses' station and reached the night nurse. She went into the room and called me from there. She could not see a way to turn the volume up any more. She said the secretary comes in at 8 and could help see if the hospital has any different phone he can use. They also just started something new with tablets for the rooms so we can video chat. The secretary can help with that as well.

Before I hung up I asked her some questions. No responses yet on the COVID-19 test. When I asked how he's doing she said "He's doing okay," which sounded conditional and when I pushed was based on his mood. With assistance they got him to the bathroom, but it was still frustrating for him. She'd spent the night frequently chatting with him to cheer him up. He currently has no TV access. She thought the TV payment process had not yet been turned on but when she checked she got it on for him; I asked her to look for tennis, but who knows if that's available. He does not have his phone (which he could use to speak with us), his glasses to read, nor anything to read if he did.

So at 8 or soon after I will speak with the secretary or day nurse to 1. see what we can do to get a phone he can use to hear us and/or the tablet and 2. explore with her if we can get him some reading materials (many options have been paused due to COVID-19). That will then lead me to 3. work with Carol to possibly get him his phone, phone charger, glasses, and a pile of *New Yorkers*.

8:20 AM: Spoke with the receptionist at the nurse's station (in until 3). A person is now going around with a tablet, connecting with patients' families on Zoom. About 10 AM they start, so I should call back then. She will call TV and phone services to ask about a different phone.

9:00 AM: Spoke with a new nurse. I got Dad's direct number in his room. The staff that manages phones not in until 1 PM. I will follow-up with them then. He has already eaten breakfast. He's currently in the bathroom, so they suggested I call his room at 9:20; I asked for an aide to be there to help him answer and to make certain there's nothing that can't be done to make it louder on his end.

9:21 AM: I called his room but couldn't reach him. Spoke with nurses who said he's fed, cleaned and asleep. Must be exhausted, with everything, and fell asleep. I spoke with a new nurse. His COVID results are in and she said he is positive. She couldn't tell me anything else and I can't learn more until at least noon. She said she will try to call me from his room.

9:40 AM: They called me 4 times from the room. They couldn't hear me any of the times. I heard nothing three of the times. One of them I heard my dad asking the nurse if she had had breakfast yet. It was frustrating. I called the nurses' station but there's no answer. When I call his room there is no answer.

9:54 AM: I called the nurses' station again. I asked to speak with a doctor about Dad's COVID status. The nurse says they've been trying to call me. Then she put me on hold. She came back and said they were trying to call me on the tablet; I said I wanted to speak with a doctor. The nurse said the doctor is not available but a physician's assistant (PA) is checking the patients now, and I can speak with her later, at noon. I need to call back at noon.

10:04 AM: The nurse was able to reach me. She figured out how to turn up the volume. Dad and I spoke for a few minutes. He feels tired but nothing hurts. He said he slept a lot last night. He'd like his glasses and a *New York Times.*

Then the physical therapist (PT) was doing her evaluation. I spoke with her to answer her basic questions and set a baseline for her. She will make a recommendation and I can ask a nurse after 4 what she advised. So, I need to call back at 4 PM.

The nurse is trying to help me call directly into the room. When I call it just rings. Turns out Dad's direct number in his room is different from what they had told me. Now, I call and it works. The PT is still there, and says he was able to do some things with him but he's tired now and wanted to stop. So I said goodbye to them both.

12:30 pm: I spoke with the new physician's assistant who just saw Dad. She said he looks good. The most important thing to her is that he is having no difficulty breathing and is well hydrated. The PT recommended he be moved when he can from the hospital to a rehab facility. Also, a new nurse said Dad looks good. She also said everything he is experiencing is due to COVID. She says it is unlikely he has UTI. So the fuzziness, his loss of balance, and that fever that came and went are all symptoms that some seniors are having connected to COVID. But right now—and that can change—all of his vitals look good. And they will watch these on a daily basis, as they can change. If things stay like this—his breathing and hydration remain good—then they can move him early next week to a rehab. There are rehabs that have COVID wings. They can provide him with the physical therapy they can't provide at the hospital, as they are strapped. When he goes, the fogginess and weakness might last, and is what the rehab will help him recover from. I will hear from a social worker who will discuss with me rehab options and I will call Forest View Center (which Atria recommended) to see if they could take him. End of report (going to eat lunch).

We discussed his DNR status.

1:25 PM: The nurse at Atria told me which rehabs to request and in what order.

3:30 PM: Chatted with Dad for :25 minutes. They got him a speaker phone. Mostly he listened as I told him things. His responses were a word or two. I checked after every few sentences to see if he was following. He said he was. I explained his condition to him. He asked and I told him Carol was well.

FACEBOOK POST:

My dad went into the hospital late Thur night, April 9th. It was confirmed today he has COVID. He is NOT (at least for now) suffering from some of the worst symptoms we tend to hear about—

his breathing and hydration is perfectly normal—but he has other COVID-related symptoms—lack of balance, a fuzzy headedness, and being tired. He is in a great hospital in Great Neck, in a private room (after 24 hours waiting in the emergency ward). If he remains stable over the next few days he'll be moved into a rehab to get the physical therapy he will need. Carol is managing well and, while remaining at Atria, will act, and be treated, like she is positive as well (no reason not to, and no need for her to leave Atria to get the test). I'll try to post updates once a day and, while I will read and appreciate any notes below, won't be planning to respond to any as I'm overwhelmed with managing and balancing my current load of family and work responsibilities, but know I love you and we here appreciate all your support (which is why I am sharing this with you).

4:30 PM: Carol has a 102 temperature and has been taken to the emergency room of Long Island Jewish Hospital. Lily says: "Atria says if she tests positive but no other symptoms they will let her come back."

Day 3: Sunday, April 12

10:30 AM: Spoke with a new nurse. She said his confusion comes and goes, and she did not attribute that to the COVID. Otherwise she had nothing else to report. I chatted with her about Dad's phone situation. It turns out it was not a speaker phone they brought into his room yesterday. The phone by his bed, which is very hard for him to use to hear anything, is still there. When I chatted with him for :25 yesterday I had thought they had brought a speaker phone into his room. It turns out they brought a type of Amazon Echo device into his room, and that is what I was using to speak with him. It's so new most of them don't know how to use it or what to call it. I now just spoke with Raj (maybe a floor manager) and she said tomorrow they will see what can be done to get him a speaker phone. So until then 1. it will be hard for us to speak with him, 2. we will probably need to be very patient and work with the nurses to speak with him, and remind them not to hand him the phone receiver but instead to use the Amazon Echo, 3. follow-up on Monday with their TV and phone dept to see if there's a speakerphone available and 4. Carol, should we consider getting his cellphone today, as that might be something that can be used for him to speak with us (or does he not know how to turn that to speakerphone as well?). If anyone has any other thoughts, please let me know.

11:00 AM: I just spoke with Dad for 10 minutes. His responses were words and phrases, not always clear (in part because he's not able to project). So mostly I just spoke to him about the banalities of my life —I think he just wanted to hear a familiar voice—and then he said he was tired so we ended the call and I said I'd call him later. I asked if he had spoken with Carol yet today and he said yes (but I wasn't sure I believed him).

7:30 PM: Chatted with Dad for :20 minutes. He can hear me fine over the Alexa device, but I can only follow 1/3 of what he says—in part because he is having a hard time projecting and enunciating, and in part because the Alexa device muffles everything (it's hard for me to speak to the nurse over it as well). He mostly just wants to hear me talk, about anything. He has no awareness of the COVID pandemic, at all, and I have to remind him each time.

I then spoke with the nurse assistant who tells me how much she likes him, (same person who got Dad that 1/2 sandwich last night and told me that he had got mad about Trump). She said he has had a loss of appetite, which is common for COVID. He is asking for PB&J; they will look but that can be hard to find. She will look for turkey as well. He is shaking a lot too, she said. I explained he might not be getting all the regular medications he takes. She said she will contact a nurse to talk with me more about his medical condition, and to learn what medication he needs to be taking.

She also told me I need to ask the PA if there are underlying conditions they need to address. To say: He is not the same as how we left him last week. So a PA—physician assistant—can get me more in-depth information.

Finally, she told me when it gets dark he gets more forgetful. They call it sundowning. It's a thing with elderly individuals. Once it gets dark they act differently.

Day 4: Monday, April 13

7:15 AM: I called to check on Dad and to speak with a doctor. They said, Change of shift. Check in at 8.

I called back to see if there was someone there from last night who was about to leave who could track the night for me—and I named the nurse I last spoke with. That seemed to work.

Didn't work. No one knew who she was. They said they are in the transition now and I should call after 8.

8:00 AM: A nurse answered, who told me I had reached the wrong nurses' station. I did not know that was even possible. I asked who can give me an update on my dad and said I need someone's help to speak with him. She sent me to the other nurses' station, no one answered, and it went back to her. I asked her instead to connect me with a doctor. She said she would give them my number.

I called again and spoke with a nurse. She said 8:30 am is the general recommended time to call. Staff has transitioned and rounds are over by then. She told me the name of the nurse I should ask for. And I should ask her to call the PA.

8:40 AM: I called and asked for the recommended nurse. I waited :25 minutes on hold then hung up.

9:05 AM: A nurse answered. Wrong side of the floor again. She transferred me to the other side's nurses' station. A new nurse answered. Said she had spoken with me earlier. I said I did everything she told me. She said they are busy. I said, So am I. She will try to get to me through the Tablet. But she doesn't know how to use it. But she will try.

9:35 AM: Still no call. Still waiting.

9:36 AM: That last nurse called, from Dad's room, on the Tablet! Then she unplugged it and then called me back. I chatted with Dad for 19 minutes. He said he slept so-so, and was fine physically. "I am mixed-up. I want to see you," he told me. "Appetite is not good. I'm ready to go home," he said, and asked "When will you call me?" I told him dinner and he said all right.

11:12 AM: I spoke with his day nurse. "He's okay," she said. He ate some food, but not everything. She has seen patients getting confused like this, when they are low on oxygen, but his oxygen is fine. I am thinking he could be missing his regular meds. She will pass

Debby's[5] phone number to the doctor to get the updated list. Debby should ask that person who calls what their assessment is for his next steps, if vitals stay the same—would he be moved to a rehab for physical therapy?

12:14 PM: I just spoke with his social worker at the hospital. They say Dad is close to being medically stable for discharge to a rehab. Perhaps as early as tomorrow. The goal is to get him "closer to his baseline" where he can get 90 minutes of physical therapy a day. We discussed facilities and she will call me later when she has more information about their availability. I have her number if anyone needs to speak with her directly.

2:00 PM: Dad called. He said he wanted to talk. But when he reached me he didn't say anything. A nurse said she doesn't know why. I used the opportunity to have her tell him the hospital said he'll be able to leave in a day or two, and remind him I will call him after work today.

Day 5: Tuesday, April 14

7:24 AM: Nurse said to call back after 10. In 3 hours! "It's a shift change, and then they have to do an assessment." I said I just need someone for one minute to call me from his room, as I start work at 9, will be in meetings all day, and it would make a difference for his spirit. She blew me off, I think she sent me to the phone in his room, which he can't answer.

9:10 AM: Got nurse to call me from the room so I can talk with Dad while they fed him and gave him medicine. On for 17 minutes. Couldn't communicate much at all with Dad.

5 Debby is my sister. She is younger and lives in Manhattan.

3:50 PM: I spoke with the social worker. She said they don't have clearance yet from the hospital to release him. They had wanted to monitor his white blood count for a little longer. She did send referrals to rehabs but can't ask for space until he is cleared to leave. She will follow-up with the medical team, hoping she will hear back before she leaves at 5 today, and once she does she said she'd be back in touch with an update.

4:10 PM: Spoke with Dad's nurse. She shared what Deb heard earlier, that his white blood cell count increased. It was 8.19. It is now 19.53. They will check again tomorrow. Today he is more restless and agitated. I should call and ask the attending doctor how he is tomorrow morning, and if it doesn't go down ask why not discharge him, and what the concern is? I told her he likes classical music, and she said she will try to get some to play in the room.

6:55 PM: I called at 6 and asked to speak with Dad. At 6:55 they called me back from the room. For a half hour I stayed on the phone with Dad—I don't want to say we chatted, as mostly I was just keeping him company—and then his nurse came, gave him some water, and he promptly fell asleep. When he was up he said he wasn't in any pain, just exhausted. Tomorrow morning they will check his white blood cell count, and compare with today's and yesterday's. My understanding is we're hoping it goes down, if he's going to be discharged soon.

Day 6: Wednesday, April 15

7:00 AM: Called to speak with Dad, or nurse. They said they'd call me back.

10:00 AM: No one called me. I called again. They moved Dad to a new room, 422B, to get him closer to the nurses' station. Tablets are down right now. IT is working on them.

I spoke with a new nurse. His white blood count was not done for a reason she does not know. I asked her to get it done, as we understand it's the only reason he is in the hospital at this point. She will ask the provider if they want to do it and I can call after noon to ask her for the results.

She said otherwise he is okay. Stable. Keeps taking his clothes off because he is hot. So they moved him closer to the nurses' station.

10:30 AM: I asked the social worker to call the provider, and escalate it. She will do that. But she recommended I do the same. She taught me new language to use when advocating for him: he is "deconditioning" and we want to get him back to baseline.

10:48 AM: The Rehab called to check in. She gave me more recommendations on which ones to avoid.

12:38 PM: No one called me so I called and asked to speak with a doctor. They gave me the PA; he will ask Dr. J. the plan for next steps, as he is the attending doctor. Only Dr. J. can speak to the treatment plan. The PA said Dad's white blood count went down to 10.7 (from 19—he was at a healthy 8.9 two days ago). I told him that the social worker said Dad needs to be medically cleared for discharge. Doctor J. will decide if Dad needs to be held an extra day to see if count holds or if he can be discharged. Dr. J. will call me but, if he does not, then I will call the PA at 5 (he is on today until 7).

12:50 PM: The social worker has coverage for social work tonight when she is out. So a rehab ask can still be made tonight if Dad is cleared. But she also needs nurse's paperwork as well, to be updated, if a nurse is available, and won't know until tonight (if a case manager is available). And then it depends on what time the facilities will take new people. The social worker will leave my contact information for the new social worker coverage (starting at 4:00).

2:30 PM: They called me with the roving iPad and I got to FaceTime with Dad for ten minutes, and see what he sees. That was really nice.

5:00 PM: I called to speak with PA. Got a new nurse instead. She will call the PA and ask him to call me.

5:08 PM: The PA called me back. He spoke with Dr. J. He said the doctor will call me back. I told him I was about to give a public talk from 5:30 - 7. The PA said he will ask the doctor to call between 7 and 8. I asked what to do if I don't hear by 7:45. He said call the nurse on the floor and ask them to call him, insist, saying "expecting update today."

7:50 PM: Called to speak with Dr. J. They put me on hold then said Dr. J., the provider, would be calling me.

8:24 PM: Dr. J. called. (He'd had my wrong number.) Dad is doing okay, when it comes to COVID. He was ready to discharge him this morning, but then someone recorded him with a fever of 102.8, so he decided to wait. They took his temperature multiple times over the day and the fever never returned. So tomorrow he'll check on his white blood cell count and make sure there's no fever. And if that's the case, then he will discharge him. He said I should call back between 11-12 tomorrow morning, and ask for the PA, to learn the decision.

8:45 PM: The nurse tried to connect me with Dad but the Alexa didn't work. So she called me on the phone. He was super weak, but probably late in day so tired. And hard to hear him. But he said "Hi Bar" and I told him I loved him, said they are almost ready to release him, and said good night.

FACEBOOK POST

Day 6: Today Dad was set to be discharged, as his white blood count returned to normal, but then he had a fever—for just an hour or so—so they decided to keep him in. He's been fine all day and if they can say the same in 12 hours from now then they SHOULD discharge him tomorrow (once they can find a rehab to take him). Fingers crossed!

Day 7: Thursday, April 16

7:00 AM: Called nurses' station. No answer

7:20 AM: I received an email this morning, from the social worker. "I just wanted to let you know that I will not be in the building today. I don't know which social worker will be covering today. Any questions, please call the unit."

8:13 AM: I called and asked for the PA, but he is busy. I spoke with his new nurse. There was no fever overnight. Dad is on "room air"—he was on oxygen but no longer needs it. He is calm, but fidgety.

8:20 AM: Called for social worker to check on getting him to a rehab. Left message.

11:13 AM: I asked to speak with the PA to learn if Dr. J. has made a discharge decision. They said they will give him my message.

11:20 AM: I was told Dr. J. is seeing patients. He will call me afterwards.

2:10 PM: Never heard from Dr. J. Calling for him again. The nurse took the call. She said she will page him, or call me back.

2:36 PM: The nurse has not received any update. Doesn't see anything in Dad's charts about the discharge.

3:30 PM: I spoke with the nurse. She will reach out to the PA again. Their new Alexa system is no longer connecting to their wifi. They don't know why. By 3:50 we decided I will try the phone. Dad and

I spoke for 5 minutes, using the regular phone— he mostly could not communicate but if held to his ear he could hear me—and was able to start and end the conversation (I love you, bye, etc.). He eats fruits, pureed; avoids pureed proteins.

4:00 PM: I called the social work office and left a message that I had never heard back.

5:00 PM: The PA called me back. Dad medically cleared to go. He spoke to social worker mid-day, around 12 or 1. Paper work is done at his end. So we are just waiting for social worker to find a space. Once a location made, the social worker will call me. They will not send him outside the hospital without calling me. And if it doesn't happen in the next hour or two it most likely won't happen until tomorrow. He told me typically they have 300 patients in the hospital; today they have 500, and they are spread all over the hospital.

5:00 PM: Called Social workers again, as they never called. Left third message.

FACEBOOK POST

Day 7: In one hour it will be exactly one week since Dad entered the hospital. The hospital approved him for discharge today—the challenge now is finding a rehab that has a space for him. No luck today. Maybe tomorrow.

Day 8: Friday, April 17

7:30 AM: I called the Social Work Dept. Left a message. It's been 24 hours since I called yesterday and have yet to hear back.

9:43 AM: I spoke with someone at Forest View. They have accepted him, medically and financially. They will hold bed. He could be transferred this afternoon.

9:45 AM: I called the social worker. She will check in now and catch-up with me in an hour.

10:52 AM: The social worker, called. All's good. Dad is stable for discharge. Forest View will accept Dad as well, which is preferred. They are scheduling 1:00 for transportation.

12:00 PM: Spoke with Forest View. Dad will be on the 4th floor. I got the case manager's name. Once paperwork is distributed, and once they meet with him, then they will call me this afternoon around 2-3. They have video chat. We'll set times.

2:00 PM A nurse called from the hospital to let us know Dad just left to go to the rehab, to Forest View.

FACEBOOK POST

Day 8: Dad is being discharged and if all goes as planned will leave in a few hours to go to the rehab right by his home (and mine—and our preferred choice). This is great news! Once he is there I can speak with them more about his treatment plan and their assessment on getting him back on his feet and returning him back to Carol at the assisted living facility. Can't thank you all enough for your support over this past week. It's not over yet, but this was a hard hill to get over.

3:00 PM: I called the case manager at Forest View. Left a message.

5:20 PM: After two hang-ups, I was sent to 4th floor nurses desk (x134). He doesn't have a phone in his room. Dad was admitted at 2:14 today.

4th call - A nurse is looking for someone for me.

5th call - Social worker's answering machine answered for some reason

6th call - Same nurse answered again. She was finally able to connect me with Dad's case manager. Notes to self:

1. Monday we can go over the intake questions—we set up a time for noon.
2. Ask afterwards if I can speak with nurse to learn his health.
3. COVID isolation—when does that change—ask doctor. Save for next week.
4. He needs clothing. 2 weeks worth. I will collect from Carol and leave at front desk. Housekeeping will label and they will do laundry. They said they will also work with me to get our iPad connected. Just put his name on it and say what room.
5. Video calls are available—they are using a tablet. Maybe Skype or google hangout. They do it once a week, for 20 minutes, and can do it as a group call.
6. There is no phone in his room. We can set up a phone in his room through Verizon. They can ask about open rooms on 2nd floor on Monday so he can have a phone. They will take an iPad from us and will work with us so we can speak with him. We would coordinate with the nurses, who will ask a supervisor and then call later to ask for a nurse or supervisor; and Dad's case manager can help during the week (once a day).
7. He is isolated now, due to COVID, so all of his activities are in his room.
8. I need to speak with Dad's case manager next week about his treatment plan, discharge plan, and progress. She will work with his therapist. Atria will send a nurse to evaluate before he can return.
9. I learned the name of the nurse during the week, in from 7-3. The supervisor changes every day.
10. In two weeks, they'd have a care plan meeting if he's still there, to do the discharge planning. And invite me to the meeting. If he can be discharged before it they will be in contact.

Then I tried to speak with a nurse. I met the Nurse Supervisor. She had just assessed my dad (6:07). He is stable. He is now on oxygen. I mentioned his eyeglasses. He was responsive but she couldn't understand his words. He didn't touch his food. She will ask Director if short term room is available, then that might be possible for the phone. She said over the weekend I should call after lunch to get his health status.

For the family: I finally got a hold of folks at Forest View. To be honest, it was much harder than I anticipated (it was easier at the hospital). I spoke with Dad's case manager (X110). She will do a formal intake (asking me questions) on monday. I asked her a lot of questions to get the lay of the land; I won't write it all here but ask me what you want to know and I'll answer if I can. He needs clothing for two weeks. Due to availability, they put him in a long term care section; the implication of this is there's no phone in his room. And because he's in isolation they can't take him out TO a phone; so I will bring over with his clothes tomorrow an iPad, which they said they would manage for us so we can speak with him. I have not yet been able to speak with a nurse, but will keep trying.

I then spoke with the nurse supervisor. She said he was stable, and is now on oxygen (from what I saw at the hospital his need for it comes and goes, and it is COVID-related). He's not eating much, communication is hard, and of course he's tired. There wasn't much more she could share with me.

Carol, Are you able to prepare clothing for my dad, and/or work with Atria staff to do that, and then have staff bring to the front desk (as I am not allowed in the building)? I can then get from the front desk tomorrow morning once you let me know they took it from your room. And is there anything else you'd like to have go over to him?

FACEBOOK POST

Day 8: Dad is now out of the hospital, but he is not out of the COVID-woods yet, and the rehab ain't home. So this is MUCH better, for sure, but he still has a way to go. There is no phone in his room and since he is in isolation he can't leave to get one. Tomorrow I'll try to get him a tablet they can use for us to contact him.

Day 9: Saturday, April 18

8:50 AM: Called to speak with Nurse to learn how Dad is doing and tell them I am bringing over clothing and iPad. I cycled 5 times with the nurses' station not answering. Then the receptionist at the front answered and said he'd send me to the nurses' station—we tried 4 times. I reached the nurse supervisor. White blood count is stable. His blood pressure is stable. No fever. Very restless. Still on oxygen (at 94). She said 10-10:30 is a better time to call. Lunch is at 12, so that is a bad time. Evening after 7 is also better.

11:30 AM: Picked up clothing from Carol, stood outside Forest View and used their wifi to connect our iPad from the street, and dropped both off at the reception desk.

2:00 PM: Calling nurses to ask if he needs pull-ups and if we can use the iPad to speak with my dad. They have them, and we don't need to supply them! Said they were short-staffed with only two people working, but if I called back in 15 minutes they could help me then.

2:25 PM: Called iPad. No answer. Called nurses' station. I was told she asked her supervisor if she can help. So I will just sit and wait for them to call me. So now I wait.

2:30 PM: The supervisor called me. It worked for she and I. But the signal dropped each time she went into Dad's room. She will call me at 11 tomorrow with her own phone, so we can talk, and Monday we can speak with the IT staff. She said Dad is very confused.

~4:30 PM: Long story short. Around 4:30 they called to say Dad looked bad and since he had no DNR (do not resuscitate) or DNI (do not intubate) they would send him back to the hospital. I told him I would sign the DNR and DNI but they wouldn't arrange it. There was no doctor to sign-off. I realized I was not going to get anywhere with them on the phone. I realized if I got there in time I could see him, in PERSON, if I drove over in time, as he would be transferred from the facility into the ambulance. I got in my car and sped over, collected his clothing and tablet from the reception desk as I waited, worked with both Atria and the very supportive EMTs to see if anyone could do anything to keep him from going back to the hospital (nope). I prepared for my 10 seconds with him during the transfer to the ambulance. When he was wheeled out on the gurney his eyes were closed and he was breathing through something pushing him extra air, so he couldn't speak. But he didn't look much worse than our last video conference. He was breathing very fast. I had my gloves on and I asked the EMTs if I could touch him. They suggested that was up to me, not them. I found his hand under the cloth that was locked around him to secure him on the gurney. I told him "Hi Dad. It's Barry. I love you. You are being moved to the hospital to give you better care. If you think it's your time, go in peace. But if you want to fight you fight. You have had the virus now for at least 1 week, and you are actually doing really well, and for most people it passes on two weeks. So if you can hang in for a few more days you can defeat it." He moved his leg, which was strapped in, and he tried to say something, which he couldn't due to the oxygen. The rehab had been telling me he was unresponsive, which was part of the problem and why they wanted to send him to the hospital—which is why I said they needed to figure out how I could speak with him—and this suggested to me I had been right. He needed contact from people he knew. The EMTs were patient and did not rush me. I gave them his clothing and the iPad. I was upset but grateful I could see him, and touch him, and talk to him in person. As I prepared to leave one of the EMTs said I could follow them to the hospital. Before long, with lights blaring, we went through red lights and took the twenty minute or so drive on the highway to the hospital. I parked and ran around to the back of the ambulance to meet Dad exiting the back. I told him all the same things again, and that I loved him, and watched him go into the emergency room. The EMTs were so patient, so amazing. They said they'd make sure the iPad was passed over. They also said I could go with them into the emergency room. I was taken aback— I guess that's a normal place for them and they don't know about the hospital's rules that keep all family out—and had to decline.

~7:30 PM: I got back to my car, allowed myself to collapse for a few moments, then called the hospital to see if they could move him to his own wing (no luck) and to make sure the DNR and DNI was in place (and they called later to arrange it). I also told them about the iPad.

8:30 PM: An emergency room nurse got our iPad onto the hospital wifi on her own initiative, went to FaceTime, found my name, and called me, hoping I might help Dad respond. It was late now, maybe 8:30, and he didn't respond. But I got to tell him I love him, good night, and that I'd call the next day.

FACEBOOK POST

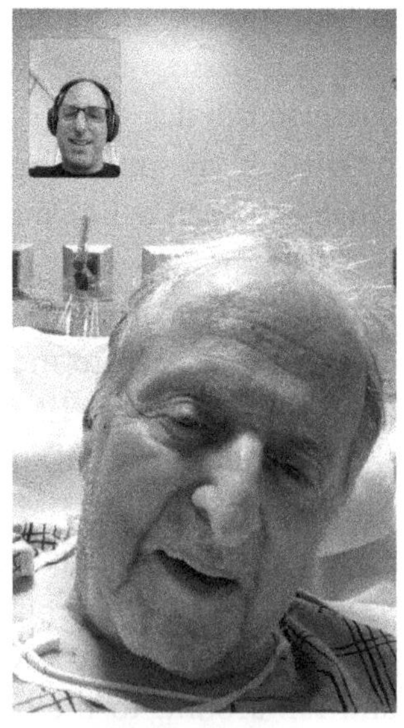

Day 9: Dad is back in the hospital. The rehab felt they couldn't give him the care he needed. Maybe, maybe not. In any case, he's made it through emergency room triage and the attending doctor said he's "hanging in there." Soon they'll admit him, and I can talk with the nurses tomorrow morning. And THIS time I got them to take the iPad I set up, so we can call him and see him. Oh, the silver lining is as soon as I heard the rehab had called the hospital I ran over in my car and made sure I could hold his hand and speak with him both when he was entering the ambulance and disembarking at Long Island Jewish Hospital.

Day 10: Sunday, April 19

8:30 AM: I called and am now waiting for a nurse to call me back, and someone else to arrange for me to speak with Dad.

10:00 AM: Called again to speak with the nurse. On hold for :15. When they returned they said she was "in a code." I asked to speak with another nurse. Given to a new nurse. He is doing okay, she said. His breathing is fast, so she notified the doctor. In a bit they will do a chest PT to loosen up chest secretions. He is on oxygen now, with mask (at 89/90). They will evaluate at the time for swallowing. No fever. I asked to speak to Dad. She said to call back in 2 hours. I said how about right now?

They got him on—his eyes were closed, his breathing with an oxygen assist. The nurse said he moved his hand, so she thought that meant he was responding to me. I told him what was going on, to rest, and to fight.

2:00 PM: Driving to Floyd Bennett Field, the former airport, to kite fly with the family (and just to get outside of our apartment while being far far away from others) the hospital called. Over the car speakerphone, the doctor said his liver is close to failing. They wanted to know if we wanted dialysis or not. They recommended not, given his age and condition. We all agreed. She recommended we call right away to say our farewells. I was driving, and still 10 minutes away from our destination, so Noemi texted my sister so she could call first. The kids were in the car, included in all of this, but what choice did we have?

Having arrived at Floyd Bennett Field, I heard from the nurse. On the derelict runway, in the wind, we walked as I spoke over FaceTime on my iPhone through the iPad with Dad—with oxygen he couldn't speak—hoping he was hearing us and understanding—and Miri cried, and Akiva with bowed head, and Noemi at my side, I said all the "right things" I could think of.

:30 minutes later those three went to fly a kite as I sat in the car and narrated which kite was in the air, and which was down, and which had just escaped, and then the mad dash after it, and the capture and the launch and again and again, just filling in the space in time, and distance, to reach my dad and surround him, or at least touch him, with my voice. During the time they gave him medicine to reduce his rapid breathing and he seemed to then nap so I got off and re-joined, to fly my own kite, recalling throughout those days I treasured as a boy flying kites with him, just he and I, when my mom would take my sister shopping for the day in the city.

7:30 PM: Got Dad on phone again. Didn't expect him to still be alive. But he was still stable. I just got off with him (on for an hour). He was in better shape in the beginning for a call. He could squeeze the nurse's hand (or so she thought) and could do one squeeze for yes, twice for no. "Do you want your son to stay or say goodnight." Stay. "Do you want him to read you poetry or just talk." Poetry. After about :30 min or so the nurse came, for the whatever they do at this time. She said he was pretty stable for everything (oxygen on bag, blood pressure, etc). But after all she did he was breathing more rapidly. So she gave him some of the same medicine they gave him earlier, which I think is an opiate. So after the nurse did that he was no longer responding when asked to hand squeeze. So I said good night to him and told the nurse that Carol might call the nurses' station and ask to speak with him. And if that worked, when they hung up with her (whenever that might be) to give me a call if he was responsive at all, so we'd be sure if he was responsive he'd have more company. I read to him from a book of poetry I took from their house when they moved—not sure if it was Carol's, Dad's, or just something he got and never read from the Walt Whitman House Association. Akiva listened along, which was really nice for me. I am SO thankful I got that iPad over to the Rehab on Saturday and worked with the EMTs to get it in with him into the emergency room.

FACEBOOK POST

Day 10: Hard day. Doctor's called and it's not looking good. Not expecting things to turn around, but I'll always have hope. He's on oxygen so can't talk but over FaceTime (never been so grateful for that iPad!) I talked with/to him for an hour this afternoon, in the context of things seeming final, and another hour tonight, where through hand squeezes to the nurse he chose my reading poetry to him—a book by Billy Collins I once borrowed from him and never planned to return.

Day 11: Monday, April 20

7:45 AM: They are in nurse transition. Asked me to call back at 8.

8:00 AM: I spoke with his day nurse. He is non-verbal. His oxygen is 93 on mask. Eyes closed. He is calm. I asked to speak with him. They said they would set it up.

8:30 AM: I connected on FaceTime but Dad was unresponsive. His nurse couldn't get him to respond before I called; then on the call, hearing my voice, she still couldn't get him to squeeze her hand. I said good morning. I told him I would call later. And I asked her to call me before the next time they give him Dilaudid, and they said they would try.

11:53 AM: Called to speak with his nurse, for an update. No changes. They took him off the fluids, as sodium was high, so doing something to reduce sodium. Cognitively, moves a bit but not much response. Said to talk with Dad I should call back 12:30, 12:45. She said I should just tell them I want to FaceTime with my dad.

1:50 PM: The nurse called so I could speak with Dad. She arranged it on his bed so no one needs to hold it. I can see him, from his torso up; almost like lying next to him on his bed. Almost, but not. I read him more poetry. The nurse took his vitals. Oxygen level is 80 to low-90s now, but dips down to the 70s at times. The nurse said he was making sounds and movement that suggested he knew I was here and enjoying hearing my voice. I read to him until 1:40. She said she felt my dad could feel my presence. After each poem I tried to use it to reflect on something about his life that I could say to bring him comfort, like the things he introduced me to as a child, or the memories he might get to recall now and hoping they brought him some comfort and reminded him of the impact he had on our lives. During it Debby texted me and said she and the others were with me and I felt that. It was such a gift to get to be with him like this and do this for him. And at the same time, his status being stable, I have to remind myself they said he is near death, because—while he's a mess—he doesn't look it, since his steady decline over the last week just seems to have plateaued.

The nurse said to try to call back at 3:30, and to ask for his day nurse, to ask for her. Maybe she is something other than a nurse, someone who is there to assist where she can. I have no idea. I thought she was a nurse.

4:00 PM: Called to see if I can speak with Dad. No one available to help. I was honest (we're told he can die any minute) but didn't push it.

6:00 PM: Called to see if I can speak with Dad. No one available to help. They said they were very busy and would call me back. But couldn't say when. Kinda rushed me off and hung up on me.

6:30 PM: Called to see if I can speak with Dad. No one available to help. They said they were very busy.

6:47 PM: Just spoke with his day nurse. She had just seen him. Dad is stable and his vitals are fine. But too busy for me to speak with him. Please call back, she asked—but I know we are just minutes from the 7pm transition, so that really pushes me to 8:30.

8:00 PM: I just got a call from Dr. W., of the night staff. Dad's liver looks stable. They look at the liver enzymes (AST/ALT). On the 18th it was 131/134. Now his liver is 75/98 - which means it has gone down a lot. "It seems pretty good." His breathing is stable. 94% "Which is amazing. Okay, good." So they are not concerned about his liver right now. Monitoring the levels. Kidney—yesterday, worried about acute kidney injury. They gave fluids, which flushes bad stuff out. CREATININE levels. On 18 it was 3.45; on 11th it was 1.71. So it has gotten worse. When it goes up they put on fluids, to flush things out. Yesterday, they decided to do that and monitor, avoiding medicine that might damage kidney. Today his sodium is high (controlled by sodium); April 18th it was at 134—then went to 147, 20th it was 169. As Kidneys get better, sodium gets better. It is not getting worse than yesterday—but Dr. W. is not a kidney doctor. Trends look the same.

8:23 PM: A nurse I spoke with earlier in the day answered the phone. Again. (Someone needs to send her home.) I said I called to see if I can speak with Dad. She told me the name of his night nurse, and that Dad's was asleep. I asked, If he woke before 11 could they give me a call and that, if not, not to worry and I'll just hope to speak with him in the morning.

FACEBOOK POST

Day 11: Hard to tell what's going on. I can't say Dad has stabilized since yesterday—and if he has it's not at a long-term sustainable place to be stable—but if does look like he's been stable since yesterday. I reached him again and this amazing person (not a nurse; not sure of her role) held the iPad for a half hour while I read him more poetry. I then tried at 4 to reach him again and, as they are short staffed with more urgent matters, 4 calls and 4.5 hours later, they were finally ready to connect us, but he's asleep. I'm glad he's asleep. And I just hope I get to spend more time with him reading him poetry tomorrow, as there's still a lot more to get to in this book.

Day 12: Tuesday, April 21

8:05 AM: Got a new nurse. Dad's day nurse from yesterday was not in today. His actual day nurse was busy, but the nurse I had reached said she would call through FaceTime for me once she got suited up and can enter the room. (It can be so easy for me to forget how much they each have to do to prepare themselves to share a space with COVID patients.)

8:21 AM: Text message to my family: the nurse, called. Said Dad was breathing a little heavy. Oxygen 92/93. Otherwise non-responsive. We set up camera on iPad so I could read to him for a few minutes but, with iPad set-up and plugged in, I just kept speaking with him and reading him poetry. At 9:24 the other patient in the room's nurse came over. I asked about my dad's oxygen saturation. At 89%. I asked if he was on Dilaudid. She said he is due for more and will ask his nurse to come give some more. At 9:50 the nurse came in and gave him the medicine, and checked his vitals. Oxygen at 90%. Dr. L. came in to speak with me at 10:00. She told me she would like to stop the blood work, since there's nothing to be done with whatever they learn. She also said his sodium has been consistently rising (due to the problems with his kidneys) and the potential solution, the IV fluids, has been keeping him hydrated but not solving the rising sodium. In other words, the IV is just maintaining him, and prolonging his suffering, but won't solve the underlying problem. So she recommended the IV be turned off. They will do the best they can now to give him medicine and keep him comfortable—so we're now in the realm of purely palliative care. She says it could take another day or two. When she called his name he opened his eyes but showed no other sign of responsiveness—she held the iPad in front of his face and I called to him, but most likely no response. So I will still call in a few hours and if awake see if it makes sense to read to him; but I also might stop—depends what I see. Reading to him today was not peaceful, like the other days, as he was now having a hard time breathing. Now, the fuck of it is, we could go visit him, as he's about to die. That would mean taking a COVID risk and then having to isolate for the next two weeks; that's a big risk to take, not knowing if he would even be aware we are there, and we each have our own situations, but I wanted you all to know that option is out there (fuck you COVID!).

Diary for myself: It was easier in some ways to rage at the pandemic for preventing me from visiting my dad as he died in the hospital from COVID. No one was allowed in, so I couldn't be by his side, holding his hand, rubbing his shoulder, looking him in his eyes and telling him I loved him. I understood the state rules, so I harbored no ill will towards policy makers, but I was shocked when suddenly, after two weeks of frustrating phone calls, iPad sessions, etc. to be told by his nurse, actually, now that he has hours left, I could come on in. Beware what you wish for.

What did that mean, I could come in? I could enter the hospital, filled with the virus, and don protective gear so I could be with my dad, filled with the virus, and stay safe while I said my goodbyes. And then what? The nurse said, well, you'll just need to isolate for two weeks? Where exactly? I lived in a NYC apt with my wife and two kids. Would I move into and not leave my bedroom for two weeks? Where would my wife go, who is also working from home while taking care of the kids and household? Would I risk their lives in the process? The last thing my dad would want would be to infect and injure his family. So yes, it was hard to be told last week I couldn't visit and care for my dad; it was even harder to be told now that, in fact, I could, and had to be the one to have to say no. I shouldn't have to choose between my dad and my family.

FACEBOOK POST

Day 12: It looks like Day 12 will be it, if not Day 13. The fluids were stabilizing him but not addressing the COVID-damaged kidney issues. We're now in the palliative care phase, and the IV fluids have been turned off. So hard since we can't visit. But I was on with him for 2 hours via FaceTime today—can't tell if he was aware of it at all, but read more poetry and just reminded him I was there—and that session ended with the doctor recommending palliative care and turning off the IV, which made perfect sense to me given how hard I saw him struggling to breathe. I am so appreciative of how hard the medical staff have worked to both care for my dad and to keep us informed; getting to spend hours on FaceTime with him through our iPad, just getting to see him and try to reach him, feels like such a luxury given how hard it is for so many right now. And given how hard COVID has struck others I feel grateful his suffering wasn't worse, and given his age and declining health, I was hopeful he'd live longer but I counted my blessings every day he was in this world—which is a long way of saying I am glad he avoided what could have been a more painful or prolonged decline and death. So... what's next? How do we prepare for a funeral, burial and *shiva* period[6] in an age of social isolation.

11:16 AM: Social worker called, to do intake form (since he returned to the hospital just a few days ago). I said, no longer relevant. She said she needs to fill it out. I said write whatever you want, and I'll agree. She accepted that.

3:00 PM: Called to ask the nurse how Dad was doing and to assess if made sense to read to him. She is on break. Check back at 5, I was told. A PC might be available then—and if available they will call me earlier.

5:00 PM: Called to ask the nurse how Dad was doing. Put on hold. 5:11—she's busy with a patient but will call me when she can.

6:15 PM: The nurse called so I could talk to Dad. They've been giving him the opioid to make things easier for him. He was unresponsive. She said, "He's still with us." I said a few words to him and that I would call him later. She said "Maybe call one more time tonight" and I said I would call after 8:30. And if he's still with us tomorrow, and is calm like this, I might read to him then.

6 In my Jewish community, *a* shiva *period is three days of mourning.*

8:48 PM: Called to see how Dad is, and maybe say good night. He is stable, and sleeping. His vitals are stable.

FACEBOOK POST

Details are starting to come together for when Dad passes, but sharing now as some of you might have some advice.

1. Funeral comes first. Will probably use Zoom and invite all who knew him or us, led by our rabbi, with eulogies. And since it's digital and I'm involved one can expect to see a slide show. I think we've got this one covered.
2. Burial. My dad has a plot next to my mom in Farmingdale. I am already in touch with them and will try to Zoom in my rabbi and the immediate family.
3. As a Reform Jew, the next 3 days are the *shiva* period—prayers, cookies, bagels and people. That's just not going to work. My current thought—developed with Noemi and the Rabbi—is to virtually recreate the *shiva* moments when the bereaved get to connect with the visitors (and leave out the cookies, home visits, bagels, and meal deliveries). We'll sit for three days, with a registration-only but open Zoom session, associated with a Google Spreadsheet. The spreadsheet will be a self-sign-up for :20 minute visits. Visitors can review and see where slots are open, put their name down, and then coordinate themselves to pay their Zoom *shiva* call. Visitors can coordinate times with others, or not—up to them. We'll have a :10 break between each session in case they run late, we want to use the bathroom, etc. Carol, Deb and I will share what times we want to be available in advance so visitors can ensure they know who they're visiting, and we can use Zoom Breakout rooms to get into smaller groups if needed.
4. I'd like an easy web site, like they have for those getting married, to share a video, share a PDF of memories people have shared with us in advance, link to a place for making

> donations, an address for those who want to write and send condolences, and instructions for the *shiva* call.

So what I am looking for is: advice on a better way to securely provide the Zoom information to *shiva* callers (should I ask someone to individually provide it after reviewing and approving Zoom registrations?), if there's a better way for them to sign up for *shiva* calls, and if there's a good web site tool for online memorials. Any recommendations?

Group Text Chain

Carol[7]:

Corn and more corn in Syosset[8] and Chautauqua[9].
Travelling alone to piano lessons upper west side age 5.
Pounding someone's head into sidewalk.
Flat tire on prom date—then jacked up wrong tire.
Chickenpox pillow fight with his brother Carl.
Meeting Marlee's[10] parents for dinner and falling asleep.
You know he wanted to be buried next to Marlee, right?
Sunday papers.
Shared pastrami sandwich with Ben Deli's fries
Hotdogs and fries at Nathan's
Frozen yogurt and pizza or hot dog at Costco.
NY Philharmonic rehearsals
Broadway shows he'd never thought he'd like.
And always tennis or skiing.

Lily:

Here's one: when Mollie[11] was little, insisting her name was Harriet and always doing a funny weird walk around her to crack her up

Carol:

Yep

---

7 With no explanation, Carol started a group text chain listing memories of my dad. Lily, her daughter, added her own. Soon my sister Debby, my wife Noemi, and I shared our own recollections. This continued over a number of days.

8 The town on Long Island where he worked.

9 The Chautauqua Institution, where he vacationed.

10 Marlee was my mom. And yes, I was aware.

11 Lily's cousin

Barry:

A well honed routine developed over decades to get kids to relax before sticking them with a needle. Worked even better once he retired and didn't need to follow the punch-line with the needle…
But Carol— "Pounding someone's head into sidewalk"?

Debby:

Yes Carol—we all wanna know about that!

Carol:

Yep. Had to be pulled off. No idea what set that off.
Fixing Miri's arm in subway when she'd pulled elbow.

Debby:

Do we know how old he was when that happened
Oh I totally remember him putting Miri's elbow back into the socket

Carol:

Nope. I think he was always stronger than his size seemed.
Movies at the Huntington Cinema.
Pancake house.
Watching Harry and Sally umpteenth time.
Swimming in pools at Chautauqua with the kids.

Barry:

IHOP!

Debby:

Watching Miri sail on her own on Lake Chautauqua. He was so impressed at her age and so proud

Barry:

Doing goofy dances.
Reading the Sunday *New York Times*

Debby:

"Snazzy"

Barry:

Keeping in contact with Meme and Poppop[12] the year Mommy wouldn't speak with them (dealing with their alcoholism).
Chinese restaurants (or did we hit that one already)

Debby:

Making hot chestnuts at night and sharing them with Barry and me

Barry:

Carol, When you're ready—and there's no rush—let me know when we can speak and I can share with you what we are currently planning with the Rabbi for the next steps. We have friends and cousins around the country who are going to help us pull this off in the grand way he deserves.
Eating those Nabisco chocolate wafer cookies with a cup of milk

Debby:

He introduced me to blue cheese

Barry:

Highlighting an upcoming movement in a piece of classical music that sounded no different to me than the one before it.

Lily:

Declaring many mangoes, pineapples, etc to be "the best one I ever ate!"

[12] My grandparents on my mother's side

Debby:

Damn Good ___________ (fill in the food in the blank space)

Lily:

Insisting everyone try "the best (fruit) I've ever tasted"

Debby:

Family trip when I was under 5. I was too small to go horseback riding and I was DEVASTATED. Mommy went with Barry and Daddy stayed with me, consoling me and got me an ice cream sandwich to make it all better
Best steak I ever had
Best lobster I ever had
2 weeks ago he had the best egg salad sandwich he ever had

Lily:

I'm sure it was. As were the 117 other best ones

Debby:

Exactly!

Carol:

Best burger. Best strawberry shortcake. Loved my brownies.

Debby:

Loved my mashed potatoes. I loved giving him the first taste b4 they went in the oven

Carol:

Yes yes. Pea soup at Regal Deli with hot dog sliced in.

Debby:

Oh, and the cream of turkey soup at On Parade diner

Carol:

Peeling potatoes and making matzoh balls.

Debby:

Going to Peter Lugers and eating everything, leaving no morsels on any plate

Carol:

Oma's[13] brisket.

Barry:

Whatever challah we happened to have at Shabbat

Debby:

Teaching Barry and me how to play tennis
Diving off his shoulders into the neighbor's pool
Doing that silly jig/dance when he was excited or anxious to get going

Barry:

Or had to pee

Debby:

Yes! Right

Barry:

When you gotta go, you gotta go

Debby:

That's what he'd say

Carol:

Mike's[14] scrambled eggs and spaghetti with meat sauce.

Debby:

Eww, really?

---

[13] Oma is the German word for grandmother, and is my mother-in-law.

[14] Lily's husband.

Barry:
His handwriting (or at least he tried to tell us it was writing…)

Carol:
Deb, not together.

Barry:
Lol

Debby:
Ooooooh.
Ha
Loving my lemonade and limeade

Carol:
Pleased when he could sign checks again.

Debby:
Doing jigsaw puzzles on the dining table

Carol:
Enjoying walks with Pam.

Debby:
Pam?

Carol:
His aide after stroke.

Barry:
Loving fresh ice tea after a Sunday morning tennis game

Debby:
Oh yes
Yes, the iced tea

Barry:

Sweeping the leaves in the yard on a fall morning and bagging them

Debby:

Playing in the pile of leaves he so carefully raked on the front lawn. Tho he was never happy about that

Carol:

Ha. Not sure he enjoyed that. Once there were 30 bags. I used to get bruises breaking up fallen branches against my thigh.

Noemi:

Washing dishes like a dish washing superhero

Debby:

OMG yes

Carol:

Yes

Noemi:

Letting the kids roll all his tennis balls down the stairs

Debby:

And losing his glasses.....when they were on top of his head

Barry:

lol

Noemi:

Miri says: playing Rummikub

Debby:

Getting strawberry ice cream at Bemus Point

Carol:

Finding a tweed hat in Lisbon that fit him.

Barry:

Family travel vacations

Carol:

Buying ties on Canal St.

Debby:

As long as they were $3 or under
Regal Crowns Cherry & Lemon sours
Hershey's kisses

Carol:

Dove pieces beat out Kisses eventually.

Debby:

Mommy said he used to eat 3 scoops of Breyers chocolate ice cream every night b4 we were born

Noemi:

Miri says: Shabbat dinners

Debby:

Mallomars!

Carol:

Yes

Debby:

Coke

Carol:

Nap on sofa

Debby:

Mommy's polychenken
Grilled cheese and tomato soup on Sundays

Lily:

In general, laughing so hard that he'd be in tears

Debby:

Going to the bagel store in Syosset and watching them treat him like a king

Carol:

Yes

Lily:

Nova, nova, nova

Debby:

Him cracking himself up

Lily:

More nova nova nova (and red onion)

Debby:

And not knowing until prob 10 years ago that plums are sweet since he always ate them before they were actually ripe

Barry:

really? lol

Debby:

Yes
Concord grapes
The time I was too small to get off the chair lift at Stratton and he skied underneath me the entire way down as I went back down on the chair lift without the arm over me. He

kept yelling at me the whole time that everything was ok and to remain still
Mets games

Barry:
and peanuts

Noemi:
Being so early to Yom Kippur services.

Debby:
Flu shots in the house at Thanksgiving

Carol:
Apples
Clean shirts from laundry after work Sat mornings

Barry:
Vaccine shots at the Roxy in the bathroom for my trip to Thailand

Carol:
Paris tie and vest for wedding[15]

[15] Their wedding

Day 13: Wednesday, April 22

6:15 AM: Spoke with the nurse. She said she gave him opiates twice during the night. He is due for more now, but isn't in any distress, but will be sure to give him more before her shift ends this hour. She said he seems startled when seeing her but otherwise not responsive. No reaching out, no attempt at verbalization.

8:36 AM: I spoke with the day nurse today. She was the one, the day before, helping the other patient in Dad's room who then moved my iPad around for me. She said Dr. L. will put him on a drip for the pain medication shortly. And will call me on FaceTime so I can say good morning.

9:20 AM: I chatted with Dad for a moment. He was calm but unresponsive. So I just told him I loved him and that I would call him back later.

FACEBOOK POST

Day 12: Okay, things are starting to get a little surreal. My dad's assisted living facility just called to express their condolences at my dad's passing. I couldn't help but erupt in laughter. As Monty Python said "Not dead yet!" And he's not, but we expect him to pass soon. Which led me to the following reflections on one of the unexpected outcomes of grieving and preparing to grieve during a period of social distancing.

I feel like I am wrapped in a warm blanket of ubiquitous support. I think in the regular context, showings of support are deep and contained—a letter, a phone call, a visit. They are short and constrained by time and space. With gaps in-between that need to be emotionally navigated. But with EVERYTHING now forced into the virtual they are no longer constrained by space or time. People are reaching out to offer support, in heart-felt and often quite practical ways, from all over the country. Yes, no one will be able to bring over a fresh cooked meal for us, but I have a cousin in Atlanta preparing a video montage, which they will be able to see when they come to the virtual funeral (something they never could otherwise have attended). I have a friend in L.A.—who recently ran a Zoom-based memorial with 300+ participants—walk me through her process. I have a friend in San Francisco who will trouble-shoot Zoom host settings with me and is preparing to coordinate virtual *shiva* volunteers. I would never have welcomed their support if it was all local and in-person; I would have just said I had it all covered (whether I actually did).

And with time—well, I'm finding the traditional out-reach of support … extended. Text chats can go on for hours, asynchronously, with immediate family members sharing stories of my dad, each adding to the one before it. Comment threads like on Facebook fill like a thin stream over the day that I can dip into whenever I need a sip. As a result, it can be hard to remember at times that I have been isolated at home with just my wife and two kids as, if I close my eyes, I feel like I am connected with scores and scores of people, reaching out and supporting my family and I.

I would trade it all in a moment to hold my dad's hand, or to hug you, but in their absence something wonderful and remarkable has been taking its place.

2:41 PM: Called to talk with the nurse. Not much changed. She was just in there. His eyes were open. She said she'd call back shortly so I could speak with him. She did and I got towards the end of the poetry book. Around 3:30 I noticed his breathing was slowing down, by watching the clear bag he breathes into filling and collapsing. He stopped breathing, at 3:45. He was calm. At 3:55 I called the nurse to check on his breathing, while I stayed on FaceTime to watch. She said he had no pulse. I had been reading him the poem *Where I Live*, on page 96, of *Picnic, Lighting*, by Billy Collins. I stayed on until the doctor came to officially declare him deceased. She tried to figure out what time he died. I told her I knew. 3:45 PM. I knew because I was there with him when it happened.

FACEBOOK POST

At 3:45 today my father passed away. He was not alone. I had spent the past hour, over FaceTime through his iPad, reading him more poetry. He stopped breathing as I was reading the second to last poem in the Billy Collins collection and by the end of the last poem he had calmly slipped away. I feel less rage at COVID taking him from us and from preventing us from being there in person and more blessed that I got to be present at his passing and imagine the sound of my voice helped him to make his transition. Scores if not hundreds of you have been supporting my family in the past week, and I can't thank you enough. So what's next? A funeral and a *shiva* period. To learn how you might remotely attend either or both, learn about donations that can be made in his honor, see how you might volunteer to help us pull this all off, or just read stories and view photos from throughout his wonderfully long and rich (and often hilariously unlikely and hilarious) life—and post your own memories—please go to: http://tinyurl.com/PaulJosephRIP. I look forward to seeing many of you there.

Email: Atria Forest Hills-COVID-19 Update

From: Atria Senior Living
Subject: Atria Forest Hills- COVID-19 Update
Date: April 23, 2020 at 4:31:09 PM EDT
To: Barry Joseph

Dear Atria Forest Hills Residents and Families,

I have a few updates to share with you today. First, I am sad to share that one of the residents who was diagnosed with COVID-19 has passed away. Please keep the family in your thoughts at this difficult time.[16]

We've also had one additional resident receive a positive diagnosis. They are currently recovering at the hospital. I will keep you informed of any new developments.

...

As always, please don't hesitate to contact me if you have additional questions. Thank you for the stream of support so many of you have shown us.

Sincerely,

Executive Director
Atria Forest Hills

[16] I received emails like this from Atria throughout COVID. They could never say the name of the residents. But this time I knew who it was. The family they referred to, of course, was my own.

July Interview Continued: COVID-19 Oral History Project

… Q: It's really interesting to hear you talk about this, given that you had extensive contact, it sounds like, with doctors and nurses. We've also interviewed a lot of doctors and nurses who have talked about it from the other side.

Joseph: I haven't told you anything about his two weeks in the hospital. That's its own kind of thing.

Q: So I'm mindful of your time, and I think I said we'd talk for an hour, maybe a little bit more. I'm pretty flexible.

Joseph: I don't mind spending some more time, but I know you have your own purpose for these videos and how long you need them to be, and I don't want to take more time than I should be taking.

Q: No, no, you have nothing to worry about in that sense because the way oral history works, the power of the interview is shared with the person being interviewed. So whatever you're interested in talking about, we're interested in hearing about.

Joseph: Well, he was in the emergency room until Saturday morning because there was no space in the New Hyde Park-based hospital. They were looking for a room for him.

I'm trying to think of how I talked to him. Oh, the hospital had an iPad. Someone was going around using it, which was something new that they were trying out. So I got to talk to him, and it was just like you and I were talking right now. That's the state that he was in. We could talk and he was fine. He was weak, but that was it. We were quite hopeful that whatever he was dealing with might pass, and that it was not COVID.

Over the next few days, he got weaker and weaker—things that are now obviously due to COVID. But we thought he was just depressed being in the hospital. After a week, he was unable to have lengthy conversations. Maybe a word or two, and it was hard to understand what he was saying.

I don't want to spend too much time complaining about the system, which I could, but I would spend two or three hours every day trying to get him on the phone in the morning. And then two or three hours in the afternoon or two or three hours at night, right? It was so exhausting. Everyone worked hard and everyone was trying to help, but when you're dealing with someone in a hospital and you can't physically ever go in, you have to learn what it's like to work there and understand the schedules. The only way to get people to do what you need is to understand when they're available and how they become available.

I knew what time the transition was in the morning, what time it was in the afternoon. I knew what they did when they came in—not the individual people, but what they all would do—when the transfer would be, when they would gather the new daily staff in a room and the people who were there at night would tell people in the morning what was going on. And when they would be doing feeding and medication. I needed to know that hour by hour, or otherwise, I didn't know how to connect with them. If I wanted to talk to someone to find out how he was doing, I could either call the half-hour before they were going to leave for the night or wait three hours later for new people to come in, get the new information, and then get someone to talk to me, which is a big gap of time between when I get up in the morning and I'm now in the middle of my workday in meetings back to back.

The stressful part is figuring all that out and how to negotiate it, because no one's going to tell you. It's like doing an escape room without being able to touch anything in the room. It was incredibly stressful.

Q: You're also lucky if you have the resources to understand that you're going into this structure and that this is what you need to figure out.

Joseph: And how to talk to people nicely when you just want to yell at them.

Q: Because if you're someone who doesn't speak English or something or doesn't know what a hospital is like, then—

Joseph: Yep. And how to negotiate with people to get what you need. Because they say they'll call you back, and then they don't. What do you do then? Do you call back or not call back? And if you call back, what do you say without pissing them off? I had the privileged background to learn how to do those negotiations and help them feel appreciated. They are the ones working in the life-and-death situation. It was awful for them. And yet, I still needed to get information about my dad, and if I really felt like he was declining because he was depressed because he was isolated—that connecting with him was the only medicine that was really going to make a difference. That wasn't true, but it was a piece of it and it was how I felt.

So doing that every day meant that I could really appreciate how much the devices were the lifeline for my dad and for me to be able to connect.

So after about a week-and-a-half, they released him. They said, "The urinary tract infection seems gone." And we were like hooray! He's going to be released.

Q: He hadn't been intubated in that time.

Joseph: No. None of the things you think about when you hear about someone having COVID was he experiencing. He was becoming more tired, he stopped eating. His liver function was not great, but it wasn't that bad—just a thing to be somewhat concerned about. He was breathing on his own, right? But in the last few days before he left, they did start putting him on oxygen. But I could still talk to him. And they released him, on a Thursday.

They released him to a rehab, which is close to where he lived. I couldn't go there, of course. You're not allowed in. But I spoke to them on Friday and it became really clear that what I did while he was in the hospital to keep a connection with him was not going to happen in the rehab. They had put him in a room with no wifi connectivity and no telephone, in complete isolation. Within thirty-six hours, they called me and said they were sending him back to the hospital. They didn't think that he was going to survive and that he needed help, and that they couldn't get permission on a Saturday from a doctor to agree for him to be there if he was going to die. That was when I realized that it wasn't a urinary tract infection—that things looked really bad.

What I also realized was that they were going to put him in an ambulance to go back to the hospital. I drove over there. The two EMTs who brought over the ambulance spoke with me. And at first I tried to get them to keep him there—not take him. They helped me to figure out what was possible, and to realize it wasn't—they couldn't not take him. And then I negotiated with them for me to spend time with him. Remember, I hadn't seen him since he went in the hospital. Forget that. I hadn't seen him in weeks beforehand. They went inside to get him and when they came out with him, before they rolled him into their ambulance, they let me spend time with him while he was on the gurney. He still had his airbag on, but I had dressed myself so that I could safely interact with him and still go back home to my family.

Q: You put on the mask and gloves and everything.

Joseph: I had gloves on, right? I could touch him and put my hand on his shoulder and tell him I loved him.

Q: It's so amazing that you were able to do that and it's so exceptional.

Joseph: And then I gave the iPad to the EMTs and said, "Can you keep this with him?" They were amazing. They understood what was going on.

Everything was different from then on for connectivity because now there was an iPad, which I gave with the power cord. No one had to figure out anything with the system, other than, "Can you please go set up the iPad? I will call it. You just have to answer and set it up."

Two things happened now. On one hand, by Sunday, they called us and said, "His liver's too bad. This is COVID. Do you want to put him on dialysis?" They said that didn't make much sense at this point, and I agreed. That meant that he was going to die soon and they would just do things to keep him comfortable. That was when we transitioned from "we think he's coming out in a week or two" to "this is it, actually. This is COVID. Any day could be the last day." It ended up being Sunday, Monday, Tuesday, Wednesday.

What I would do is, I would call the nurses and ask them if they could set up the iPad. Sometimes, I would just be there while the nurse was doing all the things they were doing. But most of the time, they would just leave, and I could spend hours with him now. He couldn't speak, but I could talk to the nurses when they were there. I would say, "Dad, squeeze her hand if you can hear me." And in the beginning, he would, so he was getting an awareness that I was there. Eventually, he might fall asleep and I would call the nurses' station and say, "Hey, just letting you know that he fell asleep, so I'm off the phone. You can put it away when you like." Before they'd come back in, they'd say, "I think he's asleep."

In a one-way conversation with no feedback you can only say so much. So eventually, I realized what I needed to do was read to him. I think all he really needed was to hear my voice. I'd like to think the things I was saying were meaningful, but if anything, if he knew my voice was there, that would be meaningful enough.

I grew up on Long Island, not far from the Walt Whitman Birthplace Association, which is Walt Whitman's house. Dad was on the board at some point, and while he was on the board, one of the guest poets who came in and read was Billy Collins.

When my dad moved into his assisted living facility, we got rid of most of his books. One of the things I decided to keep was one of Billy Collins' poetry books, which he had autographed for him. I started reading them to myself after my dad moved. His poems are incredibly accessible. They're often about writing that very poem, so they're self-referential, which I like. And they're often very meaningful or funny. I'd never really read a book of poetry like that before. I had it by my bedside, reading one or two every few nights. Eventually, I finished it and I put it on the shelf. When I was sitting by that shelf, trying to figure out what to read to Dad, I thought oh, I'll read that book of his poems, and I can share which ones I liked.

Once I started reading them, I realized I was going to need a lot to read because it was going to be a lot of days. For each poem, I could tell him not only what I liked about it, but it often created moments to reflect with him about how much I loved him or what I appreciated about him or things about his life that it made me think about. It became a vehicle to say the things I'd want to say to him before he died. It was weird in this pandemic way. I'm sitting on the couch in the living room while my son's over there doing his schoolwork and my wife is behind him on her desk doing her work and I'm talking to my dad who's dying and telling him how much I love him. On Wednesday, I got to talk to him around eleven or so in the morning. We were towards the end of the book.

Q: You're making me cry, but it's okay. [laughter] It's usually the opposite, but it's so moving, what you're describing. But don't let me interrupt you.

Joseph: Thank you for letting me tell the story. When I was reading the book earlier to myself in bed I had never actually finished the book. As it turned out, the ones at the end are all about death, all about letting go.

So now, with my dad, I think I was up to the third to last poem in the book. So here's what I see on the screen: I see my dad's head and the top of his chest. He's not intubated, but he has a bag that is giving him extra CO2. So when he breathes in, the bag collapses and then it fills up again. And then it collapses as he breathes it in and then it fills up again. I'm not seeing his chest going up and down because I don't have that angle. Maybe it was the fourth to last poem, but definitely by the third one, the rate at which it was filling and emptying was slowing down. I don't really technically know what's going on, but I'm just guessing what that's about. Maybe he's going to sleep. I don't really know. Does he even need it to breathe? Maybe it's just helping, but not essential. I don't really know.

I think it was in the second to last poem the bag just stopped. It just stayed full. Has my dad stopped breathing? Has he died? I don't know. But I finished that poem and then I started the last poem. It was pretty clear to me by the end of the last poem that everything seemed to have stopped.

My biggest fear and my expectations had been that he was going to die alone in a hospital room, because the chances of a nurse being there were pretty slim. I couldn't be there because of their rules. And then suddenly the last day, they said I could come in. But I couldn't be there without putting my family at risk. Where am I going to go to isolate for two weeks somewhere? So I had to choose not to go, which was even harder.

But then I got to be there with him, when he died, over FaceTime.

To the extent that I could hope he could hear me—even if he couldn't understand me—he got to hear my voice and he got to use my voice and the poems as a bridge for him to let go and know that it was okay to let go. I finished the poem and called the nurses' station on my phone. I said, "Can someone please go in? I think my dad's passed away." And they came in, and I'm now watching all of this on the iPad. They confirmed it. I waited more, and then the doctor came to do the official pronouncement. I'd seen enough movies to know what she needed. I told her what time he died. They put that down, what I told them...

FACEBOOK POST:

Day 14: Thursday, April 23

The funeral, *shiva*, and donation details are now finalized for my dad, Paul Joseph. They are posted both below (and THANK YOU to the more than 2 dozen people who informed this process and are volunteering to pull this off):

1. FUNERAL: The funeral service will be held this Friday, April 24, 2020 at 11:00am EST. All who knew Paul or his family are invited to attend. It will be available ONLY over Zoom, a video conferencing service.

2. *SHIVA* VISITS: *Shiva* will be held on Friday afternoon April 24, Saturday April 25, and Sunday April 26. *Shiva minyan*[17] services will be on Saturday and Sunday at 7:30pm. They will also be held over Zoom. A sign-up sheet is now available to select a :20 slot to meet with Debby and Barry during this time, along with other mourners. If you would like to connect with Carol, please call, text or email her directly.

3. DONATIONS: (Due to an overabundance of caution, the families will not be accepting food deliveries[18].) Paul passed away

---

[17] A *minyan* is ten adults.

[18] A typical *shiva* involves a LOT of food.

peacefully listening live to poems read by his son on a video call. This was only possible due to the availability of an iPad in the hospital. If you are moved to, please go to http://gf.me/u/xwf88s to donate in his honor to a fund bringing iPads to connect COVID-19 patients with their families.

July Interview Continued: COVID-19 Oral History Project

... Joseph: The burial at the cemetery was super bizarre—other than my wife and kids, and my dad's casket, there was no one physically there in the entire COVID-blockaded cemetery! No other guests, no clergy, even the workers all kept away.

My rabbi and immediate family were all Zoomed in—the rabbi lead, with us leaning down towards my iPhone to hear (attached to a tripod), holding umbrellas over the phone. My daughter acted as a shovel surrogate[19] for those who were remote. Even with all that, I got to be present for the occasion and see a conclusion to a story left unwritten 30 years ago when I first visited that plot to bury my mother.

Q: What is that story?

Joseph: I wrote about that in a different piece for the *Forward*. Give me a moment to find it. Here we go. I'll read two paragraphs:

> Last week, we buried my father in the Long Island cemetery plot that had been waiting three decades for him to arrive. When I recall my mother's 1990 funeral, in the pre-COVID era, I can still feel the love that came from the crowd surrounding us, and the support I drew from the Hebrew prayers collectively chanted. This time, however, standing before his open grave, the absence of a crowd was deafening. My iPhone was

---

19 I made that up. This is not a thing. At a Jewish funeral those in attendance can shovel dirt onto the casket, as a sign of respect.

> on a tripod, allowing my sister in Manhattan, my step-sister in Jackson Heights, and my cousin in Pennsylvania to look along as my rabbi Zoomed us together from his living room. My 11-year old daughter shovelled dirt onto the casket as I stooped to hear their final farewells over the traffic from the adjacent highway.
>
> When the Zoom call concluded, and I looked up to see no one beyond my wife and children, I was left marveling at how we were adapting our death and mourning traditions for a period of social isolation.

After the burial we got in the car, drove back home, turned on the computer, and logged into Zoom. It was time for the funeral.

We sat on the couch in the living room. I had printed out in advance the eulogy.

To be honest, I've actually been writing his eulogy for more than half my life. When I was in college my mom died. I was unprepared to lose a parent. I decided then I would be ready for Dad's. Over the years, lines would flow through my mind that captured the essence of my dad and I'd file them away.

I'd imagine saying, "Growing up, my dad couldn't always make it to a ball game. If someone asked, 'Where's your dad?' I'd say 'He's at the hospital.' Oh no, they'd respond. What's wrong? And I'd say, 'No, he's AT the hospital, not IN. He's a doctor.'"

But when COVID took my dad, he *was* in the hospital. Had been for two weeks. And in all those decades of planning I never considered that my family would be honoring him like this, a Zoom call for a man who never once owned an email address.

I would not have expected more than a dozen people to come to his funeral. When he died, just shy of turning 88, most of his friends and family had since moved to Florida, or passed on. Those who survived were the least likely to travel for the occasion. But it didn't matter; none of us could mourn in person.

Instead, I put out a call to my friends and together they provided back-end support for a Zoom-based funeral. On a Friday morning in April, funeral participants logged in from all over the country, topping 120. The rabbi and cantor, each at their own homes in Forest Hills, welcomed everyone and led the religious components of the service. Two of my father's oldest friends, a married couple both in their 90s, shared a few words in his honor. In their 90s! On Zoom!

And that eulogy I'd spent decades nurturing? I threw it all out. I saw we were in a new world, one I could never have anticipated, with new ways to honor him.

The eulogy came together for me the night before, almost in a flash. I'll put it in my file so you can read it. Next, we shared a video that covered his life in reverse through a collection of photos edited together by a cousin in Atlanta, which my sister and I narrated.

Of course, I wish we could have been together, so I could have held my step-mom and comforted my sister. But live-streaming the funeral meant we were able to bring so many more of us together, at one time, to memorialize my dad. That was awesome.

It made me realize COVID is like a super-villain in a Marvel movie. Its evil mission is to keep apart the people it can't outright kill. And there are two types of superheroes in this movie. Of course there are the heroes fighting to keep us alive, doctors and nurses and frontline workers. But there are also the other heroes fighting to oppose the forces of social distancing. And these heroes are called Team Technology. Let's call this movie Zoom vs. COVID-19. I'd like to take comfort from watching how Team Technology defeats evil and brings us all together.

Eulogy for Paul Joseph

Thank you all for coming. And looking at the participants list, of over 100, at each of your names—I can't tell you how much comfort it brings us.

I have to acknowledge—I know this is all rather odd. I never pictured myself eulogizing my dad over a computer screen. Nor that when I did I'd not be wearing any ... shoes. But what's strangest to me is our reliance on technology—and an army of amazing friends and family supporting it behind the scenes—for a man who lived with computers in his home for nearly 40 years (he got me my first for my Bar Mitzvah[20]) but who STILL never once had his own email address. Truly a wonder.

This is also odd because you can see me but I can't see you. So please feel free to respond in the chat, in any way you like. If you haven't yet please find that chat button now and share something, like where

[20] When I turned 13.

you are right now. Go ahead. … One of the upsides of this is that so many of you were able to join us today.

I want to begin by sharing a poem my dad loved, framed above his toilet, published by the Walt Whitman Birthplace Association, where he once proudly sat on the board. It's called Salt and Pepper.[21]

> Here and there
> white hairs appear
> on my chest -
> age seasons me
> gives me zest -
> I am a sage
> in the making
> Sprinkled, shaken

Yes, my dad WAS a sage in the making, but not just due to age. He lived a life of integrity, and compassion, and he would often share his wisdom in unexpected ways, at just the right time.

I love celebrating my dad, which should be news to no one. And I'm also the family archivist. So when it came time to create his memorial web site with my sister this week we just turned to all the other books of his life we'd made for him as presents over the years. Someone posted yesterday on the memorial the following: "I think it's the genetic code that enables all Josephs to move through the world collecting friends as they go." Debby and I loved documenting those collections of Dad's. His friendships were piled into a 70th birthday present nearly a foot high and two feet long filled with pages of documents and interviews with all those he touched over the decades. The words of those he touched professionally were combined into a collection of toasts from his retirement party after 39 years in private practice. And his adventures were captured in letters sent to his

[21] Samuel Menashe, "Salt and Pepper" from *Samuel Menashe: New and Selected Poems*, edited by Christopher Ricks, published by The Library of America, 2005. Copyright © 2004 by Samuel Menashe.

mom when he was 16-years old camping across America with his high school baseball team.

My dad was not just a friend and doctor to so many, but he was also son, brother & cousin, a husband, a father, an uncle, and a grandfather. His life was rich, and varied, and often went in unexpected directions.

Paul Joseph was born and grew up in Jersey City, son of a town doctor—his dad—and his mom's family were the local department store magnates. Her name was Reina. It meant queen—as she'd be the first to tell you. She'd winter in Florida with her parents, leaving Paul with his dad and the Hungarian nannies back in New Jersey. In a letter, Paul's dad wrote Reina, "I can not impress upon you the pleasures and comfort our precious boy gives me."

That precious boy was soon followed by another, his brother Carl. Dad once told me "Carl I used to beat up, until he got to the point when he was a little bigger than I was and could beat me up, and that was the end of the fighting." And the two boys had a crew of cousins—and they would spend the summers together—the whole families—dozens of them—in a seaside mansion on the Jersey shore, building relationships that would last a lifetime; the experience imprinted upon him an appreciation of the importance of family that was clear to any who knew him.

My dad spoke often, a tale hard to believe, about his weekly piano lessons. He'd say something like: "At five years old, my mother decides she's going to make a concert pianist out of me. So, I would take a bus from Jersey City to Journal Square then take the tubes to the city, then the subway from about 35th street up to 72nd street. And usually I'd go to the Automat on the corner of Broadway and 72nd street and have the mashed potatoes and the gravy and all the good things"—you picturing this, this little 5 year old boy on his own with his dime?—"THEN I'd go to Miss Feinstein's. I'd play for an hour, then I'd have to go home."

But as a teen he was having no more of it. "The first time I stood up to my mother I was thirteen years old, and the question was either piano lessons or baseball practice. I've had enough of piano lessons, I told my mother. Why? Because I want to go out and play baseball in the Spring. Mother said, "No." And I said, "Yes." And after a battle, she finally said, "Okay", cause she saw I wasn't giving in. You know, I was never afraid of speaking my mind, but I can't remember right now anything else as traumatic as that."

And with that baseball team, at 16, he not only got to play ball but in the summer of 1948 he saw America, coast to coast, camping across the country; he visited pig slaughtering plants in Chicago, the grand canyon, radio shows in LA, and a new city called Las Vegas. He wrote home daily. "I'm glad to get away from New York's cheap money-making, fast-talking bourgeoisie crowd." These letters would stay in a shoe-box, treasured by his mom, undiscovered until she passed in the 1980s, revealing to us a father my sister and I had never known. "Fast-talking bourgeoisie crowd"?

Dad went to Yale, then NYU for medical school. After a stint in the army, working in Iran, he was discharged and, in his own words: "drove from San Antonio to Atlanta, Georgia, the home of the Center for Disease Control. The CDC housed the elite corp of physicians that made up the EIS—the Epidemic Intelligence Service. I went to the director of EIS and said I wanted a job. Do you have any special expertise? No! Did you win any awards? No! Have you published any papers in peer reviewed journals? No! Do you have recommendations from an outstanding scholar in Epidemiology? No! Did you get any prizes during your internship? Yes, I said. I took first prize in the hospital tennis tournament by beating the chief of Radiology."

So no job. But he found one with the federal government to fill out his resume and, a year later he got that job he wanted, finding himself in the Philippines in charge of an American effort by the CDC to study a vaccine trial for Cholera in the midst of a significant epidemic in the region. After battling monsoons and endless bowls of fish soup, he returned to America and left the CDC. His former boss in the Philippines would congratulate Dad on completing his pediatric residency that followed, saying "Pediatric's gain is Public Health's loss". His private practice—serving the children of Long Island—would last the next 39 years.

I won't fill in all the details but during those years he settled into Long Island with my mother, had my sister and I, lost my mom, found Carol, and retired. Along the way there was serving the Walt Whitman Birthplace Association, the North Shore Synagogue Continuing Adult Education Program, and getting published in the New England Journal of Medicine. He became a grandfather to Akiva and Miri, and through Lily with Eva and Delia, and with Carol leaves Long Island for Forest Hills and eventually moves into Atria. And in recent years, on most Fridays, he was over for Shabbat dinner, eating half the challah, and passing me bills to be paid—I treasured every one of those visits, well aware they were in limited quantity and we were counting down (but from what number I couldn't know).

In recent years he began to slow down. But what never stopped were the many things we all treasured about him:

We treasured his great sense of humor, whether making us laugh or making himself laugh so hard, at his own jokes, that he'd double over clutching his stomach.

We treasured his thoughtful advice. In a letter to Debby in summer camp: "I hope that you will explore as many different activities as you can... Don't be afraid to try new things and experiment." To me in college: "All I care about is you learn to read, write, and speak publicly." Or his three point plan in his 2002 commencement speech to the graduating Residents at Winthrop University Hospital: "1. Go For It, 2. Ask Why, 3. Have Fun."

We treasured his voracious appetite for food. "That was the best [fill in the blank] I ever had" came at the conclusion of many of his meals.

We treasured his voracious appetite… for non-fiction books, preferably about the Civil War, a president, or anything by David McCullough. And not just books, but Chris Cuomo on CNN or Rachel Maddow on CNBC. For years we'd have fights if we called between 9-10 pm. "Hello? Rachel's on! Stop calling me!"

My dad had many struggles over his life, with manic depression, with losing a wife when she was 48 to cancer, at remembering the details of the last book on Lincoln he just read. As his physical health declined in recent years, and the circle of his life grew smaller and smaller, Carol was the rock he leaned on that kept him going.

But he never stopped engaging his mind, using humor to connect with those around him, and taking time to live in the moment. As one person shared with us this week: "There was a wrap-around covered porch at Chautauqua[22] that Paul loved because even when it rained, he could sit outside, relax and read a book with a tall glass of ice tea."

It's always hard to lose a loved one. Many of us are learning a new kind of hard in the age of social distancing. None of us could visit my father for the two weeks he lay dying in the hospital, cared for by so many heroic health care workers I could never thank enough. But thanks to a family iPad, and FaceTime, even once he couldn't speak due to the virus and the strapped-on oxygen bag, we could still see him, and speak with him, and observe him, and listen to the sound of his breathing as the oxygen bag would compress then expand, and just be with him.

I would spend :30 minutes with him, an hour, two hours, just sitting with him. And after I ran out of stories, out of words of encouragement, out of all the things I needed to tell him, all I had was poetry. Specifically a book of poetry by Billy Collins he and Carol got him

[22] The Chautauqua Institution, in Western New York, a place we often took summer vacations.

to sign. When Dad moved into Atria I claimed it as my own, reading one or two poems a night before bed. They became a type of meditation, and a gift from him that kept on giving. So I was saddened when I finished it. But over this week I read them all to him, over the video conference like I am speaking with you now. I read them to him cover to cover, with breaks in-between poems as I talked about what they made me think about his life, or my life with him, and how much he meant to me. On Wednesday, when I was reading the third to last poem in the book I noticed there were gaps in time between the oxygen bag collapsing and refilling. And in the second to last poem I noticed the bag fill then freeze—a captured breath waiting to be taken. And after I read the last poem, I called the nurse on the phone and they arrived to confirm he had passed. I had seen it with my own eyes, that moment, and how peaceful it was for him, without pain or struggle. And I felt lucky to be able to be there with him, that maybe my voice had provided the bridge he needed, and maybe he found guidance in those final poems, which happened as it turned out to be about death, about the fear of it, and about accepting it. I'd like to share with you the last few lines I read to him:

> This is the end
> what we have all been waiting for
> what everything comes down to
> the destination we cannot help imagining
> a streak of light in the sky
> a hat on the peg, and outside the cabin, falling leaves

Now, I could stop there. And I probably should. But... that's not what my dad would want. He'd want me to keep going, to go for the laugh. I can hear him telling me to end by reminding you of a phrase he used to say, that would often lead him to stand before that other poem I told you about, about that sage in the making. He'd say "When you gotta go, you gotta go."

We didn't want him to, but my dad had to go. And we will always hold him in our hearts.

July Interview Continued: COVID-19 Oral History Project

… Joseph: As a Reform Jew, in my tradition, *shiva* means opening the house for three days to anyone who wants to come in. Friends, neighbors, anyone in the community. We'll often bring plates of, you know, cold cuts and bagels and Italian cookies.

There are some religious rituals during that time but most of it is just socializing and letting the community come and care for us and giving us that social space to mourn. Then it ends like the opposite. It's like a storm that's going for three days and then just stops. Everyone's suddenly here and suddenly they're gone. In some ways, that's the point where you can start mourning, because you're suddenly alone and you can start feeling some of those feelings if you're not used to doing it with other people.

Of course, during the time of social isolation, we couldn't do that. People couldn't bring food. People weren't going to come in. Given my background with digital gatherings, I knew what could work and the resources it would take to pull it off in the planning. I called my friends—many of the people I've worked with over the years, who have become my close friends—and just said, "I need your help. Can you drop everything you're doing and help?" And it was very moving. One of them was actually one of the high school students in that summer camp from 2006. What I didn't mention at the time was anyone in the world could participate because it was virtual. She was a high-school student in Mexico City who has since gone on to get a graduate degree at MIT. She was one of the people who stepped up.

Before it even happened, it was very moving for me. Because these people who I consider my colleagues who I've been working with all these years stepped up to help me leverage the tools for me and my family. We set up what we call breakout rooms—that's the technical term in Zoom—where you can put people together in a separate room and no one else can see them. We can just see each other. I describe it as, there's a hallway when you walk into a house. That's the beginning of the Zoom. And then it was as if we were in a separate room that people can be sent into and pulled out of.

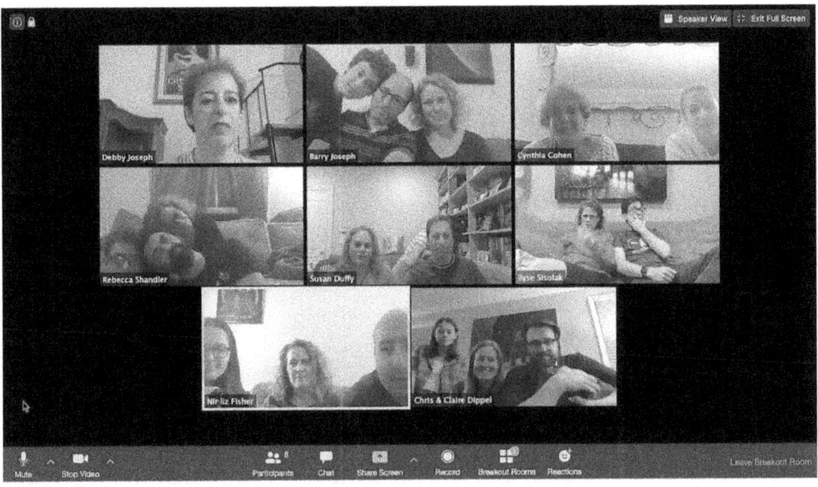

We crowd-sourced the *shiva* calendar in advance through a Google Spreadsheet, which we shared widely. Anyone interested in paying a *shiva* call could browse predetermined times and type in their name. It turned a *shiva* visit into a V.I.P., reservation-only event. I would periodically review the schedule, move people around (Do I want those cousins together? Those friends might make an interesting combination…), and, once approved, a team of volunteers, composed of two dozen close friends and family, would email the Zoom link to the day's visitors.

We arranged each visit to be twenty minutes long, with ten minutes between sessions to protect ourselves from becoming overwhelmed. We then strung them back to back, from 2:00 -9:00 pm, ending each day with a *minyan* service led by the clergy.

Our volunteers would greet people as they arrived into the Zoom room, as if they had opened the door to our apartment after hearing the doorbell. Once their video and audio was deemed to be in working order, the volunteers made sure their names were visible on their account (as I'm bad with names), and when the call was ready to begin, the helpers used the Zoom "breakout room" function to send the visitors into the private room where my sister and I were waiting. I was never in the "lobby", a virtual version of the *shiva* living room in which everyone in attendance chats with everyone except the mourners. Instead, my sister and I had our own secluded space, knowing in advance who to expect, in a number we could handle, for 20 minutes at a time. A helper would show up after 18 or 19 minutes, remind the visitors the session was almost up, then reappear a few minutes later to escort them out, leaving my sister and me behind to debrief about the crazy story we just heard or grab a quick bite or bathroom break. Then we did it all over again.

In the end we met with over 150 people. Visitors came from all over the country, and from all over our and my dad's life. During each visit, we could focus on our small group without distraction from doorbells or new visitors. I could concentrate on a story from an old friend, or take the space to grieve. Knowing who was coming in advance eliminated a certain level of social awkwardness, as did having our volunteer formally end each visit. And the *minyan* service was supported by people across four generations, from all across the country, as the clergy lead us in the traditional mourning prayers (with all but the clergy on mute, to prevent what I call the Zombie Choir effect from audio lag).

At the end of each day, my sister and I felt renewed and connected. Yes, there were no leftover bagels or cookies, but also no cleaning. We missed the physical contact and the hugs, but we were able to deeply connect with family and friends who otherwise would not have been able to attend. We experienced my dad's *shiva* not as an uncontrolled waterfall of compassion and social commitments but as a personalized cycle of visits that better matched our need to mourn during this tragic time.

Part of what I took away from that experience is that there are things we're having to do now because we have no choice during the pandemic. And I'm grateful for all we're able to get to do. Many of the things we'll drop as soon as we can when we can go back to normal. Yet, at the same time, I ask: Are there things that maybe we shouldn't drop so fast? There are things that we'll want to keep and hold onto—for my dad's funeral, for the *shiva* period. There are at least 100 people, maybe 200, who were able to participate who otherwise would not have. We would never have set up that technology beforehand. We wouldn't have thought it was reasonable to do that, maybe even appropriate to do that. Maybe after this, it's going to feel inappropriate not to make those options available. Maybe we would do *shiva* in person for three days, then have the fourth day virtual, right?

Whatever it is, there are things we're learning that are possible once we can get past that social discomfort around the technology. Now that we've broken through that, I hope that we can enhance the traditions that are being challenged right now through the pandemic and find new ways to expand them.

There are hundreds who participated in the funeral or shiva who would not have come in person. It's this really weird way where we lost something, but we gained something at the same time. It's hard to know if I could change things, what would I change? Other than the fact that I wish he wasn't dead, you know? So much went so well in the process, better than I could have ever hoped for. And I feel super fortunate and so grateful.

And yet at the same time, my sister is not ready to get together with me in a social-isolation context because unless she can hug me, it'll break her heart too much...

A few days later, I went and I picked up what little he had with him at the hospital, which included the iPad. My sister, meanwhile, had heard of someone who, out of nowhere, created an opportunity to get peoples' iPads into hospitals to do exactly what we were doing. So this organization took iPads, erased them, set them up for use in the hospitals, and donated them to hospitals. Have you come across this yet?

Q: Yeah, I mean, I haven't come across an organization that does it, but I have spoken with a lot of people working in hospitals that are using iPads.

Joseph: So this organization has raised thousands of dollars. For every $50 raised they can get and retool a used iPad. I erased the information and we donated to them the iPad we used for my dad. It is now used in hospitals. But more importantly, we chose that as the charity for people to donate to who wanted to honor my dad. Thousands of dollars have been raised from family members and friends who are still contributing to the fund to help them buy the devices and allow people to connect with their loved ones during this time.

Q: I can confirm from the perspectives of the nurses and doctors that we've spoken with that that's the toughest thing for people in the hospital—not being able to communicate with other family members. That kind of isolation is just the worst. What a privilege for you and also for your father that you were able to figure things out so that you could stay in contact with him.

Joseph: It's amazing. So yes, I lost my dad and that's sad. And yes, it happened in the pandemic, which is awful and crazy. But at the same time, there could have been no pandemic and he could have had an awful death six months from now as he continued physically deteriorating and would have been depressed and died by himself in a facility. He could have died in the hospital and it could have been due to something else and no one could have been there. Because you can't stay there all day.

Instead, I got to be with him. He got to have me there in some capacity, right?

For the doctors and nurses, they see this need for people to connect and are watching people suffering in isolation. They know they can take out their phone and make a phone call. And they can't. It's against the rules. That is so hard for them. There were a few times when people did that, where the nurse was like, "I'm not supposed to do this, but I'm using my phone." It's so unfair for them to have to be in those situations. Being able to get the technologies into the hospitals is not just great for the patients and their families and helps them in those ways, it also helps the doctors and the nurses and the aids to not have to be in this emotional bind they shouldn't have to be in.

Q: It's interesting because that's one of the underlying themes that we're finding in our interviews with people who work in hospitals. Hospital personnel end up breaking rules left and right in order to bypass regulations they think are either not ethical or not humane. We're seeing that over and over again—people making all kinds of exceptions to take care of their patients. It's a power struggle between hospital administrators and the people who are actually on the front line with the patients. From my own sociological perspective, it's really fascinating, right? Just about structures and how they transform and don't transform. How people follow and don't follow rules.

Joseph: You know, David Brooks, who writes for *The New York Times*—part of his signs of hope throughout all this was that whether cities chose to close down or not and whether schools chose to be open or not, people stepped up and did what they needed to and often did the right thing, at least during the first few months. We're not seeing that now, but it was true then. I think part of what you're able to document here is the ways that people on the ground figured out how to make life and death a little bit more humane, and not let the rules that were often based around protecting people legally or maximizing profits be the things that determined how people were going to live and die during the pandemic...

MAY 2020

In which celebrities carry messages… a community changes… buses have bubbles… at 7:00 PM we give thanks…

July Interview Continued: COVID-19 Oral History Project

... Q: I'm wondering—just going back a little bit to your experience with this sort of alternative approach to sitting *shiva* and also the experience with your father dying and also the fact that you wrote about it and published in a medium that a lot of people read—have you seen other people adopting your practices? Or have you heard from other people in response to your experience?

Joseph: I wrote a number of pieces and was interviewed as well about our experiences in my family thinking about how to manage the situation once my dad had passed. Doing that, for me, was part of what I needed to do. Everyone found their own way to do something, either to learn a new skill or expand a skill during this time, to keep them engaged. My son started learning some programming and my daughter got really into Roblox and my wife started baking new things. For me, it's writing. I always like to write, and this gave me a chance to really use my writing as an opportunity to get a better understanding of what I was experiencing. And one of the beauties of writing is getting to publish it and hear from other people who have read it—people I know in my life and through that writing, felt more connected to me and I felt connected to them.

I also heard from people who I don't know—people who wrote to editors who kindly forwarded this to me who were in the same exact situation. "How do we do a *shiva* like this? How do we bury my loved one who just passed?" It was just a reminder that I wasn't alone, that we were all dealing with this. A few weeks later, *The New York Times* ran their cover article that were excerpts from all the obituaries to mark when 100,000 people had passed. It spread off the front page to three more pages inside. It was amazing. The numbers must have been 1,000 people, so they chose one of every hundred obits that they found, and they were all listed in chronological order, because they thought there was something interesting in the obit. And there was my dad. There was him.

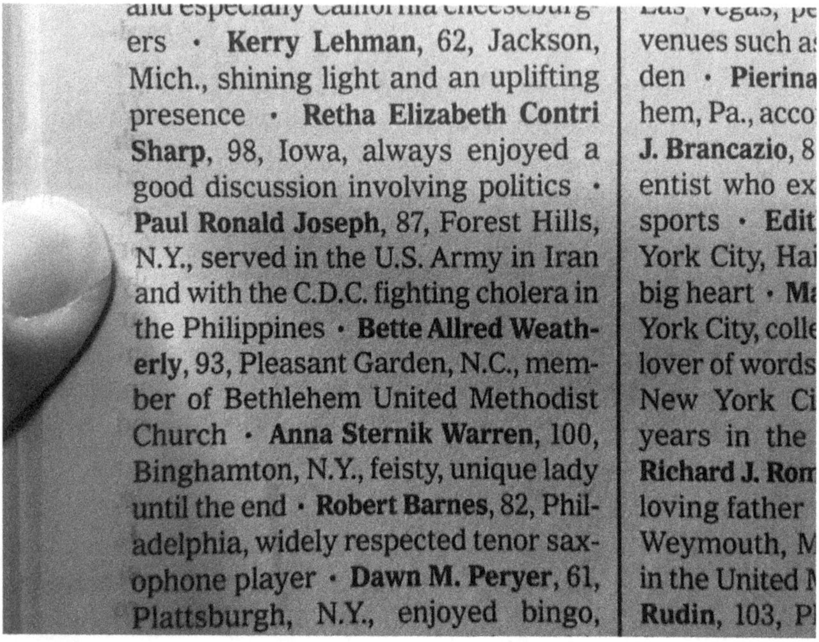

> ers • **Kerry Lehman**, 62, Jackson, Mich., shining light and an uplifting presence • **Retha Elizabeth Contri Sharp**, 98, Iowa, always enjoyed a good discussion involving politics • **Paul Ronald Joseph**, 87, Forest Hills, N.Y., served in the U.S. Army in Iran and with the C.D.C. fighting cholera in the Philippines • **Bette Allred Weatherly**, 93, Pleasant Garden, N.C., member of Bethlehem United Methodist Church • **Anna Sternik Warren**, 100, Binghamton, N.Y., feisty, unique lady until the end • **Robert Barnes**, 82, Philadelphia, widely respected tenor saxophone player • **Dawn M. Peryer**, 61, Plattsburgh, N.Y., enjoyed bingo,

So again, I have very specific experiences around my dad passing, that are personal, just mine. I somewhat feel apologetic if I talk about it. Yes, he died from COVID, but he was old. He was going to die soon anyway. He wasn't in the best health, you know? He has his own story. But seeing him be one of the thousand, representing one of the 100,000, forced me to recognize and really accept that he's a part of this larger social climate that we're all experiencing. All of us—all of the 1,000 printed, all of the 100,000—all had to deal with these incredible challenges and almost Sophie's Choice-type decisions:

"Do I see my sister or not, and then if I do, do I risk my family? Do I isolate for two weeks? Do I go to the hospital on his deathbed? And if I do, again, am I risking the health of my family going to a hospital where everyone's got COVID?" These are awful, challenging situations and what's being felt by millions of people around the country.

Q: Have your relationships with your friends changed or not changed?

With friends, what's been really fun is watching how different individuals and different groups have come together to create ways to regularly connect on Zoom. When we first started, another group of friends of ours started doing dance parties every Saturday night. We'd just invite other people to come and I would DJ, and we would just dance for an hour. That was super fun.

I have a supper club of friends who get together once a month. All of our kids go to school together, so this would be our time away from them, to be with just the adults. We've been doing it for four years. One Saturday a month, we get together and have dinner. And now, instead, every Wednesday night, we get together for an hour. No food, but we get to be together. And we've been doing this since March, and no one's even suggested that we need to stop. It's clearly part of what we need to do with each other. And other configurations of friends have also said, "Hey, let's get together," because one person says let's make that happen on a weekly basis and a biweekly basis.

And there's people who I love, but just never made the time for, or didn't make as much time as I would have liked. Now I'm seeing them on a regular basis and I'm more deeply connected to them and their lives. That feels great. There are other friends who I am still close with in the city, I'd still rather see them in person and get together. But it's fun. It's like we have little cocktail parties. Not to say we're drinking during it, but it's like, let's just socialize and share our lives with each other on a regular basis. It's nice.

Q: So your social life sounds like it is pretty much completely online. Have things shifted at all for you with these phases of reopening that we're going through?

Joseph: Yeah, completely. Completely changed. Let me put this in context: I bought a bagel in the beginning of March and otherwise have not been in any store since. My wife really organized well and became a master of coordinating all the different delivery services so we could have stuff delivered to us. There were a few times that a supermarket needed to be entered and she ended up doing that. By the end of May, I still hadn't been in a store, I hadn't been in a restaurant, hadn't seen a friend in person. It was just us in the house.

While we've been socially distanced, one of the aspects that's been super hard was dealing with the things you can only do in person. Not being able to do that, I started using Cameo.com to hire celebrities to have the kind of impact that I couldn't have in-person anymore and deliver things for me.

Q: The Cameo experience.

Joseph: Yes, I started using Cameo.com to hire celebrities to have the kind of impact that I couldn't have in-person anymore and deliver things for me.

Q: Just for people who aren't familiar with Cameo, can you briefly explain what it is?

Joseph: Sure. I actually just had a short piece published about my experience...

Article: *How I hired Jackie Hoffman to be my pandemic celebrity Cyrano*

An excerpt. Originally published in the Forward June 25, 2020

What's your pandemic guilty pleasure? My wife is cooking up a storm, my son is bingeing all 222 episodes of "Phineas and Ferb" and my daughter is posting dances to TikTok. Me? I've hired actress and comedian Jackie Hoffman ($20) as my personal avatar.

You know how it is: My cousin graduates and we can't have a party. My father dies and I can't hug my sister. I think we all need a virtual Cyrano to keep us connected in this age of social distancing. I found mine on Cameo.com.

A few years ago when I first heard of Cameo I was embarrassed to even know it existed. As Ice-T ($350) explains on the site, "What you do is… you book me… and I send a shout-out to one of your good friends, or tell one of your enemies you don't give a [expletive] about them…" In the world of Cameo, every celebrity has a price, commodifying their status into a service for hire. "I handle your business," Ice-T explains, "For you." When did the price of fame fall so low?

When I next heard of Cameo, they were in the news. And I could make little sense of it. Brett Favre ($300) was antisemitic. Wait, that wasn't right. Okay, Favre said he was "distressed" that the things he said in a video for Cameo—the coded hate-speech he read on behalf of two antisemitic groups that hired him—would be seen as an endorsement. So he would be donating his fee to fight hatred and bigotry. I am not one to admire antisemites (being quite Semitic myself) but I couldn't fail to appreciate their having done it for the LOLZ. That is, they used Cameo to turn a celebrity into a ventriloquist's dummy, unaware of his complicity in weaponizing the power of fame.

Then came COVID-19 and the world was turned inside out. Or more like, outside in, as now we all lived in a state of infinite isolation. When my daughter's 5th grade performance was cancelled, I recalled Cameo. Was there a performer she admired who could give her a pep talk? I searched Cameo for Disney's *High School Musical: The Musical: The Series*. I found Julia Lester ($40.99), who starred in the show. "I am thinking about you," she told my daughter. "I love you. Appreciate you. And am cheering you on." My daughter loved it. It made her day. I was hooked.

Hooked, but not yet addicted. That arrived later when I discovered the availability of Jackie Hoffman. I've seen Jackie Hoffman on Broadway, in both *Hairspray* and *Charlie and the Chocolate Factory*. She always makes me laugh. And on Cameo, she's a riot. Cameo is not social media. You can't scroll an endless feed of "I want to wish you a happy birthday…" But many celebrities offer up to six of their most recent.

Jackie had starred in the Broadway take on the movie *Xanadu*. I almost cried, from laughter, watching her hilarious and sweet video for the musical teacher whose high school *Xanadu* was cancelled, to share with his 100+ crushed teen thespians. It's an odd type of virtual voyeurism, like going into people's homes and reading their Hallmark cards. And her price was just right for me. Instead of one Joonas Suotamo ($100, Chewbacca in *Star Wars*) I can get five Jackies; instead of one Debbie Gibson ($200) I can get ten Jackies!

My weekly habit began with my sister. I hired Jackie through the standard request form, which allows a mere 250 characters to provide context for the video. An enhanced Twitter message doesn't provide a lot of space to explain that your dad died of COVID-19 and that you can't see your sister who lives 20 minutes away so can you please make her laugh because living alone it's heartbreaking and if you can work in these bizarre references to our time with my dad she's going to love it.

Requesting a Cameo is like an improv show, where a performer riffs on words shouted-out by an audience. Jackie is perfect for Cameo because, as a comedian, she knows how to work so hard with so little. I couldn't be there with my sister but Jackie could handle my business for me.

For my son's birthday I combined voice celebrities he loved like Deedee Magno Hall ($65) (voice of Pearl from *Steven Universe)*, and John DiMaggio ($100) (the voice of Jake from *Adventure Time*), with Jackie pretending to be the voices of the celebrities I couldn't find (or afford) into a 9-minute movie. "I play the voice of Malcolm Gladwell on his podcast," she said. "I play all the voices on *Gravity Falls*." Jackie in fact does neither.

A week later she made a video thanking my friend for running the online funeral for my dad, and the *shiva* that followed ("That's a lot of Zoom white fish. My yarmulke is off to you."). And when my colleagues sent me a condolence basket, I thanked them with a message from Jackie. She roasted my friend who escaped the city to a farm in the Berkshires. And when it came to my cousin graduating from college, Jackie helped me draw outside the lines, bending Cameo to my will.

Like with my son's birthday, I decided my cousin would appreciate a video, as he heads to Hollywood to follow his dreams. Along with a new one from Jackie I combined big ticket prizes, like comedian Gilbert Gottfried ($150), with the budget options, like reality show contestant Lili Davies ($10). And using the mobile app Acapella, my sister and I collaborated on creating a late night talk show format as context for our "guests" coming to cheer my cousin on.

The challenge was my asks were growing increasingly obscure. I couldn't explain all the in-jokes I wanted referenced, nor how I wanted to weave the videos together in a debate about whether my cousin should become the personal dishwasher for either Gilbert Gottfried or Louie Anderson ($149). Eventually I found myself just sending lists of words and phrases, asking the celebrities to work them into any sentence they could imagine: debt, Disney World, dirty sneakers, Hollywood dreams, five guys in a basket eating a donut. I was no longer just offering quick cash; I was inviting celebrities to take a leap of faith. They had to trust me. If I abused that trust, I was no better than the trolls making sports figures spout coded hate speech. When I received my first decline (which was far from my last) I took it as a sign of hope. Some celebrities had lines they wouldn't cross.

a
Five Guys
in a Basket
Eating a Donut
production

And for those who took that leap, who accepted my absurd requests, they often made sure we knew they were in on the joke, not the butt of it. As Jackie said with a straight face at the end of her video for my cousin, "I am being held captive and being forced to say these things against my will." Captive by an economic system that melds performance and celebrity into a commodity, indeed, but one in which she can find power to make comedy gold, personalized for the hapless souls that need her voice during these chaotic times.

As long as she is willing to play this game with me, I'll continue to ask Jackie to celebrate on my behalf, to mourn on my behalf, to offer a pep talk on my behalf. And when the pandemic is behind us, when

I can manage my business on my own, I can't yet imagine how I will look back on the new relationships I've formed, with those like Jackie Hoffman, with those who have been my celebrity doppelgangers for hire. But I know I'll have the video record to show for it.

July Interview Continued: COVID-19 Oral History Project

... Joseph: Cameo has become a really wonderful way for me to touch people and make a difference for them in a way that is unique and special, at least right now. I can do something special for them that will be somewhat ephemeral. You can always watch it again, but it's giving them an emotional experience.

That's what I want to do. I want to touch people and be able to give them an experience. Having celebrities give messages to other people has been an unusually satisfying and super-fun way to do that, from my kid turning fourteen to my cousin graduating from college to someone who resigned because of COVID who I worked with to giving a message to my sister because I haven't been able to hug her since my dad died.

Q: That sounds really hard. So I wanted to go back just a little bit to your neighborhood because you started talking about it in the context of this camping trip. I don't think we've spoken to anyone from Forest Hills yet, at least that I know of. What has your neighborhood been like? What was it like during the worst moment in the pandemic? And also, I guess I'm interested in how your relationship to your neighborhood and the city has changed as a result of the pandemic.

Joseph: Do you have another hour? I don't even know where to begin. The first thing I would say is that I don't have perspective on it. I lived in my apartment for three months. I would go outside at least once a week to go walk around. If you don't know Forest Hills, it has a few sections, and the section I'm in has co-ops down a major transport spine. On the other side of the co-op buildings, which are these high-rises, are houses. Those are the houses that Spider-Man grew up in in the comic books. He grew up in a house in Forest Hills.

It's those houses. They're beautiful. They're very idyllic. On the other side of them is Grand Central Parkway. It's completely closed off. But between Grand Central Parkway and the Van Wyck Expressway is Flushing Meadows–Corona Park. It's this weird thing where we're isolated because of the highways, but just a few steps further, we're also in something the size of Central Park.

So I'd spend an hour and leave and just go walk. And walking around, I would see other people pretty much doing the same thing and see who was wearing masks and who wasn't—who was being thoughtful and who wasn't. I had a totally different relationship with the community, because what the hell was I doing over there? I don't usually go over there.

One Friday, I got off at 3:00, and my daughter and I put on rollerblades. I expected we would just go around the block. Instead, we just kept going, over the highway, into the park, around the park, and (3.4 miles later) back home. She's eleven years old on rollerblades. It was up and down hills. It was crazy. But the community just pulled us out. We didn't want to come back inside.

I'm also on the main spine, like I said, so I'm seeing the buses go by. So I'm always looking at the buses and saying, "Who has to be on the buses? Who has no choice but to be on the bus?" And one of those people, of course, is the bus driver. At first, bus drivers were getting sick. And then they stopped accepting payment in the front and people would walk in the back door. And they wouldn't open the front door, and there would be plastic to separate the drivers. You could see as the buses would go by, there was like this little bubble for the bus driver. The people are sitting behind them or standing behind them.

That was so upsetting to see because it was such a reminder that these bus drivers are putting their lives at risk every day and they were struggling to figure out how to get the place that they worked to make it safe for them. That meant accepting no payment, which is pretty remarkable, right? That was the right decision to make to keep them safe.

As I mentioned, the park next door closed. At first, the city said that people had to stop using the playgrounds, and they largely did. Then they said stop playing basketball, and they largely did. But it was pretty clear to us because I was not going anywhere and I could see it every day that teenagers were still coming out and playing basketball. Then they came out and removed the basketball nets. And people still came. The next day, they closed the parks all over the city. That was as clear a sign that we could not self-manage through anarchy and we needed to shut down the city if we were going to be safe. It was around that time that we started having the 7:00 PM—I'm sure many people you've talked to have spoken about it—clapping and thanks to the essential workers.

Forest Hills is a hill. My building is at the top of the hill. Our apartment is on the top floor of the building. We look out over the park, which means that we look out on the town. So most of my interactions with the town in March, April, and May were at the 7:00 going out on the balcony. And I don't know who these people are. They're far away. They're across the park. I'd see them every day or I'd hear them. "There's the guy with the bell and there's the person with the horn." We'd be out there for a few minutes and we'd be clapping and yelling. There was someone on the roof across the way who would always come out. We had that time together to both give thanks, but also give voice as a community to the people without whom we couldn't be doing what we were doing.

Especially when my dad was in the hospital for two weeks and after he died, the people I was thanking in my mind were quite specific. Whenever I was talking to whoever the nurse was on the floor that day or a doctor I was talking to, I would remind them and say, "7:00 tonight, we're clapping for you." That made it very moving and very meaningful for me to get to do that and share that with them—for the kids to get to do that, for my kids to be connected. And I'd like to think it made a difference when they heard that. I think it kind of helped cut through the insanity that they had to deal with every day at work. They were reminded that there are people out there who appreciate what they're doing...

JUNE 2020

Escape to the Catskills… the only constant is change…Juneteeth… Randall's Island LARPing…

July Interview Continued: COVID-19 Oral History Project

… Q: It's been a few months now. We started interviewing people in the last week of March. So the questions that we ask have more or less remained the same. Well, I should say they haven't, really. We still have the same interview guide, but it's hard to ask the same questions. I'm just wondering for you, now that it's been a while, how has your perspective transformed? The whole experience of your father getting sick, going through this process in this very strange time, having to make these kinds of decisions, and now having had some space? Even though, of course, mourning takes a very long time. But in the scheme of things, I think three or four months is not that much.

Joseph: Well, my dad died at the peak, if you look historically, of the deaths in New York. I hope it never gets close to that again. It was not just new for me; it was new for us in New York—it was new for us as a country—in figuring out how to think about these things. Everything's up in the air in a pandemic. What's happening four weeks from now, we still don't know. We only learned two days ago what the mayor of New York City's planning to be able to choose as options for schools this fall. But we still don't even know which of the options our individual schools are going to select for my kids, nor once they do that, which days they're going and where the overlap is between them. And we know any of that can change.

The only constant now is change. The ability to plan for the future gives comfort and gives solace to someone like myself, but I recognize that we can't rely on that anymore. We still can make plans, but we have to know that they can change and we have to look for stability where we can for as much a period as we can. Back then, it felt like, okay, how long can we hold our breath?

Once it became clear that there wasn't a vast opening up and we couldn't go back to planning things again, what's changed for me and what's helped me understand, is that I just need to plan for things not being constant and not look for comfort in that, not rely on that. I have to be more agile. I have to keep sharing with others that we're still figuring this out publicly. We're going to figure this out, but we're only by doing it together. What becomes clear might not be what we want, but we're still going to be able to figure out what we need to survive and perhaps even thrive.

Q: So it seems to me that you haven't given up completely on the idea of planning. What you're describing is a sort of process-focused approach to planning, right? So the process has certain dynamics, which include being flexible or being aware that things might change at the last moment. But it seems like you still have some sort of structure for yourself for projecting into the future. Am I putting words into your mouth?

Joseph: No, that's true. I mean, so professionally at work, I'm thinking about my Girl Scout troops during the next troop year, right? For my kids, I'm trying to figure out their camp over the summer.

And then, once summer camp ends, there's what we are planning for school. What happens that second week of September? And it is just a black box in there. We have no idea. No idea what school will look like. No idea what we should do. So for example, we left town for all of June. My wife and I are both fortunate enough to have jobs and be able to work from home. Both of my kids were at school, but weren't going in person. Sporting activities, my Girl Scout troop I lead—all closed. There was no reason for us to physically be here anymore.

So if school was closed in September and my wife and I were still both fortunate enough to be working, should we stay here? Is it safer to go somewhere else? Would we be healthier somewhere else? So while we don't know what will happen that second week in September, what we do know more and what we have clarity about that I can rely on is knowing what some of the options are. So we went away in June. We were able to find a place that we could afford.

Q: Where did you go?

Joseph: We went to the Catskills...

Catskills Diary

June 4[23]

Today was the first full day renting for most of a month in the Catskills, in a house on a hill overlooking a lake. What did I notice today? I heard more boats pass than cars. I danced around the many rooms, and couldn't stop myself. At dinner we had things to share with each other, things we had experienced during the day that the others had not. Did not hear the sound of ambulances all day. All of these things are in contrast to how it felt just a few days ago back in Forest HIlls.

June 6

This is like getting an extra month of summer. We still have to work and attend school but between and around them the activities of sun and water and trees. Didn't know this was possible.

June 7

I see the masks piled on the piano. I haven't worn one since we arrived.

June 9

There is a disconnect between how bucolic everything is in our surroundings and the social isolation, depression, and terror we are each carrying with us.

---

[23] I tried in June to keep a diary to capture that transition from extreme social isolation in NYC to a month in an enormous lake side house in the middle of nowhere. It only lasted a few days.

June 10

Being by nature and being outside without fear is what Noemi and I need—and are loving it—but seems to have little impact on the kids. Miri needs activities and peer social contact. No clue what Akiva needs.

Facebook Post: Juneteenth

So today is Juneteeth, and Girl Scouts decided a few days ago to give us all the day off "to continue educating ourselves and challenging our perspectives, and to take time for self-care [and] to thoughtfully contemplate this day's significance". Got the self-care covered—after breakfast I got in a kayak to paddle around the private lake we're at right now, giving me ample space to contemplate what I can do as a white ethnic male to recognize the significance of both this day in American history and this moment in time.

I'm fairly certain there's no one of color living on this lake (some land ownership here goes back to the 1930s), and probably no other Jews, but I imagined if I saw someone who was black I would want to say "Happy Juneteenth". I imagine them replying, "Are you saying that just to me or to white people as well." And then I thought—Ah! That's what I can do today. Greet at least five white people with "Happy Juneteenth." The idea felt terrifying, so I knew it was in the right direction.

1. A boat slowly approached me. They said hello. I said hello. They said, "Beautiful Day" and I said, "Couldn't be better." And as they passed I said, "Have a nice Juneteenth." She sounded delighted, like I'd just given her an ice cream cone. "Yes," she replied. "You too!"

I realized 1. it made more sense coming from me as a closer, not as an opening greeting, 2. I should connect with people first and 3. I should make certain there was time for them to respond (as much as I felt like just saying it then running away).

2. I paddled past a man working on his 5 foot long sandy beach. I complimented him on the beach. He complained about the

goose poop. "Have a nice Juneteenth," I said. He laughed, the kind where you have no idea what someone just said, but it might have been funny, so laughing will be a universally accepted response.

I realized saying something amongst only white people felt like popping a bubble, a thin bubble, but formed through silent consent. Raising the issue—"Hey, wanna talk about racism?"—was establishing anti-racism as the norm, or at least my norm, and inviting them in—and giving them a chance to respond (this made me feel vulnerable, which I think is part of the point of why I did it).

3. There were two paddleboarders, an adult man and his mom. "Hello Neighbor," he greeted me, thinking he'd forgotten my name (we'd never met before). We paddled together for a while, talking about a felled tree, freshwater otters, the sky. A few minutes later I left them, saying, "Have a good Juneteenth." "Yes," he exclaimed, as if he'd been trying to remember something. "Have a nice Juneteenth," he said back (it was great to hear it!) and, to his mom: "I'm off work today. Freedom!"

4. A man passed me on a rowboat, looking for another rowboat I had seen 10 minutes earlier. He told me he was looking for me, to buy that outboard motor. I told him he must be thinking of someone else. I tried to keep up and we talked about his son entering college this Fall, about his family owning their lake property since the 1930, about where I worked. When it was time for me to leave the lake, I said, "Happy Juneteenth." He said nothing. Was he confused? Did he disagree? Or did he just not hear me (when I told him I worked at Girl Scouts he had shouted back, "You're in lumber?"). I decided not to repeat myself.

5. In town at the grocery store, after checking out, I grabbed my bags and said, "Have a nice Juneteenth," and headed to the door. The employee responded with a knee-jerk, "Thanks," as

> if assuming I had said the expected "Have a nice day." A few moments later, as it sunk in, as I was almost at the door, she raised her voice to call after me, emphatically, "You too!"

I did it a few more times as well. I always had to be intentional about it, figure out how to slip it in, how to not feel so awkward or just ignore when it did, and to just do it anyway. I might try it again next year.

Then I got back to the house and watched the movie *Blindspotting*.

Interview: COVID-19 Oral History Project

… Q: I was up there a week ago, close to Roscoe.

Joseph: That's where I was! Close to Roscoe. Tennanah Lake. Ten minutes south of the town. We've never done anything like that before. We don't spend that kind of money. We don't have that kind of money, usually. We never go away for that long. And if we do go away it is only for vacation. This time we were away but not on vacation. We were working. The kids were in school. Yet we were somewhere else. This is like a whole new way of being. I can talk about that separately, but we were so fortunate to get to do that and it felt incredible.

Again, while I don't know what will happen in September, I do have a better sense now of what our family needs and what options we can trigger based on what happens in society and what society provides us.

Oh, I had been telling you earlier about starting to see our friends. Right after we got back from the Catskills we went north of the city to a park. And that felt great, just to go out to a park. We had been doing that—just places to go where we were away from folks. And I realized our friends lived nearby, the Biens. We called them and they came by. So that was our first social distanced get-together. The four of them sat over there, the four of us sat over here, and we talked. I brought some games that we could do socially distanced, so we had a structure for the interaction that would keep us apart, but still connected.

Q: Were all of you with your kids?

Joseph: Yeah, with the kids. So two adults and two kids in each family, same ages. And that was good.

Then, the week after that, our friend had a birthday party on Randall's Island. There's so much space there. It's amazing. One of the baseball fields we had, so everyone had their own circle and everyone would sit in their circle and do their thing. And the kids would run off and play, and they'd do social distanced stuff like water guns and they did some LARPing, some live action roleplaying with, you know, cardboard swords and what not. So the swords would hit each other. And that was a little bit uncomfortable. We're like, What's okay here? What's not? But the kids pretty much kept their distance. It worked...

JULY 2020

Back to NYC… a park revived… returning to stores… July 4th camping… BLM… kindness pebbles… the Columbia COVID Oral History Project…

Interview: COVID-19 Oral History Project

... Joseph: Now that we're back from the Catskills, the city's totally different. So from May to July, the park next door to me closed for at least two months. It opened up again. So suddenly, people were out. The ice cream trucks were out. I felt more comfortable going to stores. When I was up by Roscoe, I was going to stores to go shopping for food. And we're talking now like "maybe tomorrow night we're going to get takeout for the first time. So what's the restaurant going to be? Where are we going to go? What does everyone want? Maybe we won't, but maybe we will. Maybe I'll get a bagel in the morning." I'm starting to get ready for that.

Many days this week, I've gone shopping at the supermarket and bought things. That didn't feel possible in May. Or if it did, it was such a fraught experience. So that's changed a lot. In that context, getting together with folks socially feels more doable.

We went camping on July 4th. When the pandemic hit, it was like one thing after another was canceled. The things that are important rituals in our family—like the end of the school year and everyone getting together in the park afterwards—those things were all canceled. Well, for the last nine years, we've gone camping at the same campgrounds. And not just ourselves. It's with our neighborhood. We had thirty-one people last year camping together. It's all kids who are the same age. They all go to school together and they just take over the campground. It's amazing.

We didn't even know if the campground would open up this year. And then a month in advance, the state park said they were going to be open. So everyone was like, what are we going to do? Do we want to go? What would it mean for us to be there? What would each family need? Because we each have our own needs. We weren't looking to be part of each other's pods, so we had to have a socially distanced weekend together.

I wouldn't say most, but many of the families didn't come. In the end, there were twenty-one people who came across five or six different campsites. We hiked, we went swimming, and we kept our distance from each other. And there were times the kids were a bit too close in ways that I would have never been accepting of back in May or April. But now, it felt like maybe that's okay. And we would hike and keep our distance from each other.

Things have changed tremendously, but we're still evaluating daily. Every two days, I go to the websites where I track the infection rates in New York City. What are the death rates in New York City? What are the instances of people who are testing positive? And tracking them and watching them and seeing if they're going to go up. I don't want to pretend that things are fine, as I look outside, I look at the numbers, and know that the figures can be off a week or two.

Q: It's so interesting to think about the potential transformation that might come about as a result of this. I've been talking about it with people in all kinds of environments. In hospitals, things transformed in ways that people never expected they would. In prisons, in homeless shelters, everywhere. What's your perspective on that? Do you think that people really will hold onto the sense that things can transform, that it's possible to make change? Or do you think that we'll slip back into where we were before and just assume that structures are unmovable?

Joseph: We will always slip back into structures and think they're unmovable. We'll change some things and that'll be great, and then we'll forget that they were ever changed, and then we'll say, "There can't be any change." It'll be a continuous struggle. It'll never end, but this time period is not only impacting so many people unequally; it's also helping to raise awareness around it, and more importantly, getting people to want to act to change things in a systemic way.

Whether it's something within my tradition—you know, changing rituals and practices around mourning—or whether it's thinking about how to provide access to healthcare in our country, and tying that access to peoples' jobs when jobs are the things that threaten people and force people to choose between, "Do I want to risk getting sick because that's the only way I can be covered if I do get sick?" or, "Do I want to lose my job?"—those are not the options that a fair and equitable society might want to provide its citizens.

The tremendous interest in the Black Lives Matter movement in the last few weeks is part of the increased awareness of the gross racial and economic inequalities in the country that the pandemic brought to the forefront of our attention. Anyone who has been isolating is making decisions about, "Do I have Amazon deliver things to me? Do I choose to go out to the store, and who are these people who have to be in the store, versus me when I don't have to work there? Do I have food delivered and what does it mean for the delivery person?"

People have been forced to think about the economic privilege that many of us have, and people who do not have those privileges. We're seeing the data now from *The New York Times* in these last few days about the racial disparities and the impact of those who are being impacted by the pandemic—both who have been affected by it and who's been dying from it. The numbers are clearly aligned with who has the resources to isolate themselves and who has not. Every day, the decisions we're making about our lives, to keep ourselves and our families safe, have forced us to look at the inherent economic inequality and are raising awareness about it. This is very much an economic pandemic.

I think that's part of why not only the African-American community took to the streets recently around the Black Lives Matter movement, and why support for that has increased in ways we've never seen before. I would hope, as we continue to learn more about the economic impact, we keep reflecting on ourselves and our privileges as we're making decisions to keep ourselves safe—and recognize those who don't have the freedom to make the same decisions—and use this as a catalyst for change. Some of the things we're learning now will help impact what we're doing afterwards.

Q: I'm curious and wondering how old are your kids? And also, just wondering whether everyone in your family is onboard and approaching this in the same way, or if you've all gone through different processes of accepting the change and coming into this new, unstructured sort of structure.

Joseph: My son's fourteen and my daughter's eleven. I don't want to speak for them too much, but what I can share is my daughter, right now, is going to camp. They both had sleep-away camp that was canceled this summer. But my daughter was going to go to day camp before sleep-away camp. That day camp ran school programs this spring for the children of essential workers. They developed their own best practices for safety for managing it, and were able to do that successfully.

When they told us that they weren't closing the day camp this summer, but were going to adapt those practices and do a different version of what they've done in the past, we were hopeful, emotionally. But psychologically or intellectually, we thought, well that still sounds crazy, especially the way it was last April. But we were open to the idea and as it got closer to it, we realized that that's what our daughter needs. She needs to get out of the house. She's been with us every single day since March. March, April, May, June. She's super social. She needs to be with her friends. She's super physical. She needs space to move around. And camp would provide that and do it in a safe way.

And again, it's unlike anything I've seen before or experienced myself. It's small pods that are locked in with their counselors and interact with other campers and other counselors and such. She started that this week. Meanwhile, my son—he'd be happy if it stayed just like this. He's totally fine being at home, being on his computer, watching YouTube, playing video games, coding, doing STEM activities remotely, doing roleplaying games with people, running them from around the country. He's having a totally different experience than the rest of us in the family.

Q: Interesting. Have you found that your relationships with them have changed? And you can also talk about your friendships and in what ways they have changed or not changed.

Joseph: Well, I feel very fortunate with my family. We're very close and we have good communication skills, and even with all this stress, I think it's gone remarkably well. It's very hard to work in a very small space with all of us around each other, but we figure out how to make it work, and I think it's strengthened our relationship and I think we can get through challenges like this. It makes us feel good and it makes us feel resilient.

I hate being around my kids while I'm working and not being able to give them attention. That just doesn't feel right. And you know, work has been very supportive and people have been amazing as an institution—really giving the people the space they need. It's amazing being in a phone call and hearing someone in the background yell, "Tommy, put your pants on!" It's fun. However at the end of the day, it's hard to be able to focus deeply and still be really present with the needs that are around us. That's part of the reason I'm happy my daughter's at camp. She's around adults who can give her their full attention. But aside from that, it's been great being together. I love being with them and we're good together.

Joseph: I described earlier how isolating everything was during the first few months—the park being closed, how I was isolated with my family.

But now, the park's open. There aren't groups of people playing basketball, but there are individuals who are going out and doing exercises and shooting hoops. There are parents taking kids on the playground, which I'm still nervous about. I don't think I would do that. But there aren't mobs doing it.

What's been really meaningful for me has been, as I drop my daughter off on the bus for camp each morning, I take a walk around the park, and somebody has been using colorful chalk to leave messages. They're really beautifully designed, so they're not just someone writing. They look really nice. This one was, "Mask up" and the "u" is an arrow zooming up, and the mask is in red and the "up" is in green. It's really beautiful handwriting, so it just looks really nice. It's just a reminder to put your mask up.

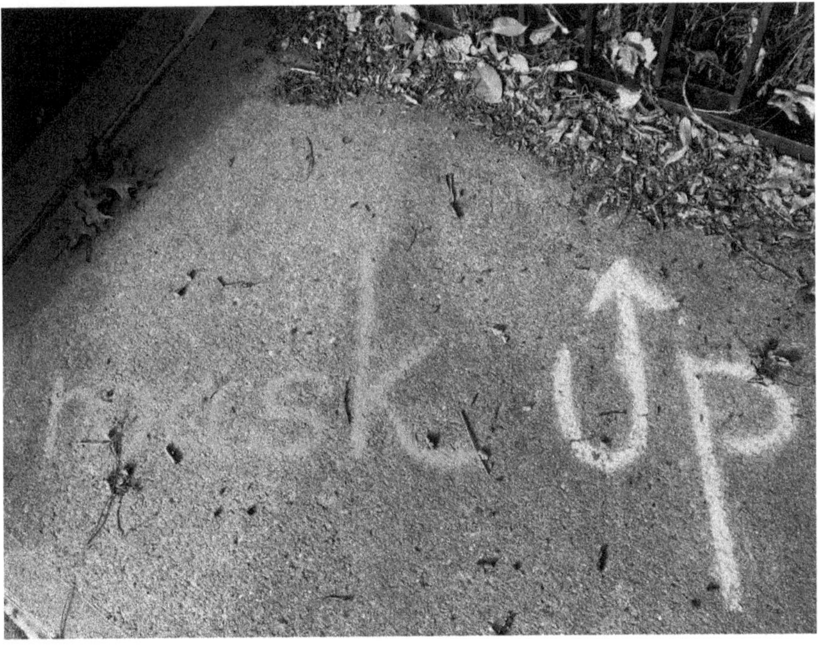

There are messages like that all the way throughout. And then today, I think someone calls them kindness rocks or kindness pebbles. I'm looking at a photo of them now. There are probably two-dozen pebbles. Let me zoom in and see if I can read you some.

One says, "Lift others up." One says, "Rise above." One says, "Look, see, feel, sigh." One says, "Mermaid grotto." And one rock has a little fish on it and it says, "Safe harbor." Another one says, "Masks are all we have." Another one looks like a bee and says "B-E-E safe." Another one says, "New York loving" and next to it, the next rock says, "United." And another one's all about Forest Hills. It says, "Forest Hills pride" and it has a gay pride flag on it. It just goes on and on and on. It's these really thoughtful things that they put on these rocks, and they made this little garden where you can go across and look at these three rows of them.

That's quite a change from a park that was closed. Someone turned it into an art gallery to share beautiful, caring messages to strangers who are walking by.

Q: It's almost 4:30 pm, so I don't want to take up too much more of your time. Our plan is to interview every narrator three times over the course of a year. So if it's okay with you, I'll check back in with you in three or four months. We'll see where things have gone. Hopefully somewhere good. We'll see about that. But before I end this, I just want to give you a chance to answer any questions you might have for me or to say anything that you think is important to say that we didn't talk about.

Joseph: I wonder who you are, why you're doing this, what the plans are.

Q: I'm a sociologist. In early March, I had a conversation with one of my colleagues about what was happening with the pandemic. We could see it coming, both of us, and he specializes in disaster management. He's been studying that for a long time. He studied 9/11. We're also pretty good friends, and we were both fascinated by how peoples' perceptions were transforming very quickly. I mean, hour by hour in early March. We wanted to find a way of witnessing it and registering it.

My work as a sociologist has been mostly ethnographic and it has been about completely different things. So I do work on accessibility to public space in the city, and I've done a lot of work on social movements and on artists as well. Very different from this. But we combined my experience with qualitative research and his expertise in disaster management, and then got together with two oral historians who run the Center for Oral History at Columbia and who had been very involved in an oral history archive that was built after 9/11. So they had a lot of experience as well.

And we started the archive. What we're doing, basically, is we're building an archive with 200 narrators, unless we get more funding. But we have enough funding to interview 200 people three times over the course of a year. And we're also gathering diary entries and conducting a survey. There's a quantitative component to it. Within, I think in a year-and-a-half, the archive will become public and it'll be held at the Columbia library, but anyone can have access to it.

Joseph: And did you get the funding once you came up with the idea, or did you already have funding from another project?

Q: No, we started out without funding. But the National Science Foundation put out a call for proposals for rapid-response grants. Within three days, they responded positively. I don't think we would have been able to do it without that. So we're really grateful for that. And we're looking for more funding now. It got big very quickly. We have thirty interviewers doing this work, so there are a lot of people out in the field and a lot of connections to community organizations. It's amazing. It's a privilege to be a part of the project.

Joseph: What has it meant for you during this time as you've been dealing with it, being able to have this project to work on?

Q: It was incredible, especially at the beginning when we were quarantining. I mean, we still are. But at the beginning, it was very, very difficult for me to be home all the time because I'm a very social person and I like to go out all the time. I live with my son, who's fifteen. And so to be able to meet new people and talk to them and to have their perspectives on what was happening in different parts of the city was just amazing.

Maybe three weeks ago, I took some time off because I had been interviewing a lot of nurses and it's hard, emotionally. I felt like I needed a break. Also, I just needed a break from nonstop work. I also teach and have other research projects going. So yeah, you're the first person I've interviewed after my two-week break. It's very nice to be back.

Joseph: Well, you did a beautiful job and made me feel very safe and gave me space to share and drew me out. You clearly had done the research, so I felt like you were listening to me and knew how to bring out the larger issues—not just about me, but about me as an example of someone living during this time. So thank you.

Q: You're welcome, and thank you for your perspective. You seem to know what people need. For me, that's the underlying theme in this interview. Also with the Cameo thing, which I didn't know about. It seems like you understand well what people need emotionally during this time, including your father, obviously.

Joseph: I remembered a crazy story that I didn't share. You want one more story or do you want to save it for next time?

Q: Sure. I have no limit for listening to stories.

Joseph: All right. You asked me about after doing what I did to mourn my dad and sharing about it publicly, if I found other people having similar experiences and needs. What ended up happening was—gosh, I didn't even think about Cameo. It's all connected. Celebrities,

Black Lives Matter, and mourning during the pandemic—it all came together.

I watched *The Wire* a few years ago. I commute an hour to the city and back, so I can watch stuff on my phone. I watched *The Wire.* All five seasons over a few months commuting back and forth many years ago. And I love it. You're a sociologist. You know why I love it. And my wife hadn't seen it, so we started watching it last year, but we never finished Season Five. We just binged Seasons One through Four, then watched other stuff. And then during the pandemic, we were like, "All right, fine. Let's finish it." So I think at the end of March, we started watching the fifth season, and we finished it.

My dad dies, we have the *shiva*, I write about it, and two weeks later, someone on Facebook who I worked with twenty-two years ago and have had no contact with saw the piece on Facebook and said there's someone who wants to talk to me. I won't name him, but he's one of the major actors from *The Wire*. And I said, "Why do you want to talk to me?" He said, "Well, George Floyd's funeral's coming up" and he wants to figure out tomorrow, online, how to bring people together to support each other and experience the funeral together as a way to connect during this time. The protests had just started. They really hadn't gotten big yet. They didn't really start having the impact at a policy level.

Remember how I told you that I had left New York in June? It's the evening I arrive there at the new house we'll be spending in for a month. We're unpacking and I'm Zooming with this guy. I can say he was one of the police officers. He's a Black man and is looking to connect with his community. I didn't know what that meant or who they were. He wanted to connect with them the next day to do this event. He said he wanted to do what I did with my dad for the funeral. And he knew nothing about how to use Zoom and do online things. So the next day, my friend who led the funeral and led the *shiva* process—we got on the phone for a half-hour to find out what he's really looking for. And when does it really make sense to hold it.

It turned out that the event would be that Monday. And there were many funerals and many memorials for George Floyd. So he would do the one on Monday, and we helped him understand what he needed to know to do it and the money and the time and how many people he would need and what kind of resources those people would need to have. He said, "Well, can I hire you?"

After we did what we did, my friend thought we should write up whatever people know so they can do it for themselves. Another friend—the one who left town—thought that I should make a business doing it; there was clearly a need and there were profit and non-profit ways to make it move forward. But where my life was at, I couldn't pursue either.

We were like, "Thank you for offering, but we can't." We told him what he needed to do, and he found what he needed. He found some people in his theatre community or dance community—his artistic community—and he invited me to join them. During the memorial, I went for the first hour. There were over 100 people from all over the world.

There were some technical issues. There always are. But he was able to use Zoom to connect with the community, and different people performed or wrote poems or sang songs and he gave opportunities for people of all backgrounds to talk about what the killing had meant for them—as an African-American woman, as a Black man, as a white woman. They mostly all knew each other. I was, because I helped them out, invited into their space to ritualize using virtual tools to collectively mourn not only George Floyd, but the recent violence against the Black community. This all came about because I knew *The Wire*. I had just watched it. Because of the killing of George Floyd. And because of my writing about how we approached my dad's ritualized mourning. It was this unbelievable combination of them all coming together. I was just blown away by the whole experience.

Also, you should know, I have not been keeping a diary. I took notes the entire time my dad was in the hospital, but not since then.

Q: The way the archive is going to work—each narrator is going to have a folder. So, for example, in your folder will be the interviews with you, the transcript of the interview, which we're going to share with you. You'll have a chance to look at it and fix any errors. If you share things with the Chronicles site, that will also be in the same folder. And before we make the archive public, we're going to send you all of the material and you can, at that point, also decide what to include, what not to include. You have a choice.

Joseph: All right, thank you, Denise. I'll consider it. Thank you for doing what you're doing. Thank you for choosing me to participate. It's an honor to get to represent whatever demographic I'm representing or voice I'm representing. And be well.

I look forward to talking to you the next time it comes around.

[END OF INTERVIEW]

PART 2

THE SEASON OF BLUR

JULY 2020

In which a diary begins… lawns are visited… beaches elude access… hugs are denied… blinds are repaired… ice cream is desired…

COVID-19 Oral History Project: January 2021

The Reminiscences of
Barry Joseph

Columbia Center for Oral History
Columbia University
2021

The following oral history is the result of a recorded interview with Barry Joseph conducted by Denise Milstein on January 15, 2021. This interview is part of the COVID-19 Oral History Project.

The reader is asked to bear in mind that s/he is reading a verbatim transcript of the spoken word, rather than written prose.

Q: Okay, so let me just briefly introduce us again. I'm Denise Milstein, and today is January 15, Friday afternoon, pretty grey winter day, and I'm in Harlem, in New York City. Can you say your name and where you are?

Joseph: I'm Barry Joseph. I'm in the same location as I was during the first interview six months ago. I'm here in Forest Hills, in Queens, under the same dreary skies as you, Denise.

Q: Okay, great. Well, thank you so much, again, for participating in this. I think it's worth maybe prefacing this interview by saying that there's an extensive archive of chronicles that you've written that whoever listens to or watches or reads this interview has access to, and so I just want to point to that. It will probably be complementary to whatever we talk about over the course of this interview.

Joseph: Just to add, I started writing it after our first interview. I hadn't been doing it before. As you know, I had earlier put in materials that I already had, which were my notes from when my dad was in the hospital for two weeks, then blog posts that I also made as well, Facebook posts, and pieces I wrote for the *Forward*. But then once we spoke the first time in July, for the interview, that inspired me to start doing a daily diary, actually, right here, at this desk, where I'm sitting now.

A daily hand-written diary, in fact. This is what it looks like.

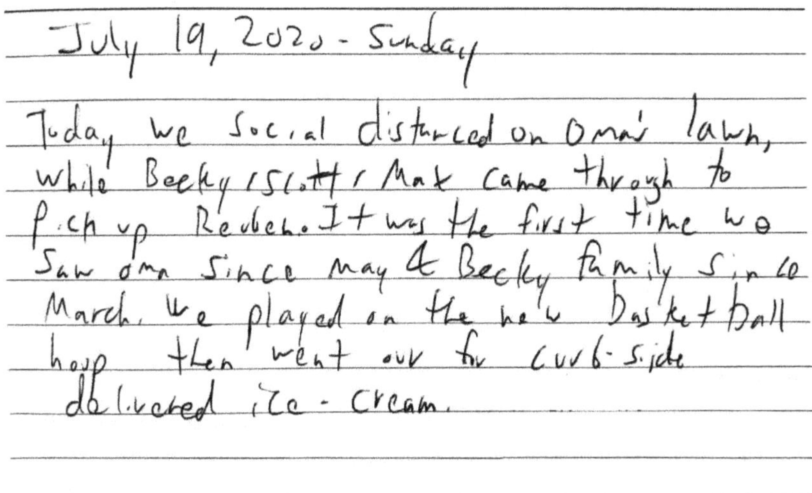

July 19, 2020 - Sunday

Today we social distanced on Oma's lawn, while Becky, Scott, Max came through to pick up Reuben. It was the first time we saw Oma since May & Becky family since March. We played on the new basket ball hoop then went out for curb-side delivered ice-cream.

Q: Oh, so we can see what it actually looks like, the real thing.

Joseph: Yes, I would try and write like a paragraph or two, every day. Not too much, because it's too much to write and too much for someone to read. But sometimes it would take a whole page.

Q: Okay, well that's great. So we can't really assume that whoever is listening has read all the entries, and so in spite of the fact that I've read them, I think some things are worth telling even if both of us know a lot of what's happened in your life over the past few months. I guess the first question I would ask you, just to start off, is how have you been since we last spoke? More or less? It's been quite a long time.

Joseph: It was July, so that's six months ago...

Daily Diary Entries

July 19, Sunday

Today we social distanced on Oma's lawn[24], while Becky[25], Scott, and Max came through to pick up Reuben (who had been grandma-camping all week). It was the first time we saw Oma since May (two months), and Becky's family since March (four months). We played a little on the new pandemic-motivated basketball hoop on Oma's garage then went out after for curb-side delivered ice-cream.

[24] That lawn is in New Rochelle, in the suburbs just north of New York City.

[25] Becky is Noemi's sister and lives in Philly with Scott, her husband, and her two children, Max and Reuben.

July 20, Monday

Today was in the mid-90s. Trump is threatening to send unwanted federal forces into liberal cities like Chicago, Detroit, and NYC. Miri has baseball practice tomorrow, then soccer Friday and Sunday... after 5 months of nobody having plans for anything, ever.

July 21, Tuesday

Every day to work I wear no socks or shoes, a t-shirt, and a weekly pair of cargo shorts.

July 22, Wednesday

Tomorrow we have to decide if Miri will drop softball, join travelling soccer for the year, and plan for full contact/no mask games starting in September. It's the risk of infection versus only one day of school turning her into a lumpy, depressed potato. Soccer appears here to have the advantage.

July 23, Thursday

Today I went into the supermarket. 2nd time in five months. Or in two weeks. Same thing. It was the start of the day so they were mostly empty. I need to plan my lunches better now. I need to stop waiting to return to eating out for lunch, for at least a year.

July 24, Friday

For Akiva's constitutional, we jogged into town down 110th Street, got rolled ice cream, and ate it unmasked in McDonald Park. Strange days indeed. At Shabbat dinner, over FaceTime, Deb said she figured out taking time off from work, getting a COVID test from her doctor, and someone to watch her cat so she can join us on vacation next month. Only then she can do the one thing she's thought about since Dad died—hugging me.

July 25, Saturday

We spent the day on the beach in the ocean, something I wasn't sure we'd get to do this year, especially as our regular Long Island beaches won't allow us city dwellers. Noemi found a beach an hour's drive away on the south east corner of Staten Island. What a hidden gem! Tons of space on both the sand and in the water from other people, on a 90 degree sunny day. What a miracle. And Paul[26] came out to join us—1st time I've seen him in person since February, but feels like not that long since we Zoom every week or two. So weird. And it sucked not getting to hug him.

July 26, Sunday

It was crazy—a 90 degree day and we couldn't figure out how to get out of the apt. City park's mostly closed. NJ beaches now require limited passes purchased on an app the day before, and usually not available. Long Beach on Long Island not letting non-residents come on weekends. Connecticut lakes just reopened—but not for us. Ended up back on Staten Island… and loving it! And ice cream curbside at Egger's. Yum!

---

[26] A best-friend from high school, a real estate agent who lives in Brooklyn with his moss.

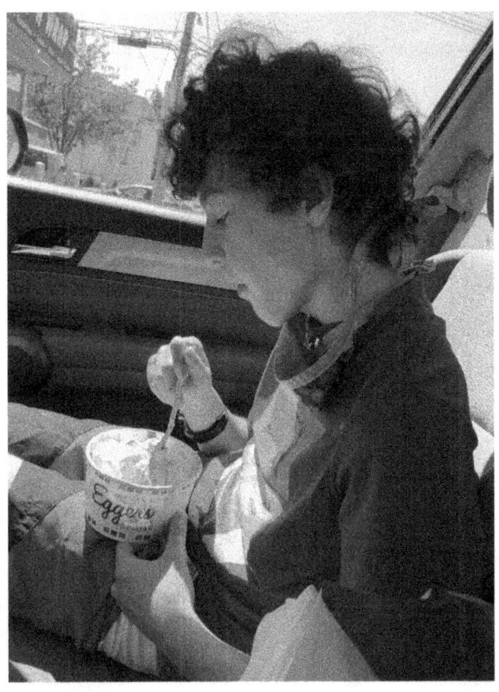

July 27, Monday

Today I left the city. Last Saturday, by a fluke of luck, we drove past Blinds To Go. That morning I'd removed our broken bedroom blinds with hope I could bring it in for repairs and had left it in the car. This morning, now two days later, at a Long Island location, they had it ready for pick up. Insanely fast. The door at the store warned masks would be provided if you weren't wearing one. That we should use hand sanitizer. That we are not to wander the store without a salesperson (all of whom kept their distance and wore masks). After putting the new blinds in the trunk I drove next door to the gas station, where my credit card got stuck in the machine. Neither of the men who worked there wore masks, nor gloves (which I wore to pump gas), and did not keep their distance. Once fixed, I pumped the gas, tossed out the gloves, and drove home. The repaired blinds brought order back to our bedroom, which came as a relief.

July 28, Tuesday

The stats, say Bridgette[27] in Boise, are that if you are in a group of 25 people your likelihood of being around someone infected is 77%. For us here in NYC it's only 13%. What the hell is going on? She blames libertarians politicizing masks.

July 29, Wednesday

I worked for two hours today sitting in the park across the street. I've been in the park for an hour or so a few times this month, but the ice cream truck ONLY comes when I am upstairs and I can't do anything about it. He came today and I was prepared—I had my wallet. On line, six feet between people in front and behind me, I strained to watch the ice cream man prepare and serve ice cream. If he was infected, what was he doing with his hands that might pass it on? And what would I do once I received it to keep myself safe? A cup was out, as I didn't bring my own spoon. Could I figure out a way to hold a cone he might have touched? If I got sick from eating ice cream how could I face my kids? Before it was my turn I abandoned the line, went back to work in the park, and cried, not for the loss of ice cream but the loss of a level of normalcy I'd hoped was in reach.

July 30, Thursday

Moved the furniture in our bedroom to install a tiny desk, as a spillover from the dining room or quiet room. It's time to start setting up the apartment—after 4 months home—to double as our office for the next year.

Akiva and I took a break and walked into town with what turned out to be $127 in loose change to deposit in our bank. When we

[27] A best friend from college.

got home I learned it had been closed for three weeks and had just opened this very day.

July 31, Friday

I planned better this time. After work I was reading in the park when I heard the sing-song call. He was wearing both mask and gloves and I watched him put a napkin around the cone then fill it with vanilla soft-serve. The ice cream touched nothing besides the top of cone and air. That I could risk. I received the cone with my left hand, reserving my right as a clean hand, and held my book and glasses in a bag so they remained untouched. I ate the ice cream top down and avoided the cone—no licking around as it melted—and sucked the last bits up and out, throwing out the empty cone. It was so cold. So sweet.

AUGUST 2020

In which Catskills homes come and go... firing decisions are delayed... COVID results are returned... New York is escaped... Debby gets hugged... kayaks are adored... Conventions are watched... the Delaware river is tubed... an offer is made...

Daily Diary Entries

August 1, Saturday

We went to Rye Beach north of the city on the Long Island Sound and rented kayaks with Andy[28] and Paul. Seemed like a perfect social distancing activity as we could talk on the water. It worked great, and the weather was beautiful. We had seen Paul last Sunday at the Staten Island beach, but this was the first time since the pandemic arrived seeing Andy in person. Which was crazy, as we talk to him over Zoom most weeks and it seemed so unlikely to have been that long in person. Kayaking was a great way to be together to chat but still far apart. Paul tried to convince us to try to buy the Catskills house from June[29]. Then we ordered take-out and found a park with a gazebo so we could eat together.

[28] Another best friend from high school. Like Paul, also lives in Brooklyn, sans moss.

[29] The place we stayed in June had just been put on the market.

August 2, Sunday

Woah. We never imagined ourselves as people who would want to own a weekend home nor could financially afford it. But we are so in love with our June rental on Lake Tennanah, and with the inheritance from my dad, we can now seriously consider it. It's blowing our minds. That seems crazy to make such a major financial decision during a pandemic, but also feels a bit crazy to let something so special get away.

August 3, Monday

The school bus is driving me nuts. We couldn't be more proud about Akiva getting ready to attend Bronx Science. But we need this private bus to get him there. And they're not thinking this through. Once we learned in-person schooling will be an expected two days a week, they refused to change their fees, still set for five days a week. It might still be worth paying for it. Then they said if we ever want to cancel, we have to do it by this Friday; afterwards we will not get our money back. That means if the city cancels in person later, after September 1st let's say, we won't get any back. They're putting all the risk on us, forcing us to cancel now and fend for ourselves.

August 4, Tuesday

I can't believe how fast and easy it has been to move forward with buying—or making an offer on—the lake house. I never imagined doing such a thing! Space, and place, is so different now. We love Forest Hills, and don't want to leave, but this investment option feels like a pressure valve. And a godsend.

August 5, Wednesday

Millions woke yesterday with no power or internet in New York City due to that crazy tropical storm. We were lucky. No problems at all. Then, after living here for a dozen years, Noemi got out some cutters to tidy up removed stray wires around the apartment. Including our current cable. Which is also our internet. Luckily our amazing super came by with some coaxial cables and fixed it, the fourth person not in our family to enter our apartment in 6 months. Masks on, of course, and I disinfected all he touched afterwards. Then, internet returned, we started our work day with only one hour delay.

The internet is the air we breathe.

August 6, Thursday

Today Noemi was in town and went to the ATM to get me some cash because I ran out. The $200 in my wallet I had used up was from the second week of March. That's how little cash I used in 5 months. I used to go to the ATM every other week.

And today, for the second time, work pushed back the deciding which of the one third of us they will let go.

Email: Queens United Soccer Club Summer Practice

From: Queensborough United S.C.
Subject: QUSC THUNDER THURSDAY SUMMER PRACTICE 8/6/20 5:30pm-6:30pm
Date: August 6, 2020 at 12:47:14 AM EDT
To: Noemi Altman and Barry Joseph

Hi QUSC Thunder,

I hope you are all having a great week. Practice for today is from: 5:30pm-6:30pm at Field 14 Meadow Lake Road West, Forest Hills, NY, 11375.

PLEASE TAKE 5 MINUTES TO READ THIS IMPORTANT PART OF THE EMAIL

We hope you're all having a great summer. We are writing to inform you that as NYC is in Phase 4 of reopening, US Youth Soccer and Eastern New York Soccer Association, who Govern our leagues, clubs and teams have moved to their own Phase 2 of Back to Soccer Activities.

This means under their guidance and protocols they have laid out that we are now allowed to do the following starting week of 7/27/20:

- We are now allowed the Full roster of players at practice please always text your coach if you can make these summer sessions, this will help him plan out the session accordingly.
- We are now allowed to have small sided games; Small sided games mean: 1v1 up to 4v4.

PLAYER RESPONSIBILITIES

- Check temperature before practice.
- Don't go to practice if:
    - You have experienced COVID-19 symptoms in the past 14 days.
    - You had a positive COVID-19 test in the past 14 days.
        - You have had close contact with a confirmed or suspected COVID-19 case in the past 14 days.
    - You have traveled to any of the restricted states or been in contact with someone who has been or is quarantined due to travel from the states on the NYS restricted travel list.
- Maintain social distancing when not doing physical activity.
- No celebrations, high fives, handshakes etc.
- Remain in your training group.
- Wear a mask to and from training.
- Bring your own equipment and don't share food and drinks.
- Wash hands before and after training.
- Wash and sanitize equipment before and after training.

PARENT RESPONSIBILITIES

- Check child's temperature before practice and don't attend if he/she has a fever of ≥ 100.4°F.
- Maintain social distancing while on the sidelines or stay in the car during practice.
- Avoid carpooling when possible.
- Wear a face covering when outside of the car.
- Ensure clothing is washed after every training session.
- Ensure equipment is sanitized before and after every training session.

- Notify the staff immediately if your child becomes ill.
- Ensure your child always has hand sanitizer.

COACH RESPONSIBILITIES

- Keep attendance for contact tracing purposes to include the following:
    - Name
    - Address
    - Number
    - Date
    - Start and end time of event

- Ask each player the following 4 questions
    - Have you experienced COVID-19 symptoms in the past 14 days?
    - Have you tested positive for COVID-19 in the past 14 days?
    - Have you had close contact with a confirmed or suspected COVID-19 case in the past 14 days?
    - Has your child traveled to any of the restricted states or been in contact with someone who has been or is quarantined due to travel from the states on the NYS restricted travel list?

- Send sick players home or prevent them from taking part in practice.
- Maintain appropriate group sizes for training.
- Maintain social distance and wear a mask when not directly involved in training.
- Make sure you are the only one who handles training equipment.
- Clean and sanitize training equipment before and after each use.
- Wash and sanitize pinnies every day if they are allowed to be used.

If you have any questions or concerns please contact me. If you don't yet feel comfortable sending your child to these summer sessions, we respect that decision, and the girls can work on their fitness plans I sent them a few weeks ago, at least twice a week.

Thank you,

Director of Coaching
Queensborough United SC

Daily Diary Entries

August 7, Friday

Governor Cuomo announced all schools will open this fall on schedule. No way. Teachers have no idea how to teach in a blended context. They will strike and all the principals are quitting. That means we have to keep our money with the bus company, even though they're putting 100% of the risk on us. So stupid.

August 8, Saturday

Today we took a family trip... to get a COVID-19 test. How fun. What a lot of hype—the swab was no big deal. This time next week we will learn if we are infected and if we have antibodies. Noemi asked the doctor, "So is this very reliable?" He replied: "Not at all." Wow! He said it's 80-85% accurate, and hopes by end of year will have something 95% accurate. But what more can we do? When we leave for the vacation spot this Wednesday, that's the only way we can form a bubble with Noemi's mom and my sister. Until then we will have to quarantine at home.

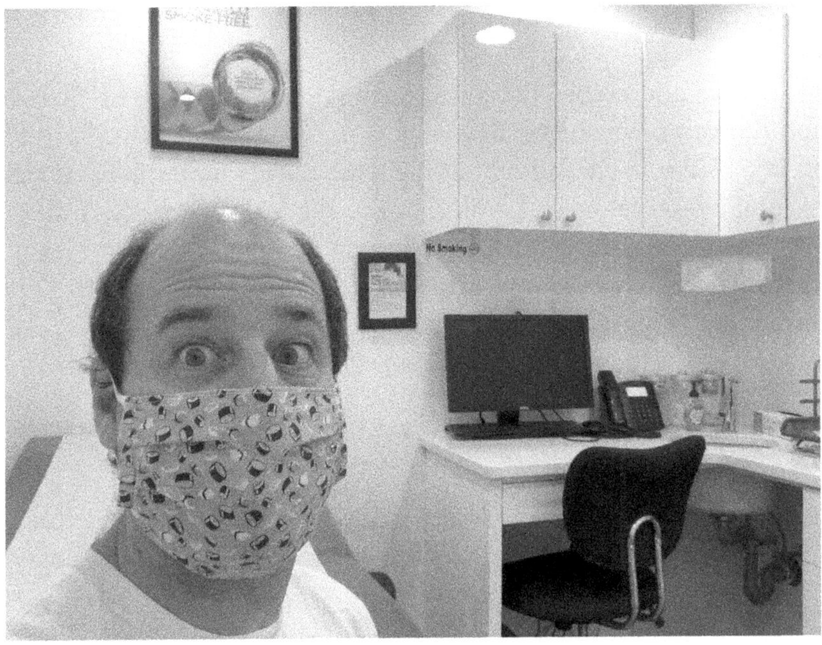

August 9, Sunday

Day 1 of quarantine until we see Oma and Debby.

A week ago we never imagined us owning a weekend home. We thought more about the lake house from June, our inheritance, and how property might not be a bad place to put money right now. Saturday the broker said we were the better buyers, and the sellers agreed. Yesterday, the broker said the other buyers made an offer the sellers couldn't refuse. Easy come, easy go. But it would have been amazing to have had a place to escape to, physically, psychologically. And how healing to have gotten to look at that lake every morning.

August 10, Monday

Our CEO unexpectedly resigned today, after being with Girl Scouts for four years. No one would say why. And our private bus company to take Akiva to the Bronx told us today there's no business model that allows them to socially distance so they're giving us back all of our money, wishing us luck, and hoping to see us next year. Noemi hasn't left the building since Saturday. Otherwise it was a mostly normal day.

August 11, Tuesday

Day 3 of quarantine. Results already back. None of us are infected. No surprise. Now we can see my sister and Noemi's mom on Saturday. No antibody results back yet, except for Miri's, who is negative.

I'm so sad today for losing the bid for the June lake home. It felt crazy and risky but something that would have been a gift to us, a source of delight we could control during a time of stress, fear, and uncertainty. We were so close to getting it, it hurts that we did not. Now it's just another thing beyond our control. But I won't let this take away my memories of being there. And the deep joy that brings.

August 12, Wednesday

The doctors called with the rest of the results. None of us has the antibodies, which comes as no surprise… except for Noemi. We are flabbergasted. We ask ourselves: How can it be? Not Miri, who just finished 5 weeks at day camp? When did it enter her system? Were there light symptoms she ignored? Was she just asymptomatic? How did she get it when living in such isolation? Was it early in February before we all needed to be afraid? And how could only one of us have it, as we couldn't be more in each other's spaces? Are her results wrong? Are our results wrong? It's all so confusing, and unexpected!

So what now? Should she be acting differently, the one among us who can be the person to go to the store, to pick up that restaurant food, to be the one who is put at risk of infection? Or does it not work that way? What are the rules of this game?

We arrived yesterday at our August home in the Sullivan Catskills (different from the June one). Such a relief to get to open a door, step outside, and not need to wear a mask.

August 13, Thursday

Today, I never wore a mask.

Today, I never wore a glove.

Today, I did not have to repeatedly wash my hands multiple times for 20 seconds because I might have touched something infected.

Today, I sat outside on the deck while I worked.

Today, after work I kayaked.

Today, we four lay outside in the dark and watched the Pleiades meteor shower overhead.

It takes days to decompress and readjust.

August 14, Friday

Tomorrow I see my sister for the first time since COVID.

It's almost unfathomable.

Unfathomable—after seeing her two to four times a month, usually for Shabbat, not seeing her for the past five months, especially after Dad's funeral.

Unfathomable—that I do actually see her, all the time, over Zoom and FaceTime, so it doesn't really feel like we've been apart for so long.

August 15, Saturday

We watched them reach the Tappan Zee Bridge on the Find Your Friends app, and the rest of their trip, then lost track, then ran out to greet them as we heard the car pull in.

Pained. That's one word to describe my sister's face when she approached me, mixed with many other emotions.

To lighten the mood, as I reached out for her, I offered "Hi, my name is Barry," to highlight the absurdity of the moment, marking the end of our longest time in our lives being apart.

We embraced and I held her while she cried, tears she'd been holding onto since my dad died in April. I burped and she laughed.

I took in her bags and then, after lunch, time being tight, we tossed the garbage in the car and deposited it at the town's waste transfer station, talking non-stop the whole way.

August 16, Sunday

Today we rescued a kayak—Hurrah!

I went into town and returned with donuts for breakfast.

We found a great farmer's market in Callicoon, by the Delaware River. Masks required, foot traffic encouraged to walk one way.

All farm tours appear to be closed due to the pandemic.

The museum at Bethel Farm, site of the 1969 Woodstock concert, is now open. No more than 25% capacity allowed in. All surfaces disinfected every night. Cafe closed. Masks required. But still, the idea of spending hours indoors at a public place... Noemi nixed that with a simple quote: "I can't risk you."

August 17, Monday

Got to go kayaking twice today! Once with Noemi all around the lake, after the rain, and once with Miri, who tried to construct her own bow and arrow (looking for "river cane" for the arrows.)

The real estate agent who made us think we'd get the Lake Tennanah house sent us new listings in the region. There's little reason to feel hopeful, but we're here a month and it's a thing to do. Saw a cute red house on a lake Noemi wanted to check out; it was filled with so many tchotchkes we couldn't see straight.

The Democratic Convention started tonight. Considering it was mostly "over Skype" and sans the convention crowd cheering, I thought it worked. It was inspiring. Great to watch with Akiva the whole time.

August 18, Tuesday

Today's eccentric archery / axe-throwing instructor[30], in a fully armed kilt, explained to us how, as an EMT, he doesn't need to wear a mask nor expected us to either. He said he saw it in the area in December and January, looking like flu, but it's been gone ever since. So there is nothing to be concerned about. Of course, we're not from this area, but, as he's the one holding throwing axes, as long as he agreed to stay far from us, nor try to touch us, and not judge our mask-wearing for

30 There was a range in a family's yard right across the street from the place we had rented for the month.

2 hours, we were happy to just get on with the lessons and try to hit the targets he provided.

We also went to the Roscoe Diner[31], which we assiduously avoided when we spent last June in this area, ordering takeout today and eating it in the town's Welcome Center benches across the street. Fried food never tasted so good.

Second Night of the DNC. Jill Biden talking in an empty classroom was both heartbreaking and so "of the moment".

August 19, Wednesday

I dreamed it was a work day after being off three days for a Jewish holiday. My schedule being off, I planned to go into the office to go

[31] World famous, or so they say.

to work. Since I had extensive leftovers planned for lunch, I needed to transport a giant oven, like those street carts that sell candied peanuts, so I took an Uber. But when I got there I realized—doh!—the pandemic. My office was still closed and now I had this oven to lug around. Seeing others on the street I realized I'd also forgotten to bring my mask. Very embarrassing. Many city streets were completely flooded—as if the current national disaster had taken a more visibly physical form, with "normally accessible" areas closed off. There was also something in the air about an increasingly oppressive police state, a memorabilia store that turned old movie posters into craft projects, and some family I was helping navigate the street. I finally bought the movie poster craft project I wanted, planned for an Uber to get back home with my lunch oven, when miraculously Noemi showed up. She found me on GPS and just wanted to be together and help me get home. Such a crazy dream!

August 20, Thursday

What a day! We went into our first cultural institution AND ate in our first restaurant.

The cultural institution is the museum on the grounds where the Woodstock concert was held. They said they disinfected it every night, and during the day multiple times where it was interactive, and limited attendance to 25% capacity. They also limited numbers in their store and bathrooms and controlled movement throughout. We went back and forth all week about whether to go, and today decided to go for it. All patrons wore masks throughout and we had no problems with people disrespecting boundaries. And we had a great time.

We planned to eat outside at a restaurant tonight, which itself is unusual for us these days. But there were no tables left. However there was one in the back, indoors. Noemi especially was unsure, but felt the pressure from the others and decided "We are sending them to school in a few weeks so…" We had no idea what to do once we sat. Masks on until food arrives or off the whole time? If off, what about giving our order, or when food arrived? There were no right answers. I tried to figure out a game where one person had to guess which one person was secretly smiling behind their mask, just to explore normalizing us six in our shared bubbles, socializing in public with masks on. Of course, once the food arrived, the masks came off.

Last night of the DNC. Biden's acceptance speech was stellar. It felt great watching it with the whole crew, including Akiva.

August 21, Friday

Yesterday our bubble went tubing down the Delaware River. The perfect socially distanced activity: no one wears masks on the river, and no one cares. And tubing is the ultimate forced relaxation. There's just nothing to do but trust the river and go with the flow. We six all held hands and took the trip as one.

August 22, Saturday

Debby returned home today. It wasn't as hard as when she arrived but it was still hard not knowing when—or exactly how—we'd see each other again. I'm hoping she can emotionally now handle getting together without hugging me, but we'll see. She certainly can't take another two weeks off in order to be with us. She wanted to start trouble—talking about her 50th birthday in late November—so I told her she can't think that far ahead. Between now and then everything can change and will.

I lost the NYU graduate student who was set to intern for me next month. I had to share with her that I can't know if I will still have my job until after the layoffs... whenever they are.

August 23, Sunday

August is going too fast! Yesterday we discovered the pristine Toronto Reservoir in Bethel. How gorgeous! This area is so magnificent. I can see why a century or so of New York Jews once turned this area into the Borscht Belt.

August 24, Monday

We found a cute river-side park west of town built around an 1880 Stone Bridge with three arches. Just to kill some time. Low expectations. I couldn't get Akiva to join us by the river but then Noemi somehow did— and soon he and I were off taking photos and traipsing up the river, in the river, exploring how the light reflected off the trees, how the arch of the bridge reflected in the water to make a circular portal framing the world on the other side. His curiosity led us further and further upstream until, an hour or so later, he said "I'm satisfied. We can go back now. This was fun." Pure gold for a father.

We looked at another potential weekend home. This one on Black Lake. At Sunset. Gorgeous. How much of our motivation to find a place is to connect with nature? How much to have a psychic escape valve from a sense of impending apocalypse and total social breakdown?

Email: Round 2 Underway!

From: COVID-19 Oral History, Narrative, and Memory Archive
Subject: Round 2 Underway!
Date: August 24, 2020 at 6:26:11 PM EDT
To: Barry Joseph

Dear Barry,

We began interviewing for the COVID-19 Oral History, Memory, and Narrative Archive in early April, 2020, not knowing what would happen next. We have now interviewed nearly 200 people for this project, and cannot thank you enough for your participation in helping to build a lasting record of this historic moment. Thanks to your generosity, this growing archive includes the stories of emergency room doctors, doulas, public school teachers, train conductors, nurses, home health aides, restaurant workers, public officials, researchers, activists, artists, and everyday New Yorkers of all kinds.

We are eager to hear from you again about what you have been thinking, seeing, feeling, and doing since your first session. This pandemic has changed people's lives, experiences, and relationships over time. It's vital to capture this part of the story, with your help.

One more thing: While we will wait until the project is completed—and you have had a chance to review your full interview sessions—before we make the collected interviews available to the public, we are already starting to think about how to share and make sense of these stories.

If you have any questions, please reach out to us. Thank you again for sharing your story with us, and with future audiences.

Thank you, and we look forward to hearing your story,

The NYC COVID-19 Oral History,
Memory, and Narrative Archive team

Daily Diary Entries

August 25, Tuesday

Today we went to the marina and tried to rent a boat. They laughed at us, for not having a reservation. She said, quite seriously, they get four to five hundred calls a day. Due to the pandemic. "What else is there for people to do?"

Last night we went to an Italian restaurant. Takeout only, which is fine, as that's all we're doing. Outside was a table. We asked if we could eat there. They said, "No problem" and all wore masks. They even offered to bring our food out. Which they did, not in a take-out bag but on their plates, with their utensils. Miri rightly asked, "What's going on here? We order takeout but are eating like we're at the restaurant?" I asked the "waitress" what she had in mind. She said, "After I bring out the last dishes, just come in if you need anything." Fine with us! It was like a sexual consent negotiation, defining our boundaries. And we did, speaking about it directly and setting clear expectations. We are six months into this but still have to negotiate these new social spaces on a near-daily basis with absolute strangers. And, while stressful, it appears to be working.

Today's outdoor waitress at lunch wore her face mask... on her wrist. I asked her to put it on when she came to take our order. She said something about it being too hot to breathe when it's on, called over a different masked waiter, and we never heard from her again.

August 26, Wednesday

We went horseback riding today. We arrived at the farm and Eleanor greeted us. She asked us to confirm we had submitted all the forms online, along with the payment. We had. It was all contactless! She directed us to the hand sanitizer and the hose to wash our hands. Once done, she got us all on our horses and led us around for an hour. She wore a riding helmet, sunglasses, and a mask that covered the rest of her face. I have no idea what she looks like. I am not even sure of her ethnicity.

Oh, and after washing our hands at the horse farm we passed around an in-ear thermometer, to take our temperatures, and were told all of this was to protect the horses from COVID-19.

August 27, Thursday

Yesterday Noemi's sister and her family[32] drove North from Philly 45 minutes to a place that could give all four of them a test, and turn the response around within the hour, and they continued the drive north, to us, gambling upon the results, which were indeed negative for all. They arrived hours later at our place, in Jeffersonville, New York, where they could at long last, for a few days, join our bubble. It was great to hug them.

Today the weather held, we took them to the Toronto Reservoir to swim. After I drove a motor boat—my first one—up Swinging Bridge Lake and saw from the water that red lake house that it's looking like tomorrow we just might try to put in an offer.

32 Becky, Scott, Max, and Reuben.

August 28, Friday

Tonight we went out for dinner and Scott said this was their first time eating out. We were outside at Lorenzo's. He wanted to know, essentially, what we do with our masks. In just a few weeks, how did our family become the experts? I shared what we figured out so far: what makes sense (no masks when eating), what doesn't make sense (not wearing a mask when ordering), and the rest which is the bulk of what we have no clue about: before ordering, after ordering, when food is arriving, after we finish eating but others are still eating, etc.

Today we actually put in an offer for the red lake house. When we return to the city next Sunday, if we knew we had a place we could always return to in the area... well, that would be beyond amazing.

August 29, Saturday

The outdoor biergarten at the local tavern is open on the weekends so we thought that would be the perfect place to take Noemi's sister's family before they leave tomorrow. When we arrived we learned it was closed, and since it had been raining all day, they only staffed for dinner inside. I spoke with the manager, explained our family would not eat indoors, and since it was literally blue skies could they reconsider. And they did! It was beautiful out on the deck and before long they filled the other tables out there as well. Then, between the appetizer and main course, the skies first darkened and then opened up with a torrential downpour. The other tables took cover, all eventually resettling inside. We stayed throughout, finagling umbrellas and such, and weathered the storm. It was a fun, if not slightly damp, adventure. The main courses arrived and my trout was delicious.

Whatever I may have written so far in this diary, for weeks only two things are constantly in my mind. In May we were told one-third of our staff would be let go—in July—then that date moved to August—then to September. Next Thursday we will be told when it will begin. At the same time, we are one and a half weeks from schools opening. When it was announced a month ago it would be blended learning—with most days home—the private bus companies cancelled all business. Miri, we learned last week, will go in day 3 and 4 in a rotating 6 day cycle; Akiva goes in one of every 5 days. Meanwhile, parents at Akiva's school are pressuring the rest of us to opt-in for the fully remote option, to increase class options, and teachers are begging / shaming us to follow.

Email: Bronx Science - Urgent Update About Learning Models

From: Bronx Sci Parent's Association News
Subject: Bronx Science - Urgent Update About Learning Models
Date: August 29, 2020 at 9:04:14 AM EDT
To: Barry Joseph

Dear Fellow Parents & Guardians,

Yesterday, the Department of Education (DOE) released guidelines about teacher assignments for blended learning and remote learning. These guidelines could profoundly affect Bronx Science, so we want to provide more information about their context and consequences.

DOE has mandated that for blended learning, each class will require **two teachers**—one teacher for the in-person component and one teacher for the remote component. **This means that since two teachers are required for each blended class, the school has fewer teachers available to teach other classes.** More blended students means fewer electives and advanced classes. Further, to make up the teacher shortfall created by the two-teacher requirement, some teachers will have to teach "out of license," i.e. math teachers might have to teach English.

Currently, 36% of the students at Bronx Science have selected blended learning. If 90% or more of the student body selects the fully remote option, the school will be able to offer more of the electives and advanced classes that our students are eager to take.

The school must complete the programming for the year by early next week. We know that many families chose blended with an eye toward switching to remote if necessary. Please understand that delaying an eventual move to 100% remote is forcing the school to make plans for a larger number of blended students. Also, please understand that taking no action—not responding to the DOE survey—means you are counted as choosing blended.

We understand and respect the decisions individual families have made, and if blended learning remains something that you feel is right for your child and/or your circumstances, then you should stick with it. However, we feel it's important that you have this new information.

We strongly recommend that families consciously re-examine their choice. **100% remote increasingly appears to be the option for our school that best preserves academically diverse course offerings and maintains teacher consistency (i.e. one teacher vs. two).** We continue to believe that all students who are in fully remote classes will be taught by Bronx Science teachers and in Bronx Science classes. It is also worth noting that the new guidance commits to a daily component of synchronous learning for all students.

Families can opt-in for fully remote or blended HERE and we ask that you do so today, or absolutely as soon as possible. Please be sure that your preference is selected.

We know the school is doing everything it can and is exploring many possible options. Together with the Alumni Foundation, we have been reaching out to many elected officials to gain further clarity and help.

Thank you again for your understanding and patience.

Best,

PA Co-Presidents

Daily Diary Entries

August 30, Sunday

Before Noemi's sister's family returned to Philly today, we took them to the Harvest Festival at Bethel Woods. When we first arrived in the Catskills 2.5 weeks ago, I read about this supercharged Farmer's Market. I had no doubt we would never go. It would be packed, people would not be wearing masks, etc. But today we went. No problem. It's not that we've grown complacent (I think) but that we've seen how well public events can set expectations and then police their rules and that largely people are playing nice. Everyone wore masks. Everyone respected the set walking pathways. We had a great time. Still, we're all figuring it out, together.

August 31, Monday

Today was my first day back to work, remotely of course, even though we're still at the rental in the Catskills. I'm working just mornings this week. In the afternoon we all left for adventures: Sticky Fingers' killer ice cream, then failed to find a new waterfall but instead a magnificent trail and gorgeous lake. Can't wait to return. Noemi and I agree that while it feels cheesy to say it, it renews the spirit. I sure hope our latest offer on the lake house is accepted. Still, they have just been so unresponsive. At times it can feel like they have no intention of selling it.

SEPTEMBER 2020

In which school goes remote… an offer is accepted… layoffs occur… bread is tossed… Yoda comes through… the dead are remembered…

Daily Diary Entries

September 1, Tuesday

School is not starting next week. Today the city canceled plans for in-person schooling, pushing it back weeks, and pushing back to an unknown date when remote instruction will begin. This week work is supposed to tell us when the layoffs will occur. We still have no response to the house offer we put in four days ago. The store I was in today had a sign that read "No bathrooms available. Thank you, COVID-19!"

Email: Bronx Science: Updates Regarding New School Year

From: Assistant Principal
Subject: Bronx Science: September 1st Updates Regarding New School Year
Date: September 1, 2020 at 5:50:01 PM EDT
To: Barry Joseph

Dear parents/guardians and students,

We have a few quick updates.

As of this morning (September 1), 86% of students had opted for 100% Remote Instruction. I know that this was a difficult and painstaking decision for many of you. Whether you have chosen blended or remote, our teachers are committed to creating an excellent experience for their students. We are working diligently on programming based on our current numbers. I know that everyone is eager to learn about their schedules for next year, but it will take us a couple of weeks to get the whole school programmed correctly. Thank you for your continued patience.

This morning, the DOE announced a delayed start to the school year. While teachers are reporting back to work next week, remote instruction will not begin until September 16 with in-person instruction beginning on September 21. This change will help ensure a smoother start to the school year for everyone.

As we continue to plan and have more definite information about the school year, we will continue to keep you up to date, including details about what day-to-day instruction will look like for both blended and remote students. This promises to be a very different year, but I know, together, we'll make it a great one.

With gratitude,

Assistant Principal
Physical Science and Engineering
The Bronx High School of Science

Daily Diary Entries

September 2, Wednesday

Sorry, I just can't.

September 3, Thursday

All I have to say is three words: Pickamoose Blue Hole. Google it. Just being up here, in this region, makes the stress of the pandemic so much more bearable.

September 4, Friday

Today at end of business we all received the email we've been waiting for since May: a week from this Tuesday the layoffs will begin, lasting two days. One day earlier, all who will be let go will receive a meeting invite, as will those whose positions might change. You won't know until you arrive at the meeting which is going to occur—being let go or having a change in position. And if you don't get an invite there is no change.

That Wednesday is currently the first day of school in New York City. Could they have picked a worse day?

Today after work (while still in the Catskills) I got in the kayak and paddled with Noemi and Akiva as far as the bridge. In the shadow of the bridge I realized, out there in nature, on our own, I could almost forget for a time that we only could be there because of the pandemic.

Email: To the owner of the lake house

From: Barry Joseph
Subject: A question about the availability of your property
Date: September 4, 2020 at 11:30:01 AM EDT
To: Property owner

I hope you don't mind my directly reaching out to you about your property. We both have agents, and I respect their roles, so I want to clarify I am not contacting you to work around them, as that would be unethical. But I did want to reach out to you to help us better get to know each other and our intentions, to ensure they are aligned.

I don't know if my name was shared, but it is my family who offered last Saturday to give you just what we were told you were looking for regarding the house lot. We never received a response to that offer. We then increased it yesterday. Still no response.

Let me tell you about ourselves a bit then ask you a question. We are a family of four from Queens. My wife was born in the Bronx, and my children are 13 and 11. I work for the Girl Scouts and my wife does research in the area of social policy. We work to make the world a better place (and on the side I give talks to promote my book on the history of seltzer water). It's been a hard year for all—my dad died from COVID this spring—and the idea of a Catskills weekend home has been one of the things that has kept us going, while being all cooped up in our tiny NYC apartment (all four of us trying to do work and attend school remotely). We love what we have seen at your place and think it will make us all very happy.

So I have just one question for you, but please let me contextualize it through a story. My parents met in the early 60s. My dad had just gotten out of the Army, where he served in a medical unit stationed in Iran, and from a stint fighting Cholera in the Philippines for the Center for Disease Control. He was ten years older than my mom, who fell in love with him on their first date. My dad's mother was very controlling and, after a few months, was frustrated that my dad had yet to propose. My parents were supposed to go away together for a trip and my grandmother counseled her to say that unless he proposed she shouldn't go. She was terrified. She didn't want to lose him. What should she do? So when it came time to pack she told my dad she wasn't going. He was surprised, and said, "Why not?" She said, "Because I love you." He laughed and replied, "And that's why you don't want to go?" She told him, "You haven't told me the same yet." He thought a moment and then said, "My intentions are honorable. And you can trust when I am ready I will do the right thing." She decided that was good enough for her, they had a great weekend, a great wedding, and until she died in 1990 a great marriage.

In many ways, I feel like house hunting is like an old-fashioned marriage. We're getting to know each other through our intermediaries. So here's where I stand: We have offered and then increased an offere designed to give you exactly what the MLS listing says you are looking for. And yet, in almost a week, we've received no response.

So what I want to ask is: Are your intentions honorable?

If so, we can wait a bit longer for your response. Otherwise, please do the right thing and let my family and I move on.

September 5, Saturday

Let's play two truths and a lie, why don't we?

Last week in New York City the DOE canceled school, forever.

This afternoon we raced rubber duckies through the river rapids.

Yesterday I wrote an email to the reluctant seller and today he accepted our offer on his lake house.

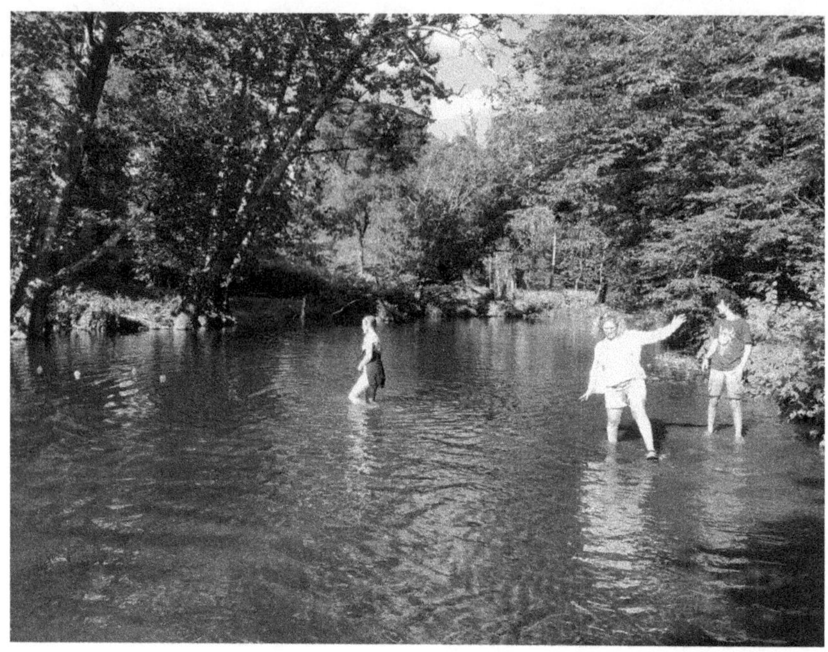

September 6, Sunday

Leaving the Catskills today, after almost four weeks away from the city. It's hard knowing we're about to return to, yes, a lovely apartment, but months upon months of being back on top of each other. It makes it so much easier knowing with our offer accepted on the lake house, we could be returning home with a piece of the Catskills (which we will be able to escape to whenever we like).

Arriving at our building in Forest Hills, I was swept by the guilt of getting the privilege to leave for so long. And I reminded myself this is normally beyond our means. We're comfortable, but not rich. We could only afford this because my dad died this spring and left me an inheritance. So yeah. But still. We are very fortunate, even in the face of such loss.

September 7, Monday, Labor Day

So I guess today is the official last day of summer, tomorrow the first day of fall. I usually look forward to this transition: the return of reliable routines for the kids—after school programs, Hebrew school, sports—looking forward to family traditions and get-togethers—High Holidays, apple picking—but this year it feels more like dread—with worse weather to keep us packed together longer, returning to working full time with our kids at home attempting remote schooling, much that brings variety canceled (movies, Broadway, Museum exhibit, festivals), so much still unknown and beyond our control (will a vaccine be found?), and will Trump return to office?, and will my kids actually start school online next week and 1 of 5 days (Akiva) and 2 of 6 days (Miri) in-person the week after?, and will I be fired next week?

Work started the day with an email from HR (promoting? warning?) that next week is suicide prevention week. The same HR that is scheduling our layoffs during this time, four months after all were told our jobs were on the chopping block. Do they taste the irony?

September 8, Tuesday

Back in June we took Akiva's laptop into Best Buy. The hinge had broken between the screen and the keyboard causing the two to separate ("coming unhinged"— a good title for a book on these times). It was our second time in four months in a store. They said the repair would take two weeks. Two months later, yesterday, they refunded our money from the original purchase in 2018 as they couldn't get the replacement parts. Their supply chain had broken down. We used the store credit to buy Akiva a new computer.

Noemi and I are pretty clear that the risk of contracting COVID is not worth us going to a dentist, or our doctors. Yesterday I took both children to the general practitioner for their annual check up, then an unexpected trip to a second doctor, then the dentist. There was no way our kids were going to miss those appointments. Where do we draw the lines between what we're willing to risk for ourselves and what we are willing to risk for our kids?

September 9, Wednesday

A few weeks ago, tomorrow would have been the first day of school. Now it's next Wednesday. We'll see. Miri is troubled that we haven't been told what time it starts. The following Monday in-person begins. We have no idea how we will get Akiva from Queens to the Bronx. Or if in-person will be canceled for him (only 15% of his school is going in and if it drops to 10% we're told the whole school goes remote).

September 10, Thursday

Where to begin? Today we received the timing for Miri's first three days of school (all remote) before the school shifts to a blended schedule. The email with instructions was insane, full of convoluted gobbledy goop, to explain four separate options—Cohort A, B, C & D—and once untangled were only relevant for those three days (and that first day of course coincides with the second day of layoffs at work).

The pandemic is like a stream of water running across a rock, seeking out the fault lines, exacerbating them until even the most stable foundations crack. That's how I understand the many friends with mental health issues emerging, either sharing their struggles with me for the first time or being revealed when they can no longer hold it together. We learned tonight that Ilyse, the founder of our supper club, my friend of a decade and mother of three, was struggling with such a severe eating disorder that she left six or so weeks ago to get into what's called a residential treatment center to seek help. Michael[33] last night said they're sending her home next week, ready or not.

[33] Ilyse's husband

Email: Important Information about our Remote Learning Opening

From: Stephen A. Halsey JHS 157
Subject: Important Information about our Remote Learning Opening Sept 16-18
Date: September 10, 2020 at 4:28:43 PM EDT
To: Barry Joseph

Good afternoon Students, Parents/Guardians,

I hope this email finds you well. As you know, on September 16, 17 and 18 **ALL students** and teachers will begin the school year on remote learning. Our first 3 days of remote learning will serve as an orientation to our new school year for our students.

During the first 3 days of remote learning teachers will be engaging students in a variety of ways:

Introducing themselves to students; ice breaker activities where students and teachers get to know each other; social emotional learning activities; discussing rituals and routines of remote learning; conversations with students on what to expect on the first days of school (both in-person and remote learning); discussing and reviewing safety procedures/protocols; discussing and reviewing the various learning platforms students will be using; reviewing and discussing students' schedules for understanding.

What you need to know for our first day of remote learning....

STUDENTS IN COHORT D FULL OPT IN RL (CLASSES ENDING IN 40/41/42/43/44/45) WILL FOLLOW DAY 1

SCHEDULE SEPT 16, DAY 3 SCHEDULE SEPT 17 AND DAY 5 SCHEDULE SEPT 18

On Sept 16, all students in Cohort A, Cohort B and Cohort C will follow their Day 1 schedule, on Sept 17, all students Cohort A, Cohort B and Cohort C will follow their Day 3 schedule and on Sept 18, all students Cohort A, Cohort B and Cohort C will follow their Day 5 schedule (SEE EXPLANATION BELOW)

SEPTEMBER 16: Day 1 Schedule all Students

All student Cohorts will follow their **Day 1** schedule on Sept 16. Normally, when we follow a Day 1 schedule, Cohort A students are attending school for in- person learning and Cohorts B and C are at home for remote learning. For Sept 16, all Cohort A students **DO NOT** attend in-person learning. **Instead, all Cohort A students will follow their day 1 schedule and log in to their classes from home on Sept 16. All Cohort B and Cohort C students will follow their remote learning Day 1 schedule.**

SEPTEMBER 17: Day 3 Schedule for all Students

All student Cohorts will follow their **Day 3** schedule on Sept 17. Normally, when we follow a Day 3 schedule, Cohort B students are attending school for in- person learning and Cohorts A and C are at home for remote learning. For Sept 17, all Cohort B students **DO NOT** attend in-person learning. **Instead, all Cohort B students will follow their day 3 schedule and log in to their classes from home on Sept 17. All Cohort A and Cohort C students will follow their remote learning Day 3 schedule.**

SEPTEMBER 18: Day 5 Schedule for all Students

All student Cohorts will follow their **Day 5** schedule on Sept 18. Normally, when we follow a Day 5 schedule, Cohort C students are attending school for in- person learning and Cohorts A and B are at home for remote learning. For Sept 18, all Cohort C students **DO NOT** attend in-person learning. **Instead, all Cohort C students will follow their Day 5 schedule and log in to their classes from home on Sept 18. All Cohort A and Cohort B students will follow their remote learning Day 5 schedule.**

Students in every Cohort will receive Google Classroom invites from each of their teachers prior to our first day of remote learning. Students must accept the Google classroom invite from each of their teachers (including their homeroom teacher)

Once students accept their homeroom teachers Google classroom invite, they can access their schedule on the morning of Sept 16. Students, on Sept 16 at 8:15AM go to our school website and follow the link to access your schedule for that day.

Next steps...More information will follow next week

Our first full day of in-person learning will take place on Monday Sept 21. We will follow a DAY 1 schedule on Sept 21 and DAY 2 schedule for Sept 22, Day 3 for Sept 23 Day 4 for Sept 24 and DAY 5 for Sept 25!

Students, parents/guardians will receive an UPDATED SEPTEMBER CALENDAR shortly.

Also, I will send another email to students (and parents/guardians) next week with specific directions for our first in-person learning day on Sept 21.

Please feel free to email if you have any questions.

Sincerely,
Principal JHS 157

Daily Diary Entries

September 11, Friday

Today is the 19th anniversary of 9/11. I almost didn't notice, less because it's being overshadowed (the horror of 3,000 dead versus 200,000+) than because it feels like we're in a temporal bubble, holding our breath as we endure a new set of norms, waiting for the bubble to burst so we can continue from where we left off. So why should the 9/11 anniversary hold relevance in a time outside time?

One response on Facebook to my post yesterday from the schools instructions sums up this whole year to a tee:

> You are being trolled.
> Can not be real.
> (I know it's real)

September 12, Saturday

Who knew there was such a thing called a velodrome?

The parks in Queens are connected in one line running east, from where I live all the way to the border with Long Island. When we go to Flushing Meadows Park through the lines left by the two World Fairs, past the remains of the Tent of Tomorrow or the glorious Unisphere, we treat it as a destination. But it's actually a starting line. And this summer we've explored it as a family for the first time by bike, past the Botanical Garden, around parks, on dirt paths intended for more rugged bikes, across overgrown ballfields, just to explore. Today we reached the velodrome, an open-air cycling arena. Open to the public, Miri and I raced around, two laps, thoroughly wiped.

We continued even further, not out of the city, but to see how close we could get. It was a boba tea place in Fresh Meadows, alongside the Northern State Parkway. The first tea place we sought was closed, not for the day but forever. I forget these days I need to call in advance. But the second was a chain, and open, and we got our tea to go (of course) and sat at the tables outside in front and drank and hydrated and recharged our muscles for the return trip, settling into the illusion, under the clear blue sky, that all was well with the world.

Recalling that perceived reality, once back home in our pandemic box after the day's adventures, and noting how easy it was to forget, to want to forget, made me cry.

Perhaps, more specifically, it's an optical illusion—squint to turn a portrait of a couple into a vase, a restless image that refuses to be fixed. The new norm during the pandemic is equally restless. We all wait for the day a combination of science, public policy, and common sense allows it to finally settle into focus.

September 13, Sunday

Morning: Usually the new year of Hebrew School begins the Sunday after the first days of public school. But since the DOE delayed a week and Temple stayed on schedule, today was the start of our post-summer year routine, with school schedules, soccer games and… who knows what else will stick. I am usually both dreading and welcoming of the return of schedules. But today I can't even trust them to deliver.

Afternoon: I finally went to Atria to clear out my dad's belongings with Carol: his clothing, photo albums, wall hangings, etc. I wish I could take my time and go through each item, consider its history and what it meant to him. The poem about his toilet included in his eulogy. The importance to him of the three ties he chose to keep. Where in Iran he found that painting.

Carol is moving out of their place, where she and my dad lived for over three years, heading to Jackson Heights a few blocks from Lily, her daughter. I went in today to help her prepare, my first time there since the lockdown in March, when it soon became clear that assisted living facilities were a breeding ground for the virus, where Carol got infected and recovered, where my dad would also get infected but never return. I had to be alone with her in the small unventilated apartment for over an hour. She carries the antibodies, but does that mean she can no longer be a carrier? I wanted to get out of there as soon as I entered.

How can these both be the same place—the home where he once lived and the virus-tinged place he now leaves behind?

Tonight: And yet life goes on! We drove as a family to pick up dinner from the Empanada Café in Corona then continued to the New York Hall of Science for our first Queens Drive-in movie: *The Wizard of Oz*. It was a blast.

September 14, Monday

Today we received the contract (at last!) on the Catskills lake house. Is this really happening?

Tomorrow I'll have my meeting to learn if I've been laid off or not, after waiting since May for this. Is this state of unknown almost over?

Wednesday, the kids each start some version of remote schooling. How are they each going to take to it?

And Friday is Rosh Hashanah[34], which we will celebrate in New Rochelle. This question belongs to a different holiday, but I've got to ask: how will this evening be different from all others?

September 15, Tuesday

Today the layoffs began. I don't know how many will be let go, just that, at 1:30 PM, I was one of them. Termination was immediate. It came as a shock, even though I knew it was possible, and after I frantically sent my personal contact info to my colleagues, racing against their efforts to close my account. I'm glad the waiting is over—since May!—as I had no control over the situation. The next steps—what jobs I look for, when and how—puts the control back in my court. For now. Before I start I just need to "catch and release"—let the feelings come, whatever they look like, acknowledge them, notice them, then let them go.

September 16, Wednesday

Today the new school year began, sort of. Depends what you mean by "school". And "began".

[34] The Jewish New Year.

Akiva went to a Google form to register that he was in attendance. He received emails, one for each teacher, with links to Google Classrooms for him to open. No live contact with the teacher. No contact at all with his classmates. We learned his school schedule for the first time. He's going in once a week to only receive in-person instruction for four periods. Is it worth it?

Miri was excited for school to start, texting with her friends and gathering her supplies around her like talismans. She, too, had a laundry list of links to Google Classrooms but each one had Zoom periods where she met her teachers, her classmates, and received some orientation.

Yesterday was the first day, first 24 hours, that I have been without a job since... I have no idea. Maybe in 25 years? I've always moved from one job to another. Even when I was let go from the museum I found my job at the Girl Scouts before I reached my last day. The response by my community on LinkedIn stunned me, people sharing job offerings I'd never find on my own. I don't know what floored me more – the warm embrace or the evidence that, holy cow, jobs still exist and there's hope for me yet. I feel very fortunate.

Email: Where Was My Homeroom Today?

From: Stephen A. Halsey
Subject: Where Was My Homeroom Today?
Date: September 16, 2020 at 12:28:42 PM EDT
To: Barry Joseph

Where Was My Homeroom Today?

Today we had a lot of emails asking where their homeroom link was.

REMEMBER: When you are a blended student scheduled to be in school (COHORT A TODAY) you would have homeroom. Cohorts B and C would not have homeroom today. Why? The teacher cannot be with their live homeroom students and the blended/remote students at the same time. Therefore Cohort A students had their homeroom class today while the other hybrid Cohorts - B and C did not.

Tomorrow we are using the Day 3 schedule which means Cohort B students would be following their in school learning schedule (just from home) while the students in Cohort A and C would follow their remote schedules. That means Cohort B will see their homeroom class while Cohorts A and C will not and will start at first period.

Friday we are using the Day 5 schedule which means Cohort C students would be following their in school learning schedule (Just from home) while the students in Cohorts A and B would follow their remote schedules. That means Cohort C will have their homeroom class while A and B will not and start first period.

THAT IS JUST FOR THIS WEEK.

Also remember this is all new and there are plenty of bumps in the road we will run into. DO NOT LET IT OVERWHELM YOU. Whatever issues pop up will be resolved.

Man, after the last 3 days, if I wasnt bald I would have gray hair right now!

Daily Diary Entries

September 17, Thursday

I couldn't take it anymore. I went into a bagel store and got a well-toasted sesame with a little cream cheese, tomato, and nova. It was pure heaven.

The thing about remote schooling at this age is each subject has its own teacher, its own Google classroom, and its own Zoom link. All day the kids are juggling the different links plus the emails from their teachers and from the school. The only tech support available is us parents. Miri couldn't log into her homeroom, and experienced the same problem later in the day. Akiva had something discontiguous at two, after hours of no courses, so, of course, he forgot about it, then once it started realized he was late and had no idea how to get in, found the email, clicked on its Zoom link, it wouldn't let him in. The email offered a Zoom meeting phone number that could be used instead. So calling that number worked and he participated, muted, audio only, for the time that still remained.

At least they'll start going in-person a few days next week... Just kidding! This afternoon the DOE announced they're canceling in person next week and pushing it back to October 1.

That's a commitment I can rely on, right?

September 18, Friday

Today I made sushi for lunch for everyone because it looks like we're going to be here a lot longer and it's time for some new lunch food.

I wrote my first job search cover letter.

Tonight, for the first night of Rosh Hashanah, we went to New Rochelle to have a socially distanced dinner celebration on Oma's lawn, four tables for four different families (Noemi's sister's family did a rapid test on the drive up from Philly so they could sleep over, but we returned home afterwards). I cut the brisket in the driveway wearing a mask.

Then Ruth Bader Ginsburg died. Will this week please fucking end already?

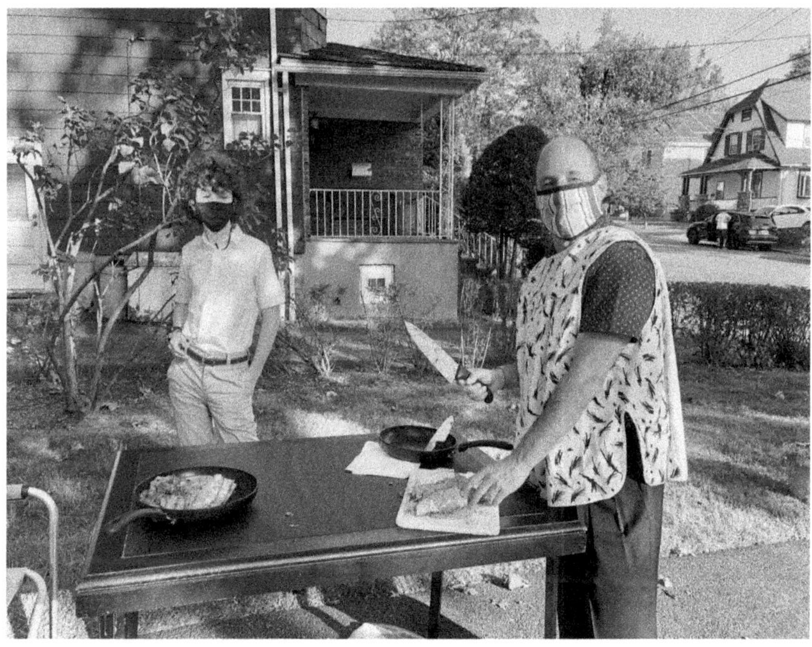

September 19, Saturday

This morning we ate apple cake for breakfast, got dressed in our best, then went to Temple for Rosh Hashanah services... in our living room. I sent my computer to the TV screen and there we watched the live Zoom feed, the Rabbi standing in front of the ark, the Cantor in her home standing in front of a Zoom backdrop of the same ark, and 200 smaller screens of homes around town, some in our building, all coming together to welcome in the New Year, listening together in the traditional way who will be inscribed in the Book of Life and who will die "by strangling, by fire, by flood, by plague" the causes now more real than ever. By strangling—George Floyd; by fire—the West Coast in flames; by flood—the hurricane in the Gulf Coast; by plague—COVID-19.

Since the Jewish High Holidays were all online this year, our Temple invited congregants to make videos in advance to promote different parts. Last month, when still in the Catskills, we volunteered to help with *tashlich*[35]. We went over to the local riverside park and filmed our portions, tossing some bread into the river. It felt good being able to make something for the community, and to see it today as part of the Zoom service. We were careful at the time not to show off how beautiful it was there, as that could distract from the *tashlich* message while drawing attention to how lucky we were to have escaped New York City for such a bucolic place.

This afternoon we invited friends in our building who live directly three floors below us, whom we haven't seen since quarantine began, to walk with us around the local Willow Lake and toss in bread for our sins. Being lost deep in the park preparing an in-person *tashlich,* I could almost imagine everything was normal.

Oh, and I submitted my first résumé for a job opening.

This morning, before the service began, I forced my head around my new situation, blogging about it for the first time, sharing my unemployed status with the world. I wrote that on the Jewish New Year we eat apples dipped in honey and wish each other a sweet new year. I

---

[35] In which we symbolically toss away our sins by throwing bread into a body of water.

asked, during this global pandemic, can there be any greater radical act of imagination than that, to collectively force ourselves to see outside the pain and dislocation of the past six months by envisioning our path together towards a better future, towards a sweet new year?

I kept my anger to myself and simply shared that I got it, that a nonprofit funded largely by young girls selling cookies to strangers was not optimized for a pandemic. Cuts needed to be made. I shared that as I entered the new year, I was thankful for the people who led me to the Girl Scouts, the remarkable people I got to work with there over the past two years, and the people (the "members"—the girls, their caregivers and their Troop Leaders) whom my work touched during that time.

And I think I meant it.

Yes, looking for work, especially during a pandemic, will be filled with pain, and disappointment, and anger, and frustration and panic. I will try not to deny those feelings when they come. But as I explore new opportunities and make new decisions about my next steps, how can I approach it in a playful way? How can I find the joy in the exploration?

How can I be open to the liberation that comes in the liminal moments between what was and what can be?

September 20, Sunday

Our trip to Glass Bottle Beach in the Rockaways on the Atlantic Ocean was abruptly canceled upon arrival when we learned they recently closed it after discovering radioactive waste (um, what?!!). We continued into Floyd Bennett Field to fly kites on the old air strips and walk the beach at Jamaica Bay.

I'm thrilled *The Watchmen* is getting the recognition it deserves at tonight's Emmys.

Tomorrow begins my first full week of no work. I'm proud of my blog post yesterday framing the job search in terms of play and seeking joy in the unknown, but that doesn't stop my still feeling on the edge of panic.

Just breathe.

So to summarize—this week I got laid off, my kids "started" "school", in-person school was delayed again, RBG died two months before the election, and I went to a beach polluted with radioactive waste. Just in case anyone wants to keep track...

September 21, Monday

Things happened.

First full week of remote school for kids began. Not much instruction yet, but I'm hopeful it will be better than last spring.

Posted my new status on LinkedIn, worked my contacts, set up interviews with jobs for contacts set up throughout the week, and kept a positive attitude.

Desperately trying to salvage the purchase of lake home by finding co-signers to secure the mortgage.

Built most of my new seltzer talk for this Thursday—"Seltzer and NYC - A Love Story."

Took Miri to soccer practice by bike and planning now for a soccer game on Long Island this Saturday, mystified as to how it will all work.

September 22, Tuesday

Akiva seems to be receiving school content in some capacity. Miri, however, still seems to be strictly on socio-emotional learning. She's yelling "I want homework!"

I had three 1st round interviews today, which I was quite pleased with, all on Zoom. In two they were wearing masks. I haven't had a video call once this year with someone wearing a mask. Both were in their offices in Manhattan. Being that close to their face (aka, my computer screen) but getting none of the information one gets from lips moving plus other facial micro-movements was bizarre. As more and more go back into offices will this become the norm—two masked people on video chats?

September 24, Thursday

Just to add to the game of "Can you believe they're pulling this on us now?" yesterday Miri's school announced some kids—after a week of school, and learning how to access separate links for each classroom—would be reshuffled to better allocate teacher resources since they now have a better idea of student:teacher load. Miri was both terrified she would be separated from her best friend yet hopeful others not with her would be moved into her class. Tonight at bedtime we got a new email from the school: no change. What's the next pointlessly stressful thing the DOE will throw our way?

September 25, Friday

I didn't leave the apartment today but I didn't feel cooped up because I chose to stay in—I had so much to do. Mostly looking for work, deciding if I should go for a big job or create a consultancy. Nice leads and opportunities emerging. Miri walks into school for the first time one week from today; Akiva, a week from Monday. Miri has her first traveling soccer game tomorrow; it still amazes me we are doing this.

I spent a half hour over video—FaceTime—telling a colleague what on my desk at Girl Scouts I want them to pack up and ship to me and what I don't need. When I last left my desk at the Girl Scouts in early March I could never have imagined I would never see it again in person—which made it especially surreal seeing it one last socially-distanced time over a video call.

September 26, Saturday

How to explain this one?!!

I woke up this morning to this text: "Great news! Your cameo from Tom Kane that expired was completed for free! Check it out!"

What!?! I wrote about Cameo in the *Forward* earlier this year, mostly about how I paid for celebrities like Jackie Hoffman to send personalized messages to people during COVID. After my dad died, my friend Rik ran the funeral and *shiva* over Zoom. To thank him I hired a number of *Star Wars*-related celebrities to express how much it meant to me. Perhaps asking on April 27th, days before May 4th—as in "May the 4th be with you"—was a mistake. When the offer that I had made to Tom Kane, the voice actor of Yoda from the *Star Wars* animated series *The Clone Wars*, expired unacknowledged, I got it. Instead I reached out to the actor who played Chewie in the last *Star Wars* trilogy. Rik loved it! I thought that was the end of the story. Now, five months later, I get this text. Tom Kane has done it? And for free? I watched it. In the brief video Tom sobs throughout—or at least close to it—sharing that his dad recently died. "Search the force," he says in the voice of Yoda, choking back tears, "and with the light side he is."

I woke up to a text message linking to a video created for free by a celebrity saying in the voice of Yoda that my dead dad is one with the force. If that's not a pandemic WTF moment, what is?

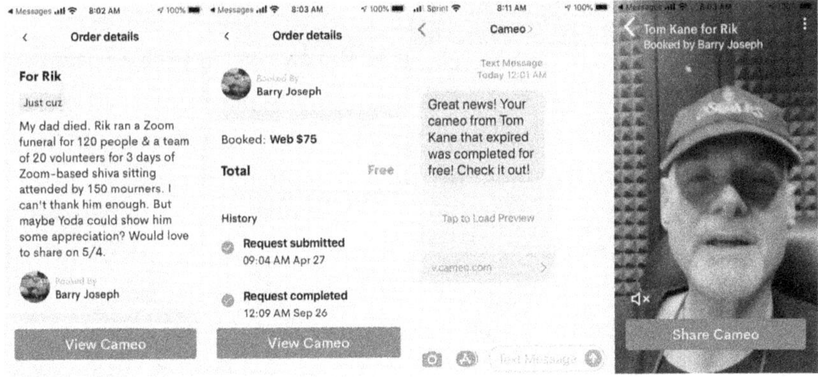

September 27, Sunday

Overheard from Miri last week:

1. At dinner. "During quarantine..." she began a sentence. When was that? What are we in now? I asked. She said quarantine was last spring, when school was from home, before we left for the Catskills.

2. "A year ago… Which feels like five years ago due to the quarantine…" said to her friend N. on the always-on FaceTime chat, as a prelude to something.
3. "Yes! I have homework!" yelled with arms raised triumphantly, Wednesday morning, after her first full week of school, as if she's been waiting for an eternity, as if she always wanted homework, as if it were her salvation, that realization how much the structured expectations of the school cycle gave order and meaning to her life, distracting her from staring into the abyss of boredom.

Miri had her first traveling soccer team game. She was never subbed-out, playing the full 2 ½ hours on a field she said was 15 times as long as what she's used to from year's past, and was amazed she had the energy to never stop running. And after six months of watching her level of at-home activities, so are we.

On Rosh Hashanah last week, the Rabbi's sermon was themed around, "Can you hear me now?" He literally played the old phone commercial and riffed on how it's the way every Zoom call now begins, how we are separated by the pandemic but we are constantly reaching out to find connections, and must not stop trying! Tonight's Yom Kippur[36] sermon was themed around "I can't breathe," at first applying it to the wildfires in the West, the suffocating isolation and stress during quarantine, then pivoting to Black Lives Matter, listing the names of the too many for whom in police custody those were their last words. It was a call to action to the congregation to recognize the systemic oppression against black Americans and our unique obligation as Jews to step up and do something about it.

It's might be worth noting—Noemi and I dressed up in our fanciest as we would had we been with the 700 other congregants in person but, as were on Zoom, we were both in bare feet.

---

[36] The second of the two High Holidays. It is a time for atonement, considered the holiest day of the year, and often marked by fasting and prayer.

September 28, Monday

Rabbi's sermon this morning at Yom Kippur services was essentially, "Why isn't everyone fucking wearing a mask, already?!!" Even when Zoomed the service was meaningful. Around 250 households participated. And it was great to see Debby's video box there, Zooming in from her loft in Manhattan, and we texted in the chat on the side. The Rabbi talked about a defiant minister who refused to cancel services and let the pandemic get in the way of his devotion to God. Two weeks later he was dead from COVID. Again, all four of us were bare footed throughout.

After the morning services was lay people's hour—usually a panel of congregants to distract us over lunch hour during our fast. Today was a panel of congregants of color talking about their experiences as Jews of color. Very smart programming.

At 1 o'clock I was on the Zoom team helping to run the children's service. I granted admin powers, ran the PowerPoint, and played the videos. In elementary school I always wanted to be on the AV team!

I left home to pick up bagels for the break fast[37]. There were a number of crowds of what I interpreted as orthodox, or Russians (perhaps both), Jews, none of whom were wearing masks. I was equally horrified, furious, and embarrassed, and not just because I was weak from fasting. Then at the bagel place, in the middle of my order, the counterman stopped listening to me, and started yelling at the person behind me who had just walked in, saying that we were in the middle of a pandemic and they had to wear a mask. He then listed bagel places she could go to without wearing one in the neighboring Orthodox communities, the same ones *The New York Times'* headlines last week highlighted regarding the recent rise in infections. She didn't argue and left, feigning embarrassment. He apologized to me. I asked if that happens often. He said all the time.

At 5 o'clock was the *Yitzkor*[38] service. Carol had a video spotlight for a time and lit a candle in memory of my dad. She read a portion until she was interrupted by Atria staff at her door yelling to her, "Are you coming down to dinner now? Are you coming down to dinner now?"

After, we broke the fast, with Debby on FaceTime. We all ate bagels together, which I enjoyed thoroughly (even though the man at the counter forgot my ¼ pound of lox).

---

37 The traditional celebratory meal held to end the Yom Kippur fast. Usually, with friends and family. This year, just us four in person.

38 The memorial prayers recited for the dead.

Email: The true heroes of RTFH HHDs

From: Rabbi Mark Kaiserman
Subject: The true heroes of RTFH HHDs
Date: September 29, 2020 at 11:12:59 AM EDT
To: Barry Joseph

Dear Zoom Team,

Moving the High Holy Days online was an ambitious feat. But it only was able to be realized because we had an amazing team at work. Simple actions in-person such as calling someone up to the *bimah*[39] became a process. Normal actions like unmuting people or moving to the next page in the prayerbook were now a thing.

Thank you for sharing with us your skills and talents.

Thank you for helping run a service with only a text chain to connect to everyone else.

Thank you for giving us your own High Holy Day service time to focus on running the service instead of your own prayer.

Thank you for your patience, your kindness, and your commitment.

Our HHD services were such a smooth success thanks to all of you. Instead of recording the services in advance, we did what our members wanted and needed—live, *hamish*[40], accessible, community based services. The response showed we made the right choice.

[39] The podium from which the Torah is read.
[40] Yiddish for cozy and homey.

Sadly we have many more services ahead and help needed. Thank you for the future and the time you give us behind-the-scenes. When we can one day, we'll have a great big in-person celebration of our Zoom Help. Until then, we offer our deepest thanks.

Shana Tova,
Rabbi Mark Kaiserman, Cantor Emily Wigod Pincus, and Faye Gilman

Daily Diary Entries

September 29, Tuesday

Tonight was the first presidential debate between Trump and Biden and Chris Wallace. (I am being intentional when I don't say "moderated by Chris Wallace" and include him in the debate itself).

OCTOBER 2020

In which an LLC is filed... Trump is positive... schools try to open... apples are picked... a red zone occurs... the lake house is in play... the Quest 2 arrives... Halloween is salvaged...

Daily Diary Entries

October 1, Thursday

September is over. Thank God.

Today, I filed with New York State to form the LLC for my consultancy. That was fast! Is this real or am I kidding myself? Three proposals requested, and two of those already submitted.

Tomorrow Miri goes into school for the first time. Noemi remarked how cute it was, how nervous she was. I said, "Yes it's only like her third first day of school this year." Then on Monday she'll go again, then remote for four days, then two days back in person.

Monday when Akiva goes in for his first day in school, it will be his first day away from us—from home or the rental place this summer—in 6 ½ months. It will also be the first time in all that time Noemi and I will be home without the kids. It's amazing that we're all pulling off this being-so-close-all-the-time thing.

I decided to write a book. Seems like a good time to re-purpose my six years writing a digital learning blog at the American Museum of Natural History into an inspirational manifesto about digital engagement. All I need now is a publisher who agrees.

October 2, Friday

Donald Trump tested positive for COVID-19!

And… good morning!

October 3, Saturday

Yesterday Miri went into school, her new middle school, for the first time. I followed her downstairs, where she met her friend N. in the park, and trailed them down Yellowstone where they picked up S. and the three then walked to school. Outside the building they lined up each on their own socially distanced circle drawn on the sidewalk, then showed proof on their phones that they passed the daily mandatory "click yes if you're going to infect your school today" survey[41], had their temperatures taken, then one at a time were admitted and allowed to enter. Welcome to your first day of school! Afterwards she said it was good to see her teachers in person, all of them, not just their heads, but the level of learning felt the same as the remote classes she had earlier in the week. Monday she will return to school (followed by four days remote) while Akiva will have his first day in his new high school.

[41] Not exactly. It's just a health screening that asks questions to determine if they are at risk of being infected.

October 5, Monday

I am starting to get a sense today, with both kids out of the house at their schools, what it has felt like to be trapped together with four people (even people I love) in a small apartment for endless days. It's like I've been steeling myself for months to resist something challenging, but then suddenly I've been invited to relax. Yet I know I dare not as momentarily I'll be returning to that defensive stance. I can't afford to widen my view but need to maintain a focused, myopic stare, not to be tempted by the fleeting promise of a taste of normally. If we did the math right, and nothing changes—neither of which are certain—the next time they are both physically in school at the same time will be mid-November, five weeks from now.

Wednesday, the Mayor is planning to return restrictions to Forest Hills due to the two surrounding neighborhoods, with large Jewish Orthodox populations, flouting precautions as infection rates spike. The Governor is fighting him, to get him to implement a more precise response. But, in either case, it's hard not to be furious at those communities refusing to take this seriously, and horrifying that it includes a subset of my own.

October 6, Tuesday

And that's why we can't have nice things. After, what? six months of things slowly opening up, with last Thursday indoor dining finally returning (not that we do that) tonight the Mayor and Governor resolved how to draw lines around communities, (communities with irresponsible people driving up the infection rate) and our house is smack in the middle of the Queen's red zone. Which means Miri's school, up the block, is expected to announce that it will be closed for at least the next two weeks. Goddamnit!

October 7, Wednesday

Yesterday, my printer was giving me a hard time printing out Miri's in-school schedule. She's on a six day rotation—going in on days four and five—and it was nice of the school to prepare a calendar for this month. This morning I found it in the printer, but I tossed it. With the school this evening formally closing in person for at least two weeks, it's already out of date. As Michael said tonight in our Wednesday supper club zoom gathering, he saw someone on the street today not wearing a mask and wanted to scream at him, "My kids are not in school because of you!" And he has three kids.

October 8, Thursday

Because of my two weeks vacation pay, only this past Monday did I become eligible for unemployment insurance. This week is the first week I'll ever in my life get it. Then by Monday, maybe Tuesday, I should have started on the new contracts. And that'll be the end of unemployment insurance. I feel very fortunate.

October 9, Friday

In July, we got a tiny desk and I put it in a corner by the window in the bedroom. We desperately needed a space of privacy for important work calls. I used it today to chat up a fellow consultant (got my first signed contract today, by the way. Hooray!) In the middle of the conversation, Noemi came in the room. I figured she needed to get something before going out for a walk. Otherwise she would have waited. She walked over to her dresser behind me, right into the shot over my shoulder. Normally I would have navigated the situation by introducing her, but I figured she'd be so quick it wasn't worth the disruption. But she wasn't. She stood there texting. I ignored it. The person I was meeting with followed my lead and ignored it as well. These are the slight household disruptions we've all silently agreed to ignore. My camera was tilted in such a way that it only showed her torso but the way she suddenly bent over told me what was about to happen before I could react: she took off her pants. It felt too late now to break our silent agreement and acknowledge her presence within the call. Instead I frantically waved my hand behind my back, out of view of the camera. She took the hint, fast, and dashed out of the room. (She had presumed, and with good reason, that my Virtual Background was turned on and she could not be seen.) I tried to maintain the silent agreement, to uphold the fiction that nothing out of the ordinary had just occurred, but it was too much, like trying not to laugh at a funeral—the harder you try to hold it in the more powerfully it wants to burst out. And it did. I laughed so hard tears ran down my face, and my colleague said with a grin, God bless him, "That's just how it is these days."

Tonight was *Simchat Torah*[42]. Normally we'd be at temple dancing. It is always such a blast in person but the idea of Zooming it all in struck me as so sad. However, Noemi insisted. And it worked! We danced the hokey pokey. We learned some Israeli line dances. We danced all around the living room, carrying the print copy of the Torah with commentary that my dad gave me as a high school graduation present. 115 households were logged in, and I was exhausted after. The Rabbi started by saying we put safety over tradition—which is why we weren't together in person—and quite pointedly called out that not all feel that way. And he used PowerPoint slides to take us on a tour of fascinating design decisions in the writing in the Temple's Torah, like the places where the Red Sea is parted, and it's spaced apart as if the words represent the Jews escaping to safety. Had we been in person he could never have shown us that. That was really cool, and enlightening.

I expect my second contract to be signed Monday and perhaps my third a week from today.

---

42 The festive Jewish holiday celebrating the conclusion of the annual cycle of public Torah readings and the beginning of the next cycle.

October 10, Saturday

Last night a piece of paper was slipped under our door: new building restrictions as we live in the red zone. This is the first time restrictions in the co-op have increased, not decreased. It pushes us back to early July—no apartment showings, no construction, no entry by building staff in apartments unless an emergency, etc. It is still upsetting to see us going backwards. And especially upsetting that it seems like it was avoidable. But to be honest we always expected a second wave in the fall; we just didn't think we'd be in its epicenter. Is that why we're trying to buy this weekend home, so if schools are canceled, we are working from home, and we feel trapped in our apartment we have somewhere to escape to, to stay safe and stay sane?

October 11, Sunday

Today we went—for the 10th year in a row—to our favorite apple picking farm upstate for the day. We went with some good friends from the supper club and it was great to see them—but our regular date, the Biens, had moved this spring to California, and we missed them as well. And I couldn't ask my dad which apples I could pick for him. And they didn't grow the corn maze this year, and Tiny Town was closed (suffering its own tiny quarantine). Usually we pick and eat apples all day, testing each batch and enjoying the best; this year we were asked not to, presumably to discourage us from removing our masks and littering the fields with potentially infected apples.

Some traditions, even in a limited or transformed way, can bring comfort in these challenging days. But today I frankly just found it depressing.

October 12, Monday

Today went better. Today we are all off for Indigenous People's Day.

Last night I was so tired I nervously took my blood oxygen level with an oximeter. Just stuck in my finger and read the result a few seconds later; I keep it in my bedside table. All fine. But scary to have felt a need to check. With no job, if sick, then no money.

Today I got my second signed contract.

I wrote my book proposal on digital design in museums, and submitted it, with a five page sample to MIT press and ETC Press.

October 13, Tuesday

Started work today on my two new clients. Felt good. Exciting.

The new Oculus Quest 2 arrived today. So exciting.

Trump-supporting relative living in the South (who I love to hear from) called to find out why the NYC mayor is being antisemitic to the ultra-orthodox communities who are refusing to observe the public health restrictions even though their neighborhoods are five times more infectious than the general public. Not so exciting.

October 14, Wednesday

Finally super busy with work, and with just two clients. Good work but I have to learn to manage my time differently.

The Oculus Quest is so awesome. Untethered VR is the best. Beat Saber. Some dancing game. Paintball. Lots of fun—Akiva and I were fighting over it.

All we can talk about during supper club was which Orthodox—the Hassids or also the Ultra—are causing the infection spike. Splitting hairs. Tonight the Governor threatened to take state funds from their yeshivas[43] if they don't close down.

October 15, Thursday

Looks like we lost the lake house. The mortgage broker, after I lost my job, managed to make us eligible for a mortgage by us adding my sister and Noemi's mom. But what he neglected to tell us was that it increased the cash down payment from 20% (easy to meet) to 60% (possible but all of our savings.) How heartbreaking. What a screw-up. What a shame. It was wonderful both knowing we have a beautiful and secure place outside the city, and that my layoff

[43] The Orthodox day schools.

wouldn't stop it. On the other hand, it might be less stressful in the short term. We'll see.

October 16, Friday

Woke up to *The New York Times* headline about the malls next to us—one open and one closed—due to the COVID red line running between them. That included a mention of local Forest Hill parents protesting the local school closing, the school both of my kids once attended. Not an ultra Orthodox yeshiva, just our public school where a week ago no one was concerned. "It's not fair," they protested to the governor. As if the pandemic itself isn't the source of what is unfair. They sound childish to me. Still, I understand the frustration.

Blog Post: *Barry Joseph Consulting, LLC is Open For Business*

After years of thinking about it, this month I finally launched my own consulting business. I couldn't be more excited. And I am thrilled to tell you about my first three clients.

My first client is the Natural History Museum of Utah. Research Quest is NHMU's premier, digitally-delivered education program used in more than 200 classrooms, offering engaging and powerful series of science investigations that improve students' critical thinking skills. I will be providing analysis and key insights to the Museum to help them identify strategic opportunities for increasing the engagement and reach of the project.

My second client is the Jewish Education Project. The Jewish Education Project empowers Jewish educators to help their students and families thrive. I will be working with them this fall to help them answer the question: "What is the future of digital learning beyond this pandemic?"

My third client is the Oakland, CA-based Spanish Speaking Citizens' Foundation. I am supporting them to launch a new games-based learning program to engage area youth who are home during the pandemic. "The results were fantastic," Executive Director Alicia Contreras told me, after applying what she learned from our first session. "The kids were so engaged and participation raised 300%."

When you look at this initial body of work, what do you see? I see: Online learning. Games-based learning. Museums. After school programming. Disruptive change. Informal learning. Digital Strategy. Data-based decision making.

What I see is the future. And I see Barry Joseph Consulting helping organizations navigate the opportunities it brings and ensure their benefits are more equitably distributed.

Daily Diary Entries

October 17, Sat

I ordered dinner from a Hawaiian place and our doorman called and said it had arrived downstairs so I went downstairs and he said there was no food waiting for me and I called him back even though I'm standing right in front of him and the man on the phone said he sure did have my food. What a head-spinner! I realized then I had sent the food to a friend's apartment in Manhattan by mistake, as I had once ordered it there during a visit. And today he just happened to be out of town. I hope the doorman enjoyed the garlic shrimp.

I took Miri to her soccer game today so she could cheer on her team—her toe is bruised after a recent practice but luckily not broken. It was one and a half hours into Long Island, passed Commack, and we arrived after the game had begun. Team families are separated due to COVID on opposite sides of the field. As we approached the game, Miri's team happened to score. One side of the field clapped so I realized we were approaching the wrong side. Arriving on the right side I shared this story, about how I had figured out which was our team's side. Someone said it's easy to tell the local Long Island team from our Forest Hills' side: no one on their side was wearing a mask. I looked across the field and it was true. Not one. And not one person on our side was not.

October 18, Sun

I unpacked my boxes from Girl Scouts today. They mailed all they could fit. That was both fun and sad. I've never in 25 years moved from one job to nowhere—so I had to decide what to do with everything.

Tonight I would have been in Chicago at the annual dinner event for the foundation[44] honoring top educators. Instead it was all over video. It went flawless but I felt bad for the honorees—they didn't get that moment in person they deserved.

Tomorrow morning I drive Akiva to school. It's the middle of October. It will be his second day in school this year. We're 1.5 weeks into our local shut down, and still don't know how or when we will hear when Miri's school reopens in person.

Miri's Girl Scout troop isn't meeting due to the pandemic—the four other leaders from last spring are too overwhelmed. But today I gave her the new Cadet guide and she was so excited to jump back in and earn new badges on her own.

October 19, Monday

Took Akiva to school today. My second time. All went well. Funny to still be getting into a school routine this late into the fall.

For one client today I'm all into learning pods and micro schools. So interesting! How will this empower interest-driven learning? How much will it reinforce economic and racial inequality? How much will it drive online learning?

October 20, Tuesday

I understand tomorrow the Governor will give a statement about our local pandemic status. How will it feel if we've beaten a second rise? How will we feel if it hasn't gone down yet and the restrictions are still in place? I want my daughter to return to school two of every six

[44] I sit on the board of the Covenant Foundation, which funds innovation in Jewish education.

days. I want her to play soccer without a 40 minute car ride in rush-hour. I want my local nonessential stores not to go out of business. I want to not die of COVID.

October 21, Wednesday

Hurrah! We're in the yellow zone now. Miri's school should reopen on Monday.

Tonight I went to the New York Hall of Science drive-in to watch *Bad Hair*, a new film that's also a horror comedy. That's also 2020 in a nutshell: a horror comedy, with bad hair.

I spoke with someone at Outschool.com today. She was saying when the pandemic hit, user demand exploded because it was like everyone jumped into the future 10 years. I corrected her. Outschool already existed when the pandemic hit. Remote and digital learning already existed. These were people who were just resisting it. And like a slingshot slowly pulled back, tightening year after year, the tension built until, boom, pandemic, snap, they were shot into the present. It's about time they caught up.

October 22, Thursday

Hey, we got in a second presidential debate. And this one wasn't a shit show. Go figure. They actually talked policy.

I went into town to mail a package at the post office, get checks at the bank, all this previously normal stuff. But all wore masks, only eight people allowed in post office at a time, and the bank made me take my temperature and berated me for coming in without an appointment.

October 23, Friday

Watched the new Borat movie. What a crazy magic trick they pulled off. I can't figure out at what point during the making of the movie the pandemic struck America and they retooled the plot to include it. A totally brilliant sleight of hand.

October 24, Saturday

Noemi said the Bukharian[45] restaurant up the block was busted a day or so ago holding an event, maybe a wedding, with 300 guests. As a result they lost their liquor license.

---

[45] Mizrahi Jews from the former Soviet Union (according to Wikipedia, "an ethnoreligious Jewish sub-group of Central Asia") many of whom immigrated to Forest Hills.

October 25, Sunday

The Supreme Court tomorrow. The Senate and presidency in one week. I can barely think straight.

October 26, Monday

Even though she doesn't get to return until Thursday, I feel better just knowing Miri's school reopened in-person. And soccer practice returned to the local park. They say infection rates are low in school so far. Will other parents decide to send more of their kids in person next month? For just a few days, will they think it's worth it until they can return every day?

I can't believe the lake house is still in play. My friend unexpectedly stepped up as a cosigner, which should work for the mortgage broker. We can afford it again. Do we still want it? How much are we motivated as a way to have a sense of control during the nonstop pandemic disruptions? How much did it just reveal something new or accelerate an existing trend in that direction? That's what Noemi and I need to decide today.

I'm enjoying both the client work I found plus the efforts to build my brand. But now I'm also feeling the stress of not knowing where my next clients will come from.

October 27, Tuesday

Only ¼ of public school kids are opting in to in-person classes, less than ½ of that at Akiva's school. The first opt-in date for switching from fully remote to partial in-person is coming up. We thought this would be the first of a series of seasonal options. But yesterday the city announced it will be the only time to switch back to in-person schooling for the entire school year. And today Akiva's school wrote to say 1. If you switch to in-person your child will likely switch to new teachers and 2. There's no guarantee if they come in person they won't just be sitting at a computer in the library in a class taught by a remote teacher. What a mess! So glad we don't have to make that decision again now. But it does suggest more disruption on the way, and lessens the chance of Akiva having his classmates all return (for the first time) to school.

Tonight Noemi and I sat down to do a risk versus benefits analysis on the lake house.

Our desires versus our fears:

1. DOWNSIDE – a. Family finances unstable. b. Work required to turn it into a rental and maintain property.
2. PANDEMIC DISRUPTIONS – Society can collapse and this will be a great escape.
3. PANDEMIC ACCELERANTS – a. Increasing access to nature, swimming, and water sports. b. Give us a place of serenity. c. Makes it easier to live in a small city apartment.
4. INHERITANCE ACCELERANT – a. Is it risking the kids' college funds? b. A place to diversify investments while markets are unstable.

In summary, the finances and the work increases our stress; having a place of serenity out of the city and in nature would reduce stress. It's an exciting risk that is also panic inducing.

What will we decide?

October 28, Wednesday

We decided to go for the lake house. We often can be very conservative in the risks we take, but this is the year for taking risks. So we're going for it.

Supper club is tonight, as it has been every Wednesday night on Zoom from 9 to 10 PM since March. Sam[46] went back to her office this week for 19 minutes—first time since March. She described how strange it was—everything on desks frozen in time from the moment schools first closed. Someone's kid's school is closed now for at least one day due to in-school COVID infections. People traded tales of waiting on line for early presidential voting—45 minutes, 90 minutes—and how joyful and powerful it felt to do it, no matter what it took. I mailed my ballot in weeks ago.

October 29, Thursday

We can hold it together.

Tonight they announced the first infection in Miri's school. All we can be told is that the student or staff is not in her class. One more infection and they will close the school for two weeks.

The election is five days away.

Infection rates nationwide have hit a new all-time high.

I'm trying to focus on my new clients but wondering if there will be new ones to follow.

We can hold it together.

October 30, Friday

Today I received the first payment from my new client. A sizable amount. I am both proud and amazed.

46 Sam works for the NYC Board of Education.

Last night school told us kids could wear costumes to school today for Halloween (thanks for the heads-up!). Miri made her own[47] and got to wear it in. Just one small piece of Halloween she'll get this year. As only 1/3 of her class gets to be in school at a time and maybe 25% are going in at all, she's lucky to get to celebrate in-person in school. Before she walked out the door this morning she marveled that it's Halloween and yet she was going into school for only the fourth time this year.

October 31, Saturday

We miraculously pulled off Halloween for the kids. We watched *Stranger Things* on Netflix over dinner then told the kids to get their

[47] Eleven from *Stranger Things*.

pumpkin buckets and go into Akiva's room. Then we each "hid" behind different bedroom and bathroom doors while they trick-or-treated to us. Each time Noemi or I played different characters in a different thrown-together costume (mostly wigs) with a different bag of candy (which we emptied with generosity into their buckets). We gathered back on the couch laughing and exploring their sweet treasures, deciding which to devour first. It was a real gift, a testament less to our creativity than how much we all need it.

Then Miri went to her room to have her Halloween sleepover over Zoom, run by her and her friend N. The six or so of them watched scary shows, showed off costumes, ate candy, and who knows what else, but she was yelling and laughing and—when it was time for Noemi and I to go to bed—finally asleep in front of a still live Zoom screen (all but one with camera off) and I flicked off her light.

NOVEMBER 2020

In which a dock is disassembled… a president is elected… a MetroCard is tossed… the Situation Room reports… a 50th is celebrated… a patio heater is secured… Macy's delivers…

Daily Diary Entries

November 1, Sunday

Today I learned[48] how one can take in a dock with just a winch, blow torch, hammer, multiple screwdrivers, lots of rope, a few nautical knots, and a lot of creativity. Up to and back from the lake house within 8.5 hours. It was nice to be there. I might just own it some day.

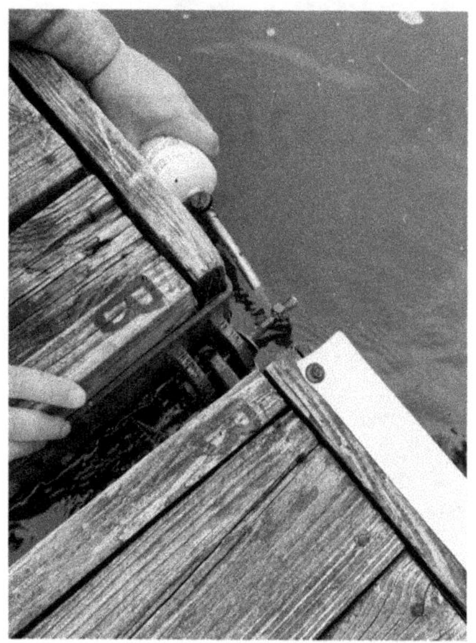

November 2, Monday

Tomorrow, whatever happens with the election, begins an historic pivot. What direction will it go in? And what disruptions will accompany it? How many lives lost? How much freedom?

---

[48] The current owner of the lake house invited me to help him take in the dock before the lake freezes so I can understand what needs to be done in the future.

November 3, Tuesday

What a nail-biter! I can't stand it. We stayed up until midnight then threw in the towel. Akiva stayed up until 11 PM. I wish it was a quick rout to show Trump how wrong he is. Now I just want to see him defeated and for us to reclaim the Senate. Both can still happen but it will just be a tighter win if it does. If not… I can't begin to imagine the despair and worry.

November 4, Wednesday

Morning, 6:40 AM. Not what was hoped for but what we feared—election is too close to call, counting will take days, Trump declares victory and threatens to use the Supreme Court to stop counting while day-of voting keeps him ahead of mail-in tallies. Now what?

Evening, 10:20 PM. I want to be excited that it looks like Biden will win—he's so close —but I won't let myself. Having most likely not taken the Senate, and Trump declaring victory, absurdly at 2 AM this morning, I just feel trepidation about the crazy new thing he or his supporters might do.

November 5, Thursday

The numbers change imperceptibly, in Pennsylvania, Georgia, Arizona, like watching water come to a boil. It was so stressful. I could barely work. At one point I took a walk for an hour.

At night Todd[49] joined me in VR—his Oculus Quest having arrived. I was surprised how high the learning curve was, but it was great connecting with him across the country. We went to a VR movie theater. I saw there were different "rooms" people made—quite a few to

[49] One of my best friends from high school. Lives in Los Angeles.

watch election returns with supporters of your candidate of choice. Instead I clicked on one watching a *Planet of the Apes* movie. I then experienced something nakedly racist. The room is a big screen theater, with people in seats holding popcorn and soda. The movie plays on the big screen while people voice chat. There appeared to be three or four friends together watching the movie and hanging out. At one scene there's a mob of apes, yelling, gesticulating. One friend said to the other, "This is what a Black Lives Matter protest must look like," and the other laughed. I said "Ouch. That is so racist." They didn't respond. Along with my popcorn I also had, for some reason, a marker. I tried to use it to make some graffiti in the air: "BLM". But it didn't work so I just left to go to the movie theater lobby. In the lobby people were standing around debating the affordances of VR. When I tried to contribute I saw I was muted. I'd always been muted, including during *Planet of the Apes*. Eventually I figured out what button to push to have a voice.

November 6, Friday

Going to bed, 11 PM, watching Biden speak for the first time since the election. Bring us together, Joe! "Let's be civil." Trump won't concede for a while, and there might be some recounts, but it looks like in any fair count Biden is the next president… and Georgia in January decides who controls Congress and how far and in what direction Biden gets to lead us over the next 2 to 4 years.

November 7, Saturday

Crying near sobs, then laughing, crying, laughing, then cheering, then laughing, more incredulous laughing, relieved laughing, then sobbing, releasing the weight we have been carrying for four years.

November 8, Sunday

Memories from yesterday:

Pulling into the pro-Trump Suffolk County parking lot for Miri's soccer game to the message on my friends' SMS chat that the election has been called for Biden by CNN. Stumbling out of my car, left hand on my chest, reading the news on the phone in my right, choking back sobs, pumping my fist in the air to the other Forest Hill parents pulling up, all aware we are still most likely in a pro-Trump community so best to be humble and keep it chill.

Videos pouring in on phones from friends of people celebrating in the streets with music and dancing in Brooklyn and Philly and Atlanta.

At the deli, watching the local news, as two senior men order lunch respond. "Is Biden for the rich or poor?" says one. The other: "I think the working class."

Listening to 1010 WINS news in the car heading home after the game just to hear the response to all the news. I can't recall the decade I last chose to listen to AM radio.

Back home our garage staff responding to my glee with an unexpected "I hate the Democrats. What they've done for my Brooklyn in 28 years. Nothing!" I said I heard him but asked him to give Biden a chance.

At night, watching Biden and Kamala give their acceptance speeches, calling for change on behalf of all Americans, followed by fireworks and an amazing drone-controlled light show.

Noemi wonders how we might get an American flag to put on our balcony. It feels like, in part, our country is back, the Democracy is back in safe hands.

November 9, Monday

Yesterday we went to New Rochelle to celebrate Oma's birthday, to sit on her lawn in this gorgeous 74° fall day, under golden leaves tinted brighter it seemed due to the pandemic spring's lack of cars. On her birthday card Miri wrote, "The pandemic has stopped us from many things but worst of all has been being with people on their birthdays. You won't get any hugs or kisses for me this year, but I hope the sentiment is in this card. You will get extra hugs next year."

Right now as I write this, both kids are in school. This is the second day this year this confluence has occurred. The school equinox, or something.

After the Bronx drop off with Akiva I headed into Manhattan—my first time since the March shut down. People wore masks. Fifth Avenue business windows are mostly boarded up, out of concern for last week's election, and concern that Trump has yet to concede. I inadvertently drove past the Trump Tower on 5th Avenue, armed police in front agreeing for who knows who to take their photo. Drove to Girl Scouts, to get everything they could not fit in a box: my beanbag chair, bookshelf and seltzer mini fridge. They had wanted me to park, sign in, and go myself into the office. No way. I didn't want to manage the emotions of returning to the place that fired me, especially while it was pandemic-emptied into a ghost town. No possible good could come of that. We met in the loading dock.

After, I drove down to Sixth Street to see Steven[50], the first time in person since the pandemic, even though we talk every day. It was good to see him. Even for the photo, on the sidewalk, he would not take off his mask.

November 10, Tuesday

Trump is a freakazoid.

November 11, Wednesday

Can it really be 8 months now working from home? It feels so normal. Being home every day, all four of us. Normal. Have I really acclimated and adapted or just stopped noticing the stress as it morphs into background noise?

November 12, Thursday

The vaccine is 90% effective, they say. That's amazing. Miraculous. Maybe we start getting it in the winter or spring. Is this the light at the end of the tunnel? I knew it would—hoped it would—come, but I didn't know what it would look like. At least, it feels that way. Of course it would be a vaccine.

Meanwhile we hit 150,000 infected nationwide in a day. We expect schools to close citywide in a few weeks, which will be such a shame. And then does it all return to like last spring? Can we hunker down like that again? Will we be better prepared for it now? And will we have the lake home by then to escape to?

---

[50] A best friend since elementary school. We text chat most days. Watch for him later in this book.

What is Trump waiting for before he concedes?

Akiva had his parent-teacher conference today. They were all glowing. Which given the pandemic situation is amazing. We knew his grades were great, but they shared how warm he is, how he always has his camera on which is appreciated. Noemi saw this as a sign of his general well-being, not just academic, reflected back to us in a hard to measure way. It's quite a relief. His inner strength and resiliency is a marvel.

November 13, Friday

I threw my MetroCard out. I realized tonight it was still in my wallet, unused for 9+ months, since the shut down in March. I paused the automatic payments from work soon after and when Girl Scouts let me go that ended that. Sometimes it takes a while to realize your wallet still carries outdated material.

I currently have nine 60L CO2 containers that need to be filled. My Sodastream soda maker only takes one at a time. We usually have three, to stay in stock. In spring with the national CO2 shortage threatening the flow of seltzer I ended up buying a few more, to keep us in stock during the dark days. Then Girl Scouts sent me the ones I kept at my desk, bringing my collection up to nine canisters. Now they are all empty, the CO2 shortage has returned, and Sodastream will not swap them out for full ones. So tomorrow I go look for a Target to see if they can make the exchange. The seltzer must flow!

November 14, Saturday

Today we went to Levittown out on Long Island for Miri's soccer game. Playing defense, she's fast like a bullet. Noemi commented on how great it is that the games and practices have gotten us out of the house so much. Next week is the last fall game. If the city closes on

Monday what happens to this game? In either case, what happens to the planned switch to a winter indoor practice regime? Miri can practice outside but indoors we draw the line. Akiva commented on the increased number of girls on the teams the further east we travel—more girls, more energy on the team, the stronger the team, due to COVID and politics: the more conservative, the less COVID concerns, the more families permit their girls to play. Thus, us being from the city, we have less girls playing and, faster to tire out, Miri's team has been losing. Hard to argue with that logic.

Akiva led us in an hour of improvisational board gaming. *Monopoly* + *Adventure Time*-themed *Munchkin* + random game pieces (dice, cubes, tiddlywinks). It was a crazy game, lots of fun and felt emblematic of strategizing survival in the world with rules in a constant state of change, but, unlike with the game *Flux*, for no discernible reason

November 15, Sunday

This morning they decided we're good! They are not shutting the schools down tomorrow. We all thought they would (and that then they'd be closed until the second or third wave passes, in months.)

That was confirmed tonight when we got our daily email from Akiva's school, then Miri's school, then for some reason from another school which neither attends, all sharing a report card of sorts that states there are not enough internal COVID cases to close any of those schools. Phew!

However five minutes ago, at 10:50 PM, Miri's school closed. There was an additional COVID case. She wasn't supposed to go in until Tuesday anyway, so will she when the day arrives? We won't learn until tomorrow night. But at least one thing's for sure… Scratch that. Nothing is for sure.

Email: Note from NYC DOE COVID-19 Situation Room

From: DOE COVID-19 Situation Room
Subject: Note from NYC DOE COVID-19 Situation Room
Date: November 16, 2020 at 7:21:49 PM EST
To: Barry Joseph

I hope today finds you and your family safe and healthy. We will be sending information directly to families on all current positive cases of COVID-19 in your school building. This means, we will be sharing updates on any new positive COVID-19 cases or any old cases that still have members of your school building quarantining. The report below is at the building level and includes information on all the schools in your building. All the information reported below has been verified by the New York City Department of Health and Mental Hygiene.

Today, between 5:30 AM and 6:44 PM, we confirmed 2 new COVID-19 positive cases

Total Number of Ongoing COVID-19 Confirmed Cases This represents all new confirmed COVID-19 cases reported between 5:30 AM today and 6:44 PM and all old cases that still have members of your building quarantining.	4

No Intervention: A member of the school building has tested positive but the school community was not exposed. **Example 1:** A student in your school building tests positive, but is fully remote and never reported to the building. **Example 2:** A staff member in your school building tests positive, but was not in the building during their infectious period or has no close contacts in the school building. **Infectious period** is the time when an individual can spread the virus to others. It typically begins two days before symptom onset or day of COVID-19 test (if no symptoms). **Close contact** is someone who is at-risk for contracting the virus due to prolonged exposure to someone who tested positive for COVID-19 during their infectious period.	Yes
Classroom Closure: A member of the school building has tested positive and members of the school community have been quarantined. **Example 1:** A student in your school building tested positive, and was in the building during their infectious period, and has close contacts who are students and staff. **Example 2:** A non-instructional staff member in your school building tested positive, and was in the building during their infectious period, and has close contacts who are also only non-instructional staff. **Please note:** Any case in this category will show up daily until that quarantine period has ended. **Infectious period** is the time when an individual can spread the virus to others. It typically begins two days before symptom onset or day of COVID-19 test (if no symptoms). **Close contact** is someone who is at-risk for contracting the virus due to prolonged exposure to someone who tested positive for COVID-19 during their infectious period.	Yes

Building Closed: Two or more unlinked positive cases in a school building. When two or more cases without a clear link are reported, a school building will be closed for at least 24 hours in order for the Department of Health and Mental Hygiene epidemiologists to perform an investigation. Sometimes there are two or more cases in a building where it is not closed. In those cases, the Test + Trace Corp has been able to identify a link between the cases, either within the building or outside of the building.	Yes

Thank you for your cooperation. Health and safety will always come first in New York City public schools, no matter what.

Sincerely,
DOE COVID-19 Situation Room

Daily Diary Entries

November 16, Monday

We learned four people in Miri's school have COVID. School is closed tomorrow. Is she infected? Do we have it? If they reopen Wednesday, do we still send her in?

November 17, Tuesday

And her school opened back up. Holy cow! I guess she's going in tomorrow.

How has Trump still not conceded?

My sister's 50th birthday is this Sunday. The Broadway show we were going to see to celebrate has been rescheduled for March, 2022—16 months from now. I didn't want to plan anything with her until this week, as we didn't know if the city would be closed down or if the weather would be good enough to meet outdoors. So far both look good; she'll take an Uber, meet us in the park downstairs, and will take a walk and hang out.

November 18, Wednesday

Miri was able to go in person to school.

In the afternoon it closed. Again. Along with every other school in the city.

We have no information on what conditions need to be met in order for them to re-open.

I'm advocating they immediately re-open the schools and run them within restaurants, as those are still open.

Email: All Public School Buildings will Temporarily Close

From: Stephen A. Halsey
Subject: All Public School Buildings will Temporarily Close for an extended time Effective Thursday 11/19
Date: November 18, 2020 at 2:41:05 PM EST
To: Barry Joseph

All Public School Buildings will Temporarily Close for an extended time Effective Thursday 11/19

Good afternoon,

As of this morning, November 18, the City has now reached this threshold of test positivity citywide and, as a result, the DOE will temporarily close down all public school buildings for in-person learning, Thursday, November 19. This action, along with other city-wide measures, is a key component to address the concerning rise in COVID-19 transmission rates. This closure of buildings is temporary; we will work diligently alongside other City agencies and every New Yorker to bring this transmission rate back down and get back to in-person learning as quickly and as safely as possible (please see attached letter from Chancellor Carranza).

Our school will be on full remote learning beginning tomorrow.

Sincerely,
Principal JHS 157

Daily Diary Entries

November 19, Thursday

Looks like Biden won Georgia. Again.

November 20, Friday

Todd (in L.A.) and I watched the new episode of the *Mandalorian* together on Disney+. Live in our Oculus Quest 2s we finally figured out how to watch together through its VR web browser. We couldn't see each other but we could hear each other's "oh no!"s and laughter. It was amazing. I used to talk to him like once or twice a year. Now we have a weekly date.

Oh, I also finally found a new co-leader of our Girl Scout Troop! We might just get it back off the ground.

November 21, Saturday

The day began with a B'nai Mitzvah[51]. My cousin was in her temple in Pennsylvania. We, and others, watched and participated from our homes over video. She kept her Torah portion and *Dvar Torah*[52] from her original May date, which as the Rabbi pointed out made this year's crop of B'nai Mitzvahs special as they all got to learn about two portions instead of one.

Then Miri's last fall soccer game (they tied).

---

[51] A Jewish coming-of-age ritual.

[52] A sermon based on that week's section of the Torah.

Then, an interactive theater piece, designed for Zoom. Like *Jackbox*, with each home audience member on a mobile website to vote on what we, Alice from *Wonderland*, would do—what she'd say to the characters, and how she'd solve puzzles, while we, the audience, strategized via group text chat.

Overall, a successful pandemic day.

November 22, Sunday

Today was Debby's 50th birthday. My calendar read "Do something with Debby today and Dad". Suffice it to say, today did not go as originally planned. No dinner at the Paris Café at the TWA Hotel—was it ever reopened? No *Music Man* on Broadway—will it still open as now scheduled in March, 2022? And not seeing Dad. But I think we all did the best we could under the circumstances, and Debby both appreciated it and enjoyed it: Ubered here, we set up a table downstairs in the park, I put on a garbage bag and hugged her, and we ate bagels and cupcakes that Noemi baked. Then we walked around Flushing Meadow lake for two hours, which was largely empty (other than friends and neighbors we kept running into, curiously). Totally low-key, just the five of us. But we were together.

Hopefully weather permitting we can see each other again for Thanksgiving this Thursday at Oma's on her lawn.

November 23, Monday

After dinner Miri took in her plate to the kitchen, began humming a tune, returned to dance around the dining room table with arms waving on her way to the bathroom, and exited with a self-referential, "You have weird children".

November 24, Tuesday

Looks like we might get Trump out of office.

Planning for Thanksgiving is becoming a logistical nightmare.

Miri said the good thing about being "quarantined" is that when you lose something you still know it's not lost since you never left home.

November 25, Wednesday

Tomorrow Is Thanksgiving. A month ago Noemi ordered a patio heater for Oma so we could celebrate at her mom's, even if it was cold out. It shipped from China. We were told it had arrived in the U.S. but it never arrived in New Rochelle. Something was fishy. Noemi asked and got her money back, but that left us with no heater. Lowe's. Home Depot. Walmart. Amazon. Everyone is sold out. Tomorrow's raining so we moved plans to Friday, figuring we could handle high 50s for a few hours. Then Debby reminded us she had a client with a 98-year old grandfather in Riverdale[53] who sells patio heaters from his garage. WTF? So guess where I'm going Friday morning?

Today I went to my general doctor. I haven't been in almost a year and a half due to the pandemic. It's more unsafe now not to go then to go. I was a little scared, but I did it, taking all the precautions I could think of. So fingers crossed. And all my standard tests came out fine. But that colonoscopy I'm due for will just have to wait until post-pandemic.

Quote of the day: "'I will not have a statement', she said," from this *New York Times*' article: "New Jersey school board member resigns after bathroom mishap in Zoom meeting".

November 26, Thursday

I don't know how Macy's pulled off both not having the parade today with it also feeling like we just watched one! It would certainly not feel like Thanksgiving without it. And Macy's went one further,

[53] Riverdale is a section of the Bronx, in New York City.

inviting representatives from the Pride parade, the West Indian Day parade, the Puerto Rican Day parade, the Mermaid parade, and so many others canceled this year—recognizing them and turning this into not just a Thanksgiving Day parade but one with the power to reach back to earlier in the year and offer some needed healing. Thank you Macy's!

November 27, Friday

We drove to Manhattan, got Debby's Thanksgiving food from her Doorman (she was still at work), drove to Riverdale in the Bronx to buy the patio heater from the garage of the 98-year-old man, drove to New Rochelle, Akiva and I put the heater together, Debby arrived by Uber, the food was ready and we sat at separate tables around the heater and had a lovely, totally normal, pandemic Thanksgiving dinner. Then, rather than sleep over, we returned home.

November 29, Sunday

A nice weekend. Lovely weather. Board games and escape rooms in a box. TV shows and movies. We even went to the Queens Zoo—which is already perfect since it's outside, in a linear circle, and the animals are far enough away to not need masks—and a walk to the Unisphere. We got take-out for dinner from the delicious Empanada Café on the way home.

New school plans in New York City arrived: elementary schools will open soon, with no blended learning, which makes sense, but the fate of middle and high schools are still unknown.

Mortgage appraisal this Wednesday on the second home. Trump says if the electoral college goes for Biden he'll step down. And this week I transitioned from my first batch of clients to my second—not yet as much money as the first, but there's still time, the work is perfect for me, and I still feel really fortunate.

November 30, Monday

My doctor's office called me today. All is well with my check-up results and blood test but he wanted to prescribe three months of daily vitamin D. How does one normally get vitamin D? Sunlight. I said forget about it. I'll just go outside.

I usually go to the dentist four times a year. After five gum grafts, I fight hard to prevent my gums from deteriorating. It's been I think a year since I went in so, along with my doctor check-up, I bit the bullet and visited the dentist. If things are getting worse and it'll be six months until the vaccine enters me, I better go now. It was terrifying. She was triple masked, so I was not a threat to her. But how did I know the previous patient wasn't positive and hadn't coughed all over the tiny unventilated room I was laying in? I hope it was worth the risk. I left feeling a deeper appreciation for the staff of the dental office and for both Noemi and I getting to work from home.

DECEMBER 2020

In which schools remain closed… a consultancy finds legs… movies are watched… holidays are celebrated… a vaccine arrives… a pandemic year in photos…

Daily Diary Entries

December 3, Thursday

It's looking like, while elementary schools will now open full-time, there's a bias against blended learning, even though I think it's working for my kids. I suspect, being in middle and high school, my kids will be forced to go fully remote for months now. We'll see. The school bus people emailed today to survey if we'd use them if schools open back up in January. Do they know something we don't? The mortgage appraisal happened yesterday on the lake house. That closing couldn't come at a better time!

December 4, Friday

I just need to take a break from work. I am floored, gob-smacked. My current project is promoting a free (with stipend even) professional development training for museum educators. This is giving me an opportunity to open my Rolodex and contact my museum network of the past decade. But this is no regular "Hey, it's been a long time." It's "Have you been fired yet or are you just heartbroken by seeing your colleagues let go and your salaries slashed?" and "Are your doors still closed like the other 1/3 of museums that haven't opened since March?" Each time before I reach out I use LinkedIn to get caught up and I just saw, yet again, someone I've known at a museum for years who had been let go in the last few months. It's a cultural slaughter. Reading his blog, and his recent experience losing his mom overnight to COVID, of the ever-present threat of layoffs erupting in an emergency all-staff meeting that led to his immediate dismissal after seven years of work, was an eerie reflection of my year. SO yeah—I needed to take a break and let it all just breathe.

December 5, Saturday

Have I shared this yet? I learned years ago from reading author Daniel Pink that my work satisfaction comes from having autonomy over my work and a clear understanding of how it advances an organization's mission. As the proprietor of my own company, hired by people who know exactly what they want from me and why, my job satisfaction is through the roof. No more office politics. No more positioning to keep my job against a threat of layoffs or someone not appreciating my value. No more having to suffer the indignity of losing control over mundane aspects of my work. Running my own consultancy has been amazing. The down side: near constant anxiety and terror that my current clients will be my last and that the marketplace is so swamped I'll never find a satisfying full-time job to replace the lost Girl Scouts' income. I keep balance through positive thinking, and patience.

December 6, Sunday

This morning was the Temple's zoom-based pre-Hanukkah[54] festivities. It was very creative and fun. I thought at the end the Rabbi gave very excellent advice about how we might pull Hanukkah off in our lives during the pandemic: try anything, no matter how outside the box; and if it doesn't work, just blame it on 2020. I thought that can not only apply to any decisions we made this year, it highlights the low stakes for taking risks, like buying a house or launching a new company. If it doesn't work, we can always blame the pandemic. But if we don't take the risks, there's no one else to blame but ourselves.

[54] Hanukkah is a Jewish holiday that marks an historic event through lighting a nine-candle menorah and the sharing of presents.

December 7, Monday

Today I drove into the city to pick my sister up after a routine medical procedure and get her back to her apartment. But there was nothing routine about it. Was this my third time driving to a destination in Manhattan since the pandemic (the first two being picking up belongings from Girl Scouts and getting Debby's Thanksgiving dishes)?

It felt so weird to be back, especially driving downtown. It was both comforting and strange to see everyone wearing masks. Then, driving around those rabbit warren side-streets heading to a garage, I found a parking spot on the street. Yes, I found a parking spot on the street downtown, just blocks from the World Trade Center!

I walked into the medical office where she had the procedure. I had a double mask on, plus gloves, just in case. But there was no one at reception. No one to ID me. Deb had just arrived in the waiting room and was groggy but fine. We went to reception to sign her out. Still no one there so we just left. I felt like I was absconding with her.

Now to get her home. No one but my family has been in our car in nine months. It was our safe space. So I ran to where I parked, drove to her, and called her a Lyft driver, making sure she got in. I zoomed to her place in Midtown and beat them there, where we said our farewells and she went into her building.

I was happy I could help but hated having to decide again and again where to put up boundaries, for both of our sakes, limiting how much support I could provide. Double guessing every decision makes me feel like I was being ungenerous, or selfish, or silly.

December 8, Tuesday

What a day! Where to begin? I returned to the dentist today to fill the two cavities they found. Two hours later I left… then returned again for another hour to fix some work that did not stick. Afterwards they said, Let's schedule your next cleaning. I said, Um, no, I'll call when the pandemic is over. I wasn't that rude of course. But it helped me to appreciate once again how privileged I am to get to work from home.

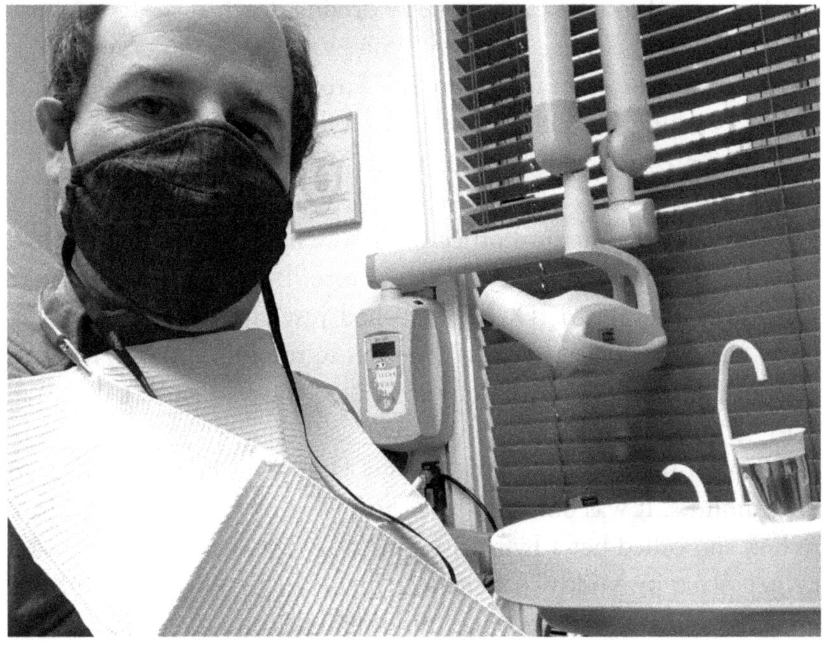

The news every day now about the coming vaccine is so positive and hopeful.

I got my fifth client today. I also concluded the scope of work with my first client who then asked me to propose the next round of work. That feels great.

Tonight at dinner Noemi asked the kids how their day was. Akiva talked about what he was learning in his after school machine learning program; Miri about how she learned in math to apply the Pythagorean theorem to calculate the distance between two points that do not share an X or Y coordinate. What was going on? Just a few weeks ago that question would be met with "It was fine" and nothing more. How can they be adapting so well to this insanity?

I imagine myself returning back in time to March and telling myself the following: in one month your dad will die; your children will not return into a school or classroom for eight months; sleepaway camps will be canceled; you will be fired along with 20% of your workplace; you will launch your own company; you will try to buy a second home. And I'd say, Who are you, how did you get into my apartment, and get the fuck out.

December 9, Wednesday

Luckily our family's healthcare comes through Noemi's job. Today, she had to choose our plan for next year: the same basic plan we have now or the enhanced plan. It was an easy decision. She said, "I don't think 2021 is the year to skimp on healthcare insurance."

December 10, Thursday

Today we received the mortgage appraisal, with an anticipated closing date. Holy second home, Batman! I think this is going to happen.

Tonight was the first night of Hanukkah. It was lively.

Normally this time of year Broadway stars greet exiting audience members at the end of shows with red buckets to raise money for Equity Fights AIDS. Since theaters are now closed NBC instead broadcast two hours of homages to the Great White Way featuring all those furloughed performers performing. It was beautiful. And heartbreaking.

December 11, Friday

The Supreme Court refused to give Trump what he has been looking for, slapping down Texas' bizarre attack on the swing states that went for Biden. That was a relief. Had it gone in the other direction, from this moment in time, it would have felt like the unraveling of the American experiment.

The movie *The Prom* was released today on Netflix, the Hollywood musical starring Hollywood stars playing Broadway actors in a Broadway show. The leap of faith it required was pretending Broadway shows were still open, and that we were watching it as intended in a movie theater, ignoring that, in fact, both are currently closed. Watching it felt so meta-meta-meta-, with a rock step and ball change. Jazz hands!

Lighting candles for the second night of Hanukkah, with people over Zoom, with people we usually never do it with, was a lovely new way to enact an old tradition.

December 12, Saturday

We had such an amazing day together taking Andy[55] for his birthday up to Storm King. It was foggy the whole time, which cast a white haze across the massive sculpture grounds, making it all feel so ethereal and magical, like fairies might pop out of the mist at any moment. Capped at 25%—and, yes, reduced attendance due to the approaching winter weather—meant we had so much space from strangers, and each other, and provided us the opportunity to wander outside for hours, hopping from one massive and awe-inspiring sculpture to another. Quite a gift in these times, and not just for our friend.

55 In case you forgot, an old friend from high school.

In the car trip back, Miri began to marvel how, once upon a time, three weeks in quarantine felt so long, then we were at five than seven weeks, and yet here we are now 10 months later, still making it work. She asked when we thought things would get back to normal. A month ago, I might have been making stuff up, but now it seems likely, as we told her, we expect sleep-away and day camp to return in the summer, in-person school in the fall, but much longer before big events like concerts. She told us she and her friend N. decided they'd become a generation that would live as depressed germaphobes. When pushed, she clarified they meant anxious germaphobes, always concerned the virus will return. We told her she might be right but we thought/hoped they'd see how well they survived this and draw strength from that when confronting whatever life faces them with in the future. So rather than make them anxious germaphobes we hope it will make them the most resilient generation ever, who feel confident they can handle anything.

December 13, Sunday

We went to Oma's in New Rochelle for the fourth night of Hanukkah. Everyone has the routine down now. Outdoor tables and chairs. Patio heater. No one in the kitchen but Oma, etc. Yummy latkes[56]! It was too windy to light the menorah outside so we figured out Oma could do it on the dining room table and we could be outside looking in. And if we were loud enough we could hear each other singing through the window. Apart but together. Whatever it takes—stay safe, maintain traditions, and keep reaching for one another. It is still exhausting having to always figure something new out, but if that's what it takes then that's what it takes.

[56] Potato pancakes, a traditional Hanukkah food.

December 14, Monday

Today was the day the first US citizens received a COVID-19 vaccine. They were healthcare workers around the country. But the first person at the first location was a randomly-selected nurse at the nearby Long Island Jewish Hospital in Lake Success.

Long Island Jewish is where my dad died.

As soon as I realized that I broke down.

December 15, Tuesday

Oh, and yesterday the Electoral College finalized the election. What a day. What a season. What a year.

December 16, Wednesday

It is day three of the vaccine. We're all cautiously optimistic. Who do we know who knows someone getting it? How does it work? When will we receive it? Tonight at supper club Chris said it's as if we all now have lived through a war (just not as bad) and for the rest of our lives it's something everything else will be compared against.

Early on last spring, Noemi and I began the practice of starting each day before work doing this web-based seven-minute workout at the NYTimes.com. It's been great for our spirit and bodies to have maintained this practice all this time. This week Akiva has joined us, every day. Previously he just was on his computer on the couch and ignored us. It feels like a minor miracle and I almost don't want to mention it for fear of jinxing it…

December 17, Thursday

Finally, a snowstorm! I stopped work so Miri and I could go outside, have a snowball fight, and make snow angels. Then we stopped playing so I could return to work and she could get back to her classes.

At least, that's what I thought at first. Then I asked myself: Did I take a break from work to go play in the snow, or did I take a break from playing in the snow to fit in some work? Being my own boss raises all sorts of new and interesting existential questions.

December 18, Friday

The last episode of season two of the *Mandalorian*, watched with my high school buddy in LA through our Oculus Quest 2…

Watching the release of the new Hollywood blockbuster *Tenet* streamed right into our homes, where we could pause, rewind, and chat about it…

Maybe 2020 wasn't THAT bad…

December 19, Saturday

It's kind of crazy that we're planning a 5 ½ hour all-Zoom New Year's Eve party. But it might just work. I'm surprised how many are RSVPing to attend. First, a fancy dinner cooked by a laid-off chef delivered in advance to our homes. Jackbox games. A caricaturist. Bring-your-own Celebrity Cameos. Personal year-in-review photos. Breakout rooms for chit-chatting, for a Photo Booth, for kids-only to play their own games. I'm actually looking forward to it.

December 20, Sunday

Between Akiva, Noemi and myself I think we played *Myst VR* on the Oculus for six hours today. Immersive, puzzle solving fun.

We dragged the kids outside out of desperation—Noemi threatened to stop washing their clothes (Akiva's response: "Well, we have to learn to do laundry some time.") And we got as far as the park next-door, joining in on the sledding fun. It felt kind of crazy all of us zooming down the hill in our masks, trying to keep the distance from other sledders, but it also felt cathartic, protecting ourselves from the virus while we threw our bodies helter skelter down the icy slope unprotected and flying like a banshee.

December 21, Monday

Last week by 4pm I was running out of steam. My cognitive load level was low. This is so unusual for me.

This week I'm hitting the wall around three. I'm mentally constipated, emotionally backed up.

December 22, Tuesday

Miri was perturbed with us this morning since she was late to school. School starts at 8:30. She wanted us to agree to wake her up at 8:25, more than enough time she felt to roll over, turn on her computer, and say "Here".

December 23, Wednesday

Yesterday we got a flyer under our door: a staff member in our building tested positive and is now being quarantined. If they think he's been in contact with us they will reach out. No one has reached out. As a result, all 20 or so staff are being tested.

Today we received a new flyer; multiple staff have now tested positive and been quarantined for two weeks. Due to HIPAA restrictions, they can't say who it is, even though over time it will be clear from their absence. But since they park our cars and handle our packages and receive our food deliveries we just can't know if we've been infected by them or not. It makes me want to isolate ourselves in our apartment again, after months of being increasingly lax in the hallways, stairwells and foyers. I don't like being scared in our own home.

On the other hand, during supper club tonight, people are sharing tales of knowing someone who knows someone who received the vaccine. When will we all know someone? When will we assume all we know are vaccinated? When will we pass through this liminal space?

December 24, Thursday

I watched Spike Lee's direction of David Byrne's *American Utopia.* It was the best concert I've ever seen here at Forest Hills Stadium. Watching this adaptation of its move to Broadway, with so many people packed into a tight space with such monumental energy permeating that theater, I almost cried for missing such cultural experiences since the pandemic and not knowing when we will feel safe enough to have that back in our lives.

As I watched I continued preparing my photos from the year, culling the garbage, rating them, labeling the faces. What a tour. My last seltzer talk in February. That March 1 sign in a Chinatown mall elevator stating myths and facts about COVID (e.g. "Don't be mean to International students"). Miri walking to school on what turned out to be her last day in person in middle school, and her last day in person in school in eight months. Our 7 PM clapping for the healthcare workers. Our socially distanced park visits with friends. On the lawn at Noemi's mom's house. Breaking the isolation with Debby (at last) in August. So much of our lives lived through Zoom: my dad's death, funeral and *shiva*, work, temple events, birthdays, socializing with friends…

Noemi is asking each guest to pick three photos each to show on New Year's Eve. I'm having a heckuva time. Which three can capture all this?

December 25, Friday

I posted 17 photos on Facebook, with the following to introduce them:

This is not my annual collection of favorite family photos from the year. Rather, this is our annotated pandemic year in photos—each one selected as it highlights something unique about 2020 that I hope STAYS in 2020. I added questions after each one. Please feel free to respond in the comments for each photo, or, better yet, consider responding with your own annotated photo.

1. Jan. March against antisemitism across the Brooklyn Bridge. The biggest rally the kids have ever been to, and their first time walking across the bridge. By the end of this year it feels impossible to imagine having ever been around and so close to that many people. What is the largest group of people you were with this year?

2. Late February - this was the last date of my SeltzertopiaLive! tour. I just wouldn't know for a few weeks that it would be my last. What is something that ended for you this year that came as a surprise?

3. Our last supper club in March - a group of friends whose kids went to elementary school together have gathered once a month for years without the kids to have dinner. The pandemic stopped this cold, but couldn't stop us. We pivoted to a weekly Wednesday night Zoom call right away and have kept it up all year. What is one group you have kept meeting with regularly this year?

4. Miri travelling with her friend N. to school, walking ahead, beginning this first leg of their independence. This day also turned out to be their last ever going into class, let alone their elementary school. This year later began middle school, but also continued the independence the pandemic could not take away, with these two walking together on their own and heading to Dunkin or a bagel shop on the way home after school. How much did the pandemic stall their development? How did it advance it at light speed?

5. Early on Miri drew a picture of me at work. She was now always around when I was working, as no one left the apartment. And working with headsets on was now the norm, as all work was done through a Zoom-like interface. How did your work practices change this year? What might someone have drawn who was observing you?

6. I had read (and written) my dad's public obituary for the death that was mine and my family's to grieve. This, however, is an excerpt repeated weeks later in the *NYTimes*, his death now representing 99 others, their collective grouped with 999 other such groups, together representing the first 100,000 American COVID deaths. Now his death was part of the history of COVID loss in America, and the world. Who was the first you knew to die from COVID?

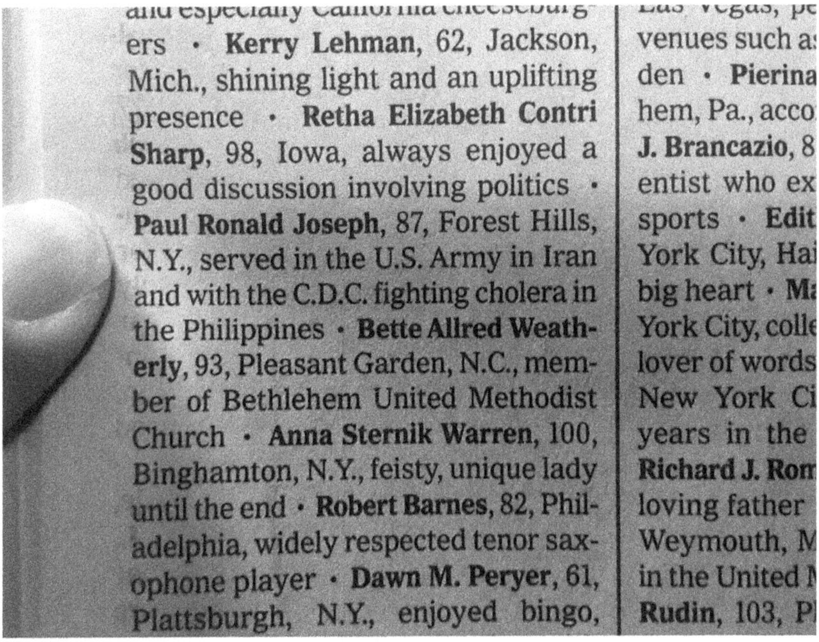

and especially California cheeseburgers • **Kerry Lehman**, 62, Jackson, Mich., shining light and an uplifting presence • **Retha Elizabeth Contri Sharp**, 98, Iowa, always enjoyed a good discussion involving politics • **Paul Ronald Joseph**, 87, Forest Hills, N.Y., served in the U.S. Army in Iran and with the C.D.C. fighting cholera in the Philippines • **Bette Allred Weatherly**, 93, Pleasant Garden, N.C., member of Bethlehem United Methodist Church • **Anna Sternik Warren**, 100, Binghamton, N.Y., feisty, unique lady until the end • **Robert Barnes**, 82, Philadelphia, widely respected tenor saxophone player • **Dawn M. Peryer**, 61, Plattsburgh, N.Y., enjoyed bingo,

Las Vegas, pe
venues such a
den • **Pierina**
hem, Pa., acco
J. Brancazio, 8
entist who ex
sports • **Edit**
York City, Ha
big heart • **M**
York City, colle
lover of words
New York Ci
years in the
Richard J. Ror
loving father
Weymouth, M
in the United
Rudin, 103, P

7. Heading to New Rochelle to figure out how to socially distance with Oma. How did you keep connected with your family this year?

8. During the quarantine doing anything we could to get outside into the biggest places we could find. Here we are in Brooklyn at an abandoned airstrip at Floyd Bennett Field. What is the biggest place you went to outdoors this year?

9. 7pm, come what may, meant exiting our apt (perhaps the first time for the day), entering our balcony, and joining our neighbors around our adjacent park clapping and yelling in appreciation of the sacrifice of local health care workers. What did you do to honor health care professionals this year?

10. We spent more time this year outdoors than ever. And less. We'd spend a full week never leaving the apt then compress our outdoor needs into weekend day excursions like these, exploring in all directions. What is one outdoor place you discovered this year?

11. This is us in a park north of the city, getting outside our apt in late June where there would not be many people, playing a socially distanced board game (*Wavelength*) with our friends, the Biens -- this photograph taken by Geraldine -- our first time seeing friends in a park since quarantine, and before they moved to L.A. the following week. Did you discover a game that works great to play at a distance?

12. This is at our June lake escape house. In the reflected window we see the mirror world of the beauty we were fortunate enough to live and work in; Akiva's stance shows the weight of the burden we still carried. How did you find a way to balance bringing beauty and good into the world this year with so much hardship and pain?

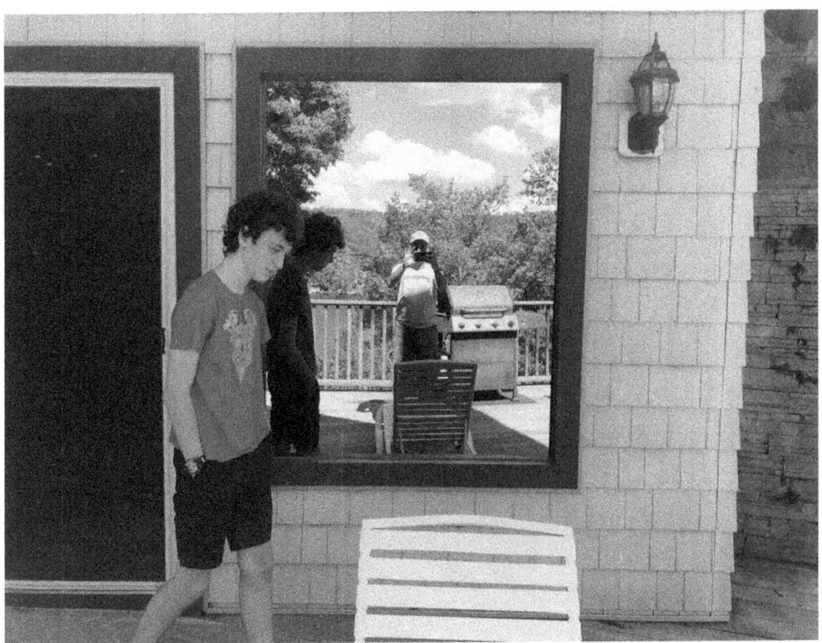

13. Everybody working to make it work, no matter what it takes. And the desire for all of this extra effort required to engage in the quotidian to just STOP already. What is something you had to work at this year to do that before you would never have given a second thought?

14. In our bubble, vacationing together, we convinced this restaurant to open its patio as we would not eat inside. We sat under a blue sky; we ate under torrential showers, undaunted, refusing to give in, and we had a blast together. What is one of the crazy things the pandemic made you do to keep connected with the people you love?

15. Miri's 1st day of middle school. In October. Welcome to school… and let me make sure you're not a threat to the lives of your classmates and teachers. How did COVID checks change your life?

16. Our annual apple picking trip. There are many traditions we got to continue this year, this being one of the many (July 4th camping, holidays, birthdays, etc.) but all had new twists - some for the better, some for the worst. What's a tradition you got to maintain this year, and what had to change to make it work (and will you keep that change in the future)?

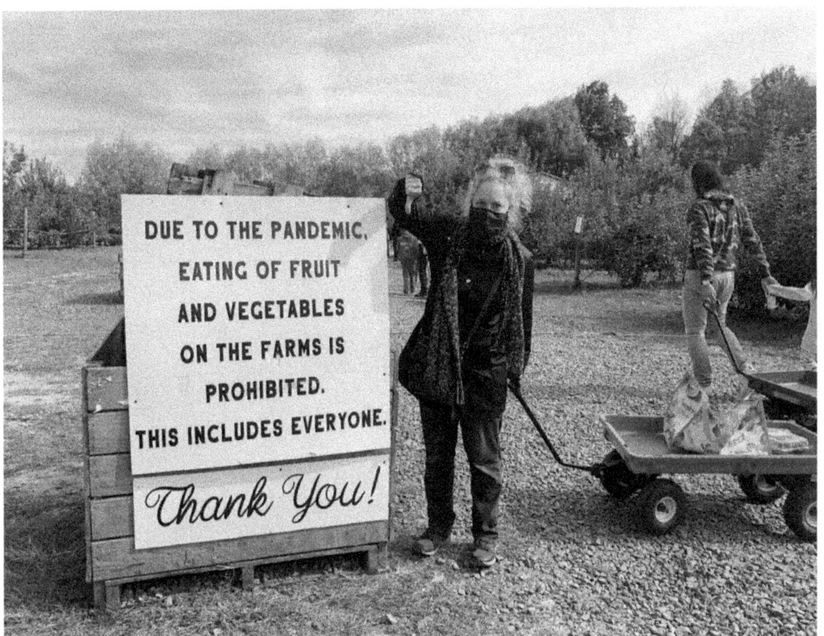

17. This to me is the pandemic year in a nutshell: a misty day at the Storm King Sculpture Park. The kids are tiny in the distance. We are celebrating Andy's birthday. This took place any day, every day, which is to say blursday. Is the mist approaching? Is it receding? This was 2020 - lost in a fog and having little clarity about what comes next. What do you have scheduled next blursday?

December 27, Sunday

Normally, as Jews, Christmas means Chinese food and a movie. Since we couldn't go out for either, on Friday and Saturday we ordered in (Saturday actually was Indonesian—yummy!) and on each day we watched what would have been new movie theater releases—on Friday Pixar's *Soul* (on Disney+) and on Saturday *Wonder Woman 84* (on HBO Max). But I think both paled in comparison for the kids to tonight's feature, on its 10th anniversary: *Inception*. Between that and Christopher Nolan's recent *Tenet*, perhaps their new taste for complex, mind-bending stories is just perfect for the pandemic.

This Sunday's *New York Times* asked the following in a piece about dealing with stress by staying in the moment: If someone had told you in March how long the pandemic would last, would you have thought you could handle it? Great question. I'd like to think I would've said yes, but not nearly as well as it's turning out.

December 29, Tuesday

Yesterday Akiva and I played the classic *Dune* board game with Chris and others over a combination of Tabletop Simulator and Discord. It only took nine hours. Super fun—the time just flew by.

Today I took Miri ice-skating. It was hard to find a rink that was both outdoors and big enough to be safe. I was prepared to leave the city, maybe go north to Bear Mountain, but the new double rink in Prospect Park in Brooklyn looked perfect. And it was. A tad small, but with reduced capacity it was not crowded and only felt a little uncomfortable COVID-wise. She said it was really a fun day, which is all I needed to hear.

December 30, Wednesday

Miri baked tortilla chips for snack.

Akiva made French onion soup for dinner.

Chris and Claire learned at 3 AM by police arriving at their front door that her sister in Denver was murdered.

Tomorrow we are somehow throwing three remote parties totaling around 70 people.

I worked on my book proposal.

Our supper club met for our weekly Zoom.

I helped Miri with her animated video about climate change.

I hold back the panic about income loss in 2021.

We started the day thinking unexpected conditions within the deed would prevent us from buying the lake house, but then those were largely resolved.

I walked into town with Akiva, to buy cheese, and was equally pleased by all I saw wearing masks yet discomforted to be around so many people.

Just another day in COVID land.

JANUARY 2021

In which a new year is welcomed… a bridge is not crossed… a coup is bungled… an election comes to a close… a mortgage is approved… Denise returns…

Daily Diary Entries

January 1, 2021, Friday

Happy New Years!

I rolled out of bed at 10 AM this morning. Too early! At least I got eight hours of sleep in. Yesterday was amazing. 71 guests across three different events and all went smoothly. First the afternoon family remote trivia face-off, led by a company we hired, with six families. Then at seven we Zoom-dined with six households, all but one with the gourmet meal we hired a chef to prepare and deliver to each of our homes. Eating the same food at the same time worked and made us feel more connected. Then from 8:30 PM to 1:30 AM it was one activity after another. The caricaturists did a lovely job. Guests taking one minute to share at least three photos from their year kept the festivities real and grounded (I used my photo of the supper club, street dining by the stop sign, and that photo of Akiva and the house window from our first time in the Catskills), balanced against the wonderful Cameo.com celebrities people contracted who brought to us roasts, jokes, music, well-wishes, and bloopers. The trivia game company then came back and our four teams did battle, ending in an epic dance off. Meanwhile the kids had their own hangout room which they used to coordinate games and declare their gender (she/her, he/him, he/him/pansexual, he/him/gay, agender/no pronouns, neogender/pansexual). We revealed the final caricature at 11:30, more guests arrived, we tuned in and shared CNN for midnight in the emptied Times Square, and finally closed down the party after 1:00 a.m.—for adults AND kids, as Noemi and I—exhausted, delighted, celebratory—were ready to call it a night and the start of a new year.

January 2, Saturday

Last month I pulled a sci-fi book off of our shelves, given to us by Carol, called *The Years of the City*, from 1984. It tells loosely-connected short stories which each jump ahead by decades to show today's (1984's) New York City transformed into a collectively–administered, germ-free, domed city. By page 300, out of nowhere, an unfrozen citizen from the past infects the city with a strain of flu unseen in decades; as a result, by the end of the day, the whole city is shut down by the resulting pandemic. "There had not been an epidemic, or the threat of one, in so long that the city didn't know how to take it." Science fiction indeed! Within two days all is brought under control, with help and vaccines pouring in from around the country and world. But until that occurred "no leper was ever singled out with more vigor than any New Yorker who, that day, happened to clear his throat out loud."

January 3, Sunday

Yesterday we headed to Brooklyn to fulfill the last item on our New Year's Eve bucket list—walk across the Brooklyn Bridge. We last walked it in winter, before the pandemic, with our temple, in a march against antisemitism. It would be so different now, without crowds packed together. But unfortunately, it still felt too busy, too crowded to feel safe. So instead we walked underneath it to the East River, where there was more space to keep our distance from the others like us, and met Andy, then Paul, and walked south along Brooklyn Bridge Park. The sky was a perfect winter blue and it was great to start the year seeing them in person, strolling the waterfront then along the Brooklyn Promenade, in our old neighborhood.

Later in the day Noemi organized us to make personal pizzas. The kids made the dough, we all made toppings, and each then created their own personal pizza. It was fun. I think Noemi viewed it as a minor miracle that we got through it together.

January 4, Monday

Today was the first day the family went back to work and school in the new year. I was so tired, getting up at 6:10 instead of 10 AM, but I finally got up to speed. I asked Akiva at dinner how school was today (on the couch) and he said the commute was bad, with no further clarification.

January 5, Tuesday

It's 11:10 PM. We can't turn off MSNBC. Watching the Senate races in Georgia. So hopeful. I can't believe that the future of Congress and Biden's presidency comes down to this.

January 6, Wednesday

Go, Georgia, go!

Yesterday I had to walk into town to buy envelopes for the Happy Holiday cards I ordered a month ago which just now arrived. It's not right to call this a ghost town—they were still people all over, masked—but what else can I call it? I'd forgotten the Walgreens had closed, all boarded up, along with the Starbucks next door and the chicken wings franchise above. The marquee at the movie theater still announces "temporarily closed", as if the word "temporarily" had been redefined to extend longer than the 10 months since that message was first announced, serving now as a type of Zen koan signifying the sound of one hand hoping. I am confident it will all return in 2021, in one form or another, but I can't predict the price paid by "temporarily" holding my breath until that day arrives.

January 7, Thursday

How shall I describe yesterday? Shall I start with the supper club? One friend couldn't join us because her sister was murdered last week in Denver and she and her family are now responsible for her nine-year-old nephew. Another friend couldn't join because her dad died this weekend. One who joined said she knew four people who died in the last week; the other said they only knew one person who died. "Only."

So maybe don't start with supper club. How about Congress?

By 1 PM or so Noemi and I were glued to the web and three 24-hour news channels watching the failed Trump coup play out, not believing the horrors we were seeing, wondering if finally Trump had crossed the line or if once again he managed to push it so far the new shape defined something other than a democracy.

So maybe don't start with Congress.

Sometime today, with little fanfare, Georgia elected a Jewish man and a Black man to the Senate, concluding the Congressional election in the state, ending the November election for the country, and putting both houses of Congress AND the White House in the hands of the Democrats.

Now THAT'S a good place to start.

January 8, Friday

Yesterday was a good day.

None of my friends came down with COVID.

No one I knew died.

No armed mob stormed the capital.

The President didn't say anything offensive.

The Wall Street Journal said Trump should resign.

And this lovely joke still holds true: A black man and a Jew walk into a bar in Georgia… and the bartender says, "What can I get you, Senators?"

January 9, Saturday

Trump has been banned by Twitter for life? Less than two weeks before the end of his term? Too little, too late.

I liked this quote in *The New York Times* from a Holocaust survivor about the concentration camp-themed shirt worn by one of the insurrectionists occupying the Capital: "Maybe this was a very good lesson for the American people. Maybe it will strengthen the will to defend democracy."[57] I always prefer to be hopeful, but when that hope against rising fascism comes from a victim of Nazi atrocities—well, that floored me.

January 10, Sunday

They have broadened the definition of who can get vaccinated now. We're hoping Noemi's mom can get it. We zoomed with Carol last night; I almost wish she were still in Atria so they could arrange for her shots. We're all scared of the new strain. We're also scared of rising fascist tendencies among Trump-supporting Republicans. But what's new? We watched the film version of the Broadway show *What the Constitution Means to Me* last night. Brilliant. Devastating. Tonight I met formally with a new leadership team of our Girl Scout troop, and I'm excited. Next week we'll start meeting once a month for six months, over Zoom, for three hours a meeting. We've all learned so much about online engagement in this last year—both us adults and the girls. I'm excited to see what we can pull off together.

January 11, Monday

I feel tired.

---

[57] "Sweatshirt Seen at Capitol Revives Distressing Memories". *The New York Times*, January 9, 2021, Page A11

Tonight we learned our mortgage was approved on the second home. We are now just waiting for a closing date—and whether they are going to insist we all sign papers together in the same room or catch up with the rest of the world and do it remotely.

Tomorrow night I'll give my first Zoom-based seltzer talk. Looking forward to it.

And tomorrow Trump might get impeached. Again.

January 12, Tuesday

Our downstairs neighbor, an elderly man, died in 2019. During the pandemic someone moved in, as we can hear them now. Normally we would introduce ourselves, but… pandemic. Finally I wrote a note of introductions, apologized for sounding like a herd of elephants, and dropped some cookies off at their door. We rang the bell, moved back 20 feet, and learned that this lovely couple moved in last August, grew up in the neighborhood (everyone loves to return to Forest Hills) and said they weren't concerned about us being loud: they are moving out for three months to do extensive renovations. In the past, we wouldn't care, as we would be at school and work all day. Now it will become the soundtrack of our lives.

January 13, Wednesday

Last night I gave a seltzer talk for a temple on Long Island that had originally been planned last spring in person. While I've given remote talks this year through a lovely company, this was the first time I got to do so over Zoom, with me in control. I didn't realize how much I missed seeing and hearing the audience. What a difference! One man laughing throughout made my night. One woman was inexplicably Zooming-in from what appeared to be a medical facility, wearing a mask, handling syringes. During the Q&A she asked a question, giving me the opportunity to politely ask back: What the hell are you doing? She showed us, holding up the COVID vaccine, explaining she's been there since 6 AM giving shots all day. I asked her how she could attend my talk while working. She said it was during her dinner break, before she went home. My talk was her way to relax after 16 hours of giving people the COVID vaccine. That blew me away.

Miri sat down at dinner and said, "I saw on TikTok that Trump was impeached again." TikTok: 1; Trump: 0.

At supper club folks traded vaccine updates. The first whose parents were vaccinated two weeks ago in Israel now got their second shot. The healthcare worker got her first and the college professor (a new approved category) got his appointment for March 22. All other parents spent these weeks calling from one place to another, many frustrated by messages of "we are booked up for the entire year".

January 14, Thursday

The bus company that was going to take Akiva to school in the Bronx, the one we had such a hard time with this summer… today they emailed that they are going out of business.

Headline in the Queens Daily Eagle: "Queens man impeached - again." An instant classic.

January Interview Continued: COVID-19 Oral History Project

... Q: I guess the first question I would ask you, just to start off, is how have you been since we last spoke? More or less? It's been quite a long time.

Joseph: It was July, so that's six months.

Q: But how have you been lately?

Joseph: If someone went from listening to the first interview to this one, it's like worlds apart. My life is so different from then, but I would say I'm good, thank you for asking. My family's good, we're healthy, thank you.

But we're still under tremendous stress. We have found lots of ways to make things work that I find remarkable. The resiliency of my children, their creativity, their ability to pivot and create a new normal for themselves has been amazing to see, as a parent. Being a parent of a child graduating from fifth grade and graduating from eighth grade last spring was a nightmare. While it certainly hasn't been easy, and the fall was very stressful, their ability to transition to new grades, new schools, for each of them, and be able to thrive, being at home almost the entire time, has been incredibly smooth. Unexpectedly smooth, at this point.

On the other hand, it's always stressful. Some of it is because I think we figure things out, like everyone has, and some of it is we've just learned to ignore certain stressors. Those become the background hum that's so constant you don't notice that they're even there. And I know that until it ends, until that hum turns off, I won't really understand how ever-present it was and how loud it actually was. I look forward to hearing that silence. Whenever I'm starting to think about how I am right now, I always know that there's this foundation that I can't even assess, that makes my mental bandwidth tighter. It makes me more irritable, it makes me have less patience, and that it's hard to assess all the time.

But there's been times during the year when there's a lot of crazy things going on. Today isn't one of those times. Last week was. The week before that was. But this week, you know, no attempted coups. No one in the hospital. No friends in residential treatment centers. No changes between who's in school or not in school. No changes of who is employed by who. None of that, which is nice, which is quite nice.

Q: Yes. Let's hope that it lasts, that we have some stability for a little bit of time. We were just talking about your kids a little bit and so maybe it makes sense to transition from there to just talking about you as a parent and what your experience has been like with teenagers. And I'm especially curious about it also because I'm a parent of a teenager. I think it's also important to talk about, because we haven't gotten to talk to teenagers, but their experience is really important to understand in this pandemic.

Joseph: So I have two children. One is about to—my daughter is about to turn twelve—and my son will turn fifteen this spring, in May. As I mentioned, they both started new schools. My youngest started middle school down the block, which she could walk to, and my oldest started high school in the Bronx.

This is the year, I thought, Miri would start to get some independence, start being able to leave the house on her own and walk around the town, go to the store, walk to school. We were planning for that at the end of last year. Back then in elementary school we would walk a block behind her with her friends and make sure she was doing the right things. Especially because the new school was just three blocks away, we thought that would happen. And it did happen, even though she only had a small number of days she actually went to school between October and November. Maybe in a six-week period she went in five or six times. But in that time she developed that level of independence we were anticipating. She'd walk out the door on her own after a few days, meet her friends downstairs in the park, socially distance, pick up a few friends on the way, go to school. Then after school maybe go to a park in someone's building, like an indoor garden, or go to Dunkin Donuts or go to the bagel shop. We would watch her on the phone to know where she was, she would text us, and then she would come home. That these things have continued has amazed us.

They each have their own challenges that they had coming into the pandemic, but they are able to adapt in ways that I find just miraculous. Like my daughter being able to reflect on it and think about it. I wrote about, in the diary, my daughter telling us that her and her friend were talking about that they were going to grow up to be a generation of, what's the phrase? Anxious germophobes.

Q: It was depressed first, and then anxious, right?

Joseph: Right, it was depressed germophobes. And then we pushed what she meant by depressed and she said she meant anxious, concerned that it would happen again. I have my own thoughts about whether they will or not, but the fact that they're talking about it and thinking about it I just think is so healthy and so important, to come up with their own relationship with what they're experiencing now. And be aware that it's temporary, and it will change and pass.

The challenges, especially last spring, was being locked in the house and not being able to be physically active, not being able to go outside, not being social. My daughter addressed that through TikTok, where she became very active. I think she has three accounts at this point, and created a whole sub-community around a book that she loves, and it's had a tremendous impact on her.

She also joined a travelling soccer team. She has three practices a week—some is in person, some is on Zoom. So she's kept herself social in that space and kept herself physically active. She also joined a youth, faith-based climate change political movement that she's been very engaged with, that she pursued on her own, that we've been supporting her to do.

She was not doing any of these things last spring. She wasn't going out on her own, she wasn't on a year-long soccer team, she wasn't part of this political movement, she wasn't as active on TikTok. These are all the natural growth and things we'd want to see, and they're still happening even in the context of the pandemic, and sometimes even because of it.

My son has his own story, about what his challenges were coming into the pandemic and how he's negotiated this period. But again, we talked to the teachers during the parent-teacher meetings. They think he's great, and he's sweet, and they get a sense of his personality and how generous he is. He always keeps his camera on, which I guess is a good thing for a teacher. His grades are fantastic, and he's going to more after school programs now than he did the last few years combined. He has a regular Dungeons & Dragons group with friends that he's known from before. They didn't used to have weekly gaming sessions but now they do. So there's ways that just as Noemi and I have connected with friends that we now meet with on a regular basis on Wednesdays or Saturday mornings, he's also done the same.

I don't know what the long-term effects are going to be, but as a parent we're always like, we're doing the best we can. We'll find out later what worked and what didn't. But we feel very fortunate and lucky, especially when we hear about other parents who can't get their kids to study, who can't get them to pay attention when they're on the computer for school. Akiva stays out in the living room, Miri stays in her bedroom, and they're both always in class. Noemi and I are able to do our work, at home throughout the whole thing, and be there for them, to have breakfast with them or make sure they eat lunch, and like that. So it's a hard time, but I feel very fortunate when I hear what other people are having to deal with.

Q: Yes, it's really wonderful to hear and also it stands out in relation to what I've heard from other parents. I wonder if you have a sense of what makes your family different. What made it so that your transition was less rocky than that of other families?

Joseph: Well, I can't say anything about other families. My son is very comfortable being with himself, so large amount of time on his own, he's fine with. I admire this. That's been required for everybody during this situation, especially if you're used to being around people in the office or around kids at school. Having kids who personally aspire to want to do well in school certainly helps a lot. We give them tremendous support towards making their own decisions around the use of technology. They came into this with the technology they already needed, and with the skills they needed, and the permission from us to explore it in new ways.

On New Year's Eve Miri wanted to have a Zoom meeting with some of the people she met on TikTok. She knew to come check with me first, and I knew to say, "That's okay," and now we have a new list of things we want to talk to her about, like you can't talk to these people one-on-one until we get to know more about them, and stuff like that. We not only empowered them around technology but have communications in place to make sure it's safe. It means they can use these tools to not be isolated.

That said, my daughter got in trouble twice this semester for texting during a test, or during class. She had been keeping in contact with her friends during school, on the side, using digital tools, as she would if she was in a classroom. So it might've been like she was caught passing a note in class. Instead it was texting, you know?

They've also stepped up. Before the pandemic, I always made breakfast for the kids and my wife made lunches for them, but now they both make lunches for themselves and Miri, who wants to sleep late, is making her own breakfast. They've risen to the challenge of this time to learn new skills.

So I don't know. Are you asking me what we did differently as parents? I just feel like mostly it's them. I want to give them all the credit for using the resources they have to make it work. But you know, good communication is important. When things first started in March, we were like, "We just have to de-stress everything, and let everyone have all the space they need." If that child was doing that thing that we're always telling them not to do, just let them be for a time. Choose not to get upset about it. Just give them lots of space. That made this incredibly stressful time much more bearable, and it felt great, actually. We weren't fighting. In fact, we were fighting less in those early days than from before the shut-down. Then by mid-summer it was like, "You know, I still need you to do that thing you aren't doing." Then we got back to holding out higher expectations and holding them accountable again in ways we had been letting slide.

Even so, the stress is less. Being able to talk about it. Making sure that we always have dinner together, keeping the kids at the table maybe longer than they want so we can talk about their days. Sharing what's going on with us and not pretending it isn't hard, I think, is helping to build some of the resiliency. We've been able to keep the connections with grandparents and cousins on Zoom, and doing socially distanced stuff up in New Rochelle, where their grandmother is, I think has helped as well. Just as they see how we're adapting, how we're figuring it out, that we're not pretending we know everything, that they actually are part of the process of us figuring it all out together.

Q: Are there moments that stand out for you with your kids that were especially meaningful over the past few months, where you were together with them? Either because they were just wonderful moments or because they were challenging moments?

Joseph: Well, let's see. We have a three-day weekend coming up, because Monday is MLK Day and the bulk of our time isn't scheduled. They'll have to do some homework, but otherwise what are we going to do? It's wintertime. When it was warm we would get on the bike or go down to the beach and stand by the water or go hiking or something. But we can't do any of that, and we can't do the alternative stuff you would do in the winter: go to a museum, go see a movie, go to someone's house. And we don't want to be trapped in here, and so having to try and figure out—what do we do together as a family? If we stay here, they'll want to go off and do their own thing; they're kind of in their groove now, and it's a deep, deep groove that the pandemic has created for them. Miri will go off and do something with TikTok or talk to friends in her room, and Akiva will go on his computer and play Minecraft or some other game, while watching YouTube. Getting them out of those grooves can feel impossible.

So right now the weekends are hard. We want to be together but we want to do it without fighting with them to be together. And what is the weather allowing us to do? What is the pandemic allowing us to do? So we're in the middle of it now. It's the middle of January.

We knew this was going to be the hardest time during the pandemic. The vaccine's coming, but right now the numbers are higher than they ever were. I was comparing it just yesterday against in April, when my dad died. The infection rates are now double when it was at its peak in April. So there's more incentive to stay inside.

Q: Exactly. Which goes a little bit to something I wanted to ask you about, which is the effort to find a place upstate to go to. How that has gone, because also as I was reading that I was following it and excited about it, and then disappointed alongside you, and then hopeful again. Just wondering how that's going, but also what your thoughts are about having a place to go outside of the city.

Joseph: We looked to buy a place when we were in the Catskill area last August. Then we found one. Coincidentally, the day that the offer was accepted was the day I was let go from the Girl Scouts. We figured at that point it was over. For five months now, it's been on and off and on and off. It was off again two weeks ago. We're expecting the closing now, next week. But they haven't given us a date. It was supposed to be today, and they cancelled it because they weren't ready. We're trying to figure it all out.

The long and short of it is, if it comes through, we're going to have a place that we can go to on weekends. It's a place to think about. That's something positive that we can control, that we can use as somewhat of a distraction from the challenges that are here. It'll be a place we can enjoy, to go to and relax. What are we going to do this weekend? We're going up to the place. And then we can just walk outside, nature's right there. If it's cold, go back inside and put some wood on the fireplace, or hop in the hot tub, right? It'll be wonderful. Closer to spring it'll be ready and we can start renting it out as an Airbnb to supplement the costs for running it. We'll be able to leverage the interest on the pandemic of people getting out of the city, who have money. The rentals up there, which normally might sit empty in the winter, are booked every weekend right now. Which actually makes it possible for us to think about owning this property.

I'm feeling excited. I'm anticipating how amazing it's going to be andI'm looking forward to the work of getting it ready for us. But the process of getting it, I had no idea what a roller coaster ride it was going to be.

Q: Yes, it does sound like a roller coaster. I wonder, just through that process, how your relationship to New York City has fluctuated.

Joseph: Hasn't changed.

Q: It hasn't changed?

Joseph: No, I love New York City. Noemi and I walked, last weekend, to get some cookies for a neighbor who moved in. We walked past this thing called the subway entrance, and I was like, "What is that strange construction on the sidewalk?" I am used to commuting every single day on the subway, for 25 years. And I haven't been into a subway station since the second week of March. The idea that it's very likely we'll spend an entire year never going on it, never going on a bus, never being on the public transportation system, that's wild. And all the cultural stuff that we can't access because it's closed, and the restaurants, the museums and the shows. If you don't do those things in New York, there's no reason to be here. They are the reason to deal with being in such a compressed space, with so many people. It's to be able to get those qualities in your life.

But we know it will all come back. Eventually. And every once in a while, we'll go up on weekends out to the Catskills, or just go out for a day hiking or apple picking or get pumpkins or something. So if anything, just like after 9/11, this just gives us an opportunity to renew our commitment to the city.

Q: How have you seen it change in this time? I'm remembering one instance of you describing, I think, driving around downtown and finding a place to—

Joseph: Parking spot.

Q: —on Wall Street, or close to Wall Street.

Joseph: Unbelievable.

Q: Yes, but also seeing buildings boarded up in anticipation of possible violence, and just interested in hearing how you've seen the city transform. The city as a whole, but also your neighborhood, would be interesting to hear more about.

Joseph: Sure. It's winter, people are out less now. My barber shop and cobbler both closed. Lost their lease. The Starbucks is closed, but moved up the block so now is open somewhere else. The CVS has closed. So many businesses closed, and it's shocking to go into town and see their absence. It's equally shocking to see new ones that have come in. I went into town yesterday and had a piece of pizza from a pizza place that's new. I went there because the Korean chicken place, that's also new, is only serving dinner right now, and our favorite noodle place is gone and it's been replaced with a Korean hibachi place. It's amazing to think, Wow, people are building new businesses, in this context.

Again, with that said, I still feel like I don't have a good sense of what's happening in our town. What I know is all within subcommunities. My friends at the temple, and what's happening with the temple. My daughter's friends at school, and what's happening with the school community. It's very micro-communities now, all disconnected. I don't see the spaces between them. I don't—can you hear the construction they're doing?

Q: No, no.

Joseph: That's great, because it's driving me nuts.

Q: Can you hear mine?

Joseph: No, I can't. They moved in—

Q: Good. Zoom is doing a good job of filtering out all the construction noise.

Joseph: Oh, thank you Zoom!

Q: When I spoke to you last, you still had your position at Girl Scouts. Things have changed since then. In your diary, that's also a thread that I followed and that I was anxious about. Then saddened, and then also encouraged by seeing the resiliency that your response revealed. So just wondering can you talk a little bit about that, your work life and what's happened over the past few months.

Joseph: From March through September, I worked at the Girl Scouts. We were told in May everyone's job was under consideration for being cut. So there was tremendous stress both from that and from how do we respond as an organization to keep this business model viable? That day that we were going to be let go kept getting pushed back, from the beginning of the summer to the end of the summer, to the beginning of the fall.

We kept losing people on the way because people were like, "I can't handle this. I'm just quitting." Or, "I'm going to look for something else to do that's more stable." Then the CEO left. We don't really know exactly what happened. A few weeks before the potential date of being told our fates that happened and it was like, "What is going on around here?!!" It just felt like there was no consistency, no foundation to rely on.

Of course, I was grateful to have the income, but I never knew what was going to happen from week to week. It seemed like, okay, given my understanding of the organization's needs to be effective during this pandemic, in a digital age, I thought I'd be the perfect person. So I was shocked when they let me go.

At the same time, I had been thinking about, for quite some time, what might be my next step? What was I learning about myself at the Girl Scouts that I could build upon, about my skills, my interests, my talents, my passions? What network was I building that I could leverage for my next step? So the pandemic just accelerated those thoughts, and then re-flavored that whole process.

But boy, it was great getting let go with 15-20% of the organization rather than, you know, at a review at the end of the year when they say, "We don't want to keep you," right? So it provided a context that was like a no-fail. No one's going to ever question what happened. I'm not saying someone should, but it was part of the interesting opportunities that this pandemic year has created, that many people have been fortunate enough to take advantage of and say, "Great,

I'm going to take the risk. If it fails, I can just say, 'Well, it was the pandemic.'"

At first I had some interesting interviews. Within a week or so, people wanted to hire me, not full-time but for part-time work. I think this was a trend accelerated due to hiring freezes while the pandemic was creating new opportunities for organizations to pivot or try something new. Suddenly I filled this niche. I could meet it very fast and very effectively.

Once I saw that I can start working part-time for a few people in contract work, I realized I might as well just formalize this and make it a business. I still send out a resume for full-time work every week or two, but I haven't had to. I've been fully employed, by clients, ever since I started.

Still, I find it terrifying! I don't like to work for myself… figure out how to get business... figure out business models... figure out the market. Those just hadn't been my strengths. There's a reason I've worked in the nonprofit space for over 20 years.

But I figured out what to do: make an LLC, make a website, get a logo, do outreach, work my networks, let people know I'm available, hang up that digital shingle, and get work. I just signed, this week, the first contract with someone that's a renewal from the first round. I'm expecting a second one, and perhaps a third one, by the end of the month as well. Which just tells me that this is working.

Now, how much of it is relying on people's unique needs during the pandemic and will it change afterwards? I have no idea. But it's been incredibly satisfying to run my own business.

It has forced me to look at the space between what I feel is expected of me, as a man, in which my job is my identity. I still need to do things to make money, but more often now I am forced to think, "How should I spend the next minute of my time? How do I spend the next hour?" If I'm not reporting to somebody higher-up in the food chain, then I have to make the decision on my own about how I spend my time.

Maybe I should go for a walk. Maybe I can hang out with my daughter for an hour. It gives me the freedom to ask questions like, Who am I? What am I supposed to do? It turns out I can decide when I work, and how, making the experience more intentional. It's been amazing to have space during the pandemic where I can take better care of myself, and take care of the people around me, in ways that I couldn't before, or at least thought I couldn't.

I have a peer mentor group. I think we're years on at this point. When we started we all were doing digital learning in museums. Now, none of us are. We meet once a month, from locations all over the country, and they've known me for all this time. When we last met in December, they reflected back to me that I just seemed so much more relaxed than I had in the last few years. You'd think I should be more anxious now, I should be more stressed, with the pandemic, and fretting over how I am going to earn money two months from now, but they said they just saw in the way I held myself, that I was so much more physically in my body and so much more relaxed.

Q: That's so interesting. So what you're describing is an improvement, in a sense, in your quality of life in a situation where a lot of people might find the lack of structure really challenging. It sounds like you found your way to sort of reorganize your priorities, or that things came into focus for you in a way that maybe weren't before.

Joseph: It's true, but I'm also very cognizant that as long as we still have the pandemic, we're going to be in a liminal space. A space between things. Liminal spaces are always the times when things that are stable become unstable. Things that are fixed become unfixed. Roles shift, relationships shift. Commitments shift. Identities shift. Those are times of stress, but they can also be times of liberation, depending on how you approach it. Your observations about me are about things that are not yet fixed. Since we're not on the other side yet, when things get fixed again, I don't know if I'll get to hold on to those gains. Or if, instead, I will just look back upon them as something temporary that helped me to survive during the pandemic.

Q: Yes. That's interesting, also, because one of the questions that we asked you and everyone in the first interview, and we have a similar version of that question now, is, what's coming next? What do you think is coming next? And your sense that the end of the pandemic, or the end of this liminal space, would be a return to things being fixed again, is in a way a response to that. But I'll ask you anyway. Where do you think we're headed? Maybe starting off in the short term. Like over the next couple of months, and then thinking a little bit further into the future toward when the pandemic might actually wind down.

Joseph: Well, I think the next few months are going to be really difficult. I think the current presidential administration has been unable to get the country on board in a consistent way with what's necessary to tackle the virus. We've created many problems on our own, and now we're suffering from them. The headlines in *The New York Times* yesterday—right next to each other—were about the challenge of getting healthcare workers to get vaccinated, even though they're priority. It mentioned the hospital three blocks from my house. It said there's seven people who do the intubating; only one of them have gotten the vaccine, as the rest are too scared to take it. In Ohio, 60% of healthcare workers are not taking it. The next article, right next to it, was how hard it is for those eligible to get vaccinated—healthcare workers, senior citizens, teachers—to get vaccinated. They're calling around and they can't get an appointment.

Both are going on at the same time. You have one group of people who are working really hard and frustrated because they can't get it, and another group, they're too terrified to take it. We're not on the same page. There's reasons why those populations are different, and some people, because of economic inequality and systemic racism and the history of medical racism, have reasons to be cautious and not want to be guinea pigs. At the same time, wow, we're just not on the same page. And that's New York. That's not even dealing with the politics of people who don't believe in vaccines, people who don't believe in masks, don't believe in what the CDC is saying, don't trust the government. So wow, we're in a bad spot.

I think we're best positioned now, more than ever, with the new administration coming in to have consistent and strong policies. That'll get us there. But we also have the new variants coming, that spread faster, and if we don't get the vaccine fast enough we're never going to bring the curve down, because the new ones will kick it up. But when can we go back inside restaurants? When does Broadway open up? When will tourists want to come back? Those are all things that are just going to be really bad for the next period of time.

It'll eventually end, unless it turns out that this thing mutates so fast. That it gets deadlier, or the vaccines can't account for it. That could happen. I don't think that'll happen, and I hope it doesn't happen, so I'm assuming that by this time next year, we'll be a few weeks out from my daughter's B'nai Mitzvah. I'm assuming we'll have people flying in from around the country, staying in hotels, coming to the temple. It'll be safe to come together without masks and party and have fun, and bring the community together and honor her during this period. My other friends are planning for a Bat Mitzvah in November. I don't know what's going to happen in November. I think there'll be some social distancing going on, that we won't be doing by February. We'll see.

I think we will learn something from this time. Some things about the inequalities that have been brought to the surface, that we're trying to address in new ways. Also the ability to be more resilient. Will we schedule less? Schedule ourselves in less? Or will we do it more because we emotionally need it? There's ways that we'll have learned to be flexible, I think. I hope that we'll shift some of the ways that we act. I'm saying we, I mean my family.

Q: I hope that you're right about, yes, people flying in to your daughter's B'nai Mitzvah in about a year. I mean, for you and for everyone, that would be amazing. I'm wondering what you understand, now, that you maybe didn't understand the last time we spoke, about what we're going through.

Joseph: Well, it wasn't so politicized back then. I never expected—I mean, it was beginning to be politicized and it had just started, in June. We all live in our own media bubble but Trump supporters seem to live in a media bubble that is more aligned with conspiracy theories and distrust in government, and distrust of science, and somewhat faith-based. Sometimes the faith is just in charismatic figures, and making connections that really aren't there. You know, QAnon and stuff like that. I never thought that would come to dominate so much of the country's response to the pandemic, as it's so self-destructive. People with guns breaking into the Capitols. I don't just mean in D.C. I mean in other states as well, months ago. It's remarkable that the political situation in the country got so bad that this life-threatening situation was being spun in a way to make people do things that would hurt themselves and hurt their community. That was shocking.

Your question was, what have we learned? No. What was the question, again?

Q: My question is, what do you understand now that you didn't understand back then?

Joseph: Oh. I didn't understand how craven so many politicians can be in doing things they just knew couldn't be true, to stay in power, and how much it would hurt people. I didn't know how smoothly school could be, remotely, for our family. How much it could work for the kids, doing it remote, how much my wife and I could still work from home, and how much we enjoy getting to see them, not just being frustrated or being stuck around them. I didn't know that could happen. I didn't know what I would do if I left Girl Scouts.

I didn't know what I would do if I was on the job market. I didn't know what would happen if I tried to build my own company, built on my reputation over the last 25 years with the contacts I've made. I had no idea how that could go.

I'm sure I could keep coming up with stuff, but those seem to be the major ones.

I guess the last thing I can say is, the abilities of individuals and communities to be creative, often using technology, to keep connected, to keep traditions, to keep rituals, to keep in each other's lives, has been amazing. I talked about the supper club, and I think it's a good example. You know, before we met once a month for dinner. We'd go out for dinner, and then in March we started meeting once a week, over Zoom. We've been meeting once a week ever since, and we don't always want to go. We're exhausted, we're tired, we want to watch TV maybe or just go to bed. But most of the time we go, and we're always happy we do. We love them; they're wonderful people. No one ever said, "We're going to meet every week, and let's make sure we do this ten months later." It just happened, you know?

I can come up with all these different examples like that. How people are like, "We're going to make this work. It's not going to be perfect, but we're going to make it work." So there's a way that people have been intentionally reaching out to each other, and that muscle, that reaching-out muscle, I might've thought, last March, would've gotten tired by now. But instead, boy, it's strong. We're all giving it a regular workout and we're keeping in shape.

Q: That's also interesting to hear, because I've heard other people talk about being burned out from Zoom and all of these kinds of things. So it's good to have that perspective on here.

Joseph: I don't believe in Zoom burnout. If you had someone reading a book for eight hours and you said, "Do you want to read another book?" They'd be like, "No, no." But Zoom, like you and

I doing right now, we're talking on the cameras, this is only one of many ways to use it. It would be as if you only watched YouTube on your web browser and you said, "I don't want to do anything else on the web. I don't want to play a game, I don't want to read *The New York Times*, I don't want to look at a recipe to cook something. Because I'm sick of looking at YouTube." Well, they're totally different things. Most people are using Zoom in exactly the same way, so of course they get sick of doing exactly the same thing. But there's nothing about Zoom that says this is the only way we can connect over live video.

You and I, right now, could be playing a crossword puzzle together, or we could be watching a movie together, or we could be playing an escape room. I think it's just that people haven't learned yet how to creatively apply the technology in different ways. That's why when we did our New Year's Eve party, which ran from whenever it was—like from four o'clock in the afternoon to 1:00 in the morning—it worked. Because the modality of engagement shifted every half hour, or every hour. We designed it that way. So this notion of Zoom burnout speaks to a lack of awareness of how to do experience design in digital spaces.

Q: Yes. I mean, I think that, in a way, answers a question I asked you earlier about what accounts for the smoother transition of your family into this life, than what I've seen among other people. I remember something that you wrote in your diary. It was something like, I think someone said to you, "We've been forced 10 years into the future," and you said, "No, we've actually been forced into the present." Which I also think is pretty telling.

Something I wanted to ask you about, as well, because you talk about it quite a bit is your religious community. Just the role that it has played in your life in this time. It sounds like your synagogue has done a lot of really creative things to keep people engaged and yes, just wondering what the life of that community and your part in it has been like.

Joseph: What to say? My daughter goes to Hebrew school Wednesday afternoons and Sunday morning, all online. The major holidays—the High Holidays in the fall, Chanukah in December—all created opportunities to engage with the community. Sometimes with the school, because the school's doing something around Chanukah, or the congregation's celebrating something, Simchat Torah, which is like you go and you dance and it's really fun, how is it ever going to translate to Zoom? Yet it did and we were in the house dancing around, being taught all these different dance moves that we were doing and watching other people's pre-recorded dance videos. It was great. It connects us with the community. It connects us with people we can go to for help if we need to. We're also friendly with them; I've spent more time with all the clergy, socially, than I have in the past—playing games with them online, going out with their kids to the park or something like that. You normally would see them at drop-off at Hebrew school, or after a Shabbat service at the Oneg[58] eating cookies or something. If I wanted to see them now, we had to get more proactive, be more intentional.

We had a Zoom memorial on Sunday, for someone who died, and a *shiva* Sunday and Monday night. There was our clergy leading it each night, with our friend who lost her parent. Our friends who were there to support them, all together. It keeps our social connections broader. It grounds our relationships in that community, and we know that they're there for us if we need them, as they were for me when my dad died.

Q: Is there a spiritual aspect to that experience, or is it primarily the social relationships that are in place for you?

Joseph: I am not a religious person, but that isn't to say that I see it strictly in secular or transactional terms, either. It is a community of people, but it's a group that, being faith-based, is about having ideals that we all aspire to as a community, that we put out into the

58 A social period after the religious service.

world. We're committed to moving towards them together, making the world a better place. It values the human side of the connections between people, versus the transactional, and is designed to create opportunities to connect with each other, connect with ourselves in those human spaces, to make something bigger than ourselves, and create opportunities to give back, make a difference, whether it's with the community doing something out in the world, or within the community, like helping to run Zoom sessions during one of the religious services. Those are things that give one a role in the world, outside one's self and family. I don't know if that answers your question.

Q: Yes, yes, that helps. I've talked to people from all kinds of different faiths, and the extent to which spirituality comes in varies quite a bit. So it's good to hear that. I was just listening to you, thinking about whether all of this will be familiar or really strange to people 50 years from now, when they encounter it, right? I guess it depends on what happens with the situation and whether we actually make our way out of the pandemic or not.

Joseph: Yes. We might get into a state of constant change. Most things are set up so we can rely on them. That's what allows us to deal with all the other stuff in our lives. What we've had to do this year is keep a certain amount of our mental space available for things constantly changing, and knowing that just because it is this way now it doesn't mean it's that way tomorrow, and we have to be flexible. It doesn't mean you can't plan for things. I'm still planning to take my sister to her fiftieth birthday party to see a Broadway show in March of 2022. Her fiftieth birthday was last November, and I'm going to plan for it! Spent the money, we have the tickets, they've moved the date three times now. You need those things to look forward to. We'll have to shift as a society to plan for the future but have structures in place to remain flexible.

Q: Yes, yes. I mean, in part it takes us back around to something you talked about in the beginning of the interview. Your daughter's prediction that her generation would turn into anxious germaphobes.

What you're talking about indicates that something is changing in our understanding of just the contingency of our lives. What it means to plan and what it means to adapt.

Joseph: What I would just add to that, Denise, is I think that's true for someone like myself, of middle income, white. I think that people who have less resources, or are under more constant threat, that's what their lives already looked like pre-pandemic. They have things changing all the time, when there often isn't space in society to catch people with safety nets. Access to resources gives you the things you need to be flexible and to pivot. But what we're also seeing is the increased inequalities, which means that people are having to live like this all the time even when there is no pandemic. I hope this raises some awareness about what we need in society to support people, to build civility where there isn't and create more flexibility for folks through understanding when things are unable to be consistent for them.

Q: Yes. Absolutely. I think that's one of the salient aspects of what we've been looking at, talking to different people and seeing the ways in which they manage different types of instability, with or without resources. It's fascinating. So, do you have any questions before we end? We've been talking for a while.

Joseph: I really appreciate, again, your taking the time to talk to me, to let me share just one particular, very particularized slice of someone's experience during this time. That I hope it gives an opportunity for people to see things that I can't even see, outside my blind spots. Or it's from a time in the future when, with hindsight, you can see things I'm talking about in new ways and this helps inform that. I hope I don't look too silly or naive in what I'm saying, but I hope that anyone can see that I'm at least trying to interrogate, you know, my assumptions and reflect on the experience and try and make it work the best that we can.

Because that's all that we're doing right now, is trying to make it work the best we can.

Q: Yes. Thanks for saying that and thanks just in general for participating. It's really rich material so it's really great to have it. I am going to stop the recording and keep talking to you for just a minute, so.

Joseph: There are few questions I wanted to ask outside the recording.

Q: Okay, great.

[END OF INTERVIEW]

PART 3

THE SEASON OF HOPE

JANUARY 2021

In which perspective is provided... a Girl Scout troop is launched... Democracy prevails... Bernie wears mittens... a publisher is secured... pandemic interviews are postponed... closings are delayed... the vaccine is negotiated...

Daily Diary Entries

January 15, Friday

Today I had my second interview with Denise, the researcher at Columbia who has given me the gift of motivation to write these words which, on a regular basis, try to capture how I am processing each day during these uncertain and unmoored times.

And today I dared ask her for, and then received, a second gift.

I am now one of 190 people in their project. I do not know who they are, their stories, the themes they focus on in their diaries, nor their daily struggles. Denise, however, knows them all. She is the archive of their lives. She is their confessor. So I saw the unique opportunity I had and reluctantly went for it. I realized due to our unique circumstances she could offer what few have now but all will get through time: distance and perspective. I told her I wasn't sure I should even make the request, that I might not want to hear her response, that she shouldn't feel obligated to respond.

I asked: "So, how are we doing?"

What she said made me both proud and embarrassed. Proud because it highlighted some of the decisions we have been making as parents, as a family. Embarrassed because I recognize that I share some of the credit with the privileges that come from our race and class, that not all have equal access to the resources we deployed in response to the challenges posed by the pandemic.

I asked Denise what themes she saw in common amongst those also doing well. She shared two thoughts:

1. The facility with which we are able to use technology, and support our children to do the same, and have an open dialogue with them about it. She said, as parents, our experiences were radically different from others.
2. She said those connected to community, any community—of faith, of political engagement, of volunteers—are faring better. And for me she saw our connections to our Temple, to which I'd add our ad-hoc community of friends, like the supper club, all contributing to our resiliency.

I thanked her and recommended, with all she now knows, that she write a book: How to Survive a Pandemic.

January 17, Sunday

Last night we held our first new Cadette Girl Scout troop meeting. Last summer my leadership team fell apart. To be honest, they fell apart in March but by summer I could no longer hold the threads together. I found one mom/co-leader and a dad stepped up to be treasurer and we were good to go.

We decided to simplify it for all willing to return remotely: three hours once a month. I honestly did not know if the girls could last three hours. But they did, and then some, easily getting us past three hours, and staying on (sans adults) to run their own Zoom sleepover (mostly spent playing *Roblox*).

I was proud to see how much we leaders have learned since spring about how to run a virtual session, and how much more agile the girls are now. And they are older, so need more leadership opportunities, which means giving them an objective and getting out of their way. They chose Financing Your Dreams and the Coding

For Good Journey. A nice pair of badges. More importantly they informed themselves, listened to each other, created a shared space to take notes, listed ideas, and refined it through discussions, debate, and straw polls until it landed on these two, making sure all the girls were bought into the plan.

It's a lot taking this on right now, but seeing how they all took to it, especially my daughter, made it all worthwhile.

January 18, Monday

Today is MLK day. We watched the 2016 film *Selma*. Powerful. Especially so now that 1. John Lewis passed just last spring. 2. Republicans are all about restricting voting access. 3. The Black vote in Georgia just gave Congress to the Democrats.

Walking into town I passed through the top of the park, which is a circle with a raised grass hill in the middle. Two adults were standing in the middle of the path talking; neither wearing masks. I approached and said, "Excuse me, I'd like to pass but you're not wearing masks." She said to me, "So go the other way," meaning to walk clockwise around the hill. He said to me, "So you want me to leave and go home?" I ignored her taunt and responded to him, "You're in a public place without a mask." He said, "Go around us," suggesting I pass him. I said, "I can't as there's no space more than 6 feet from you since you're standing in the middle of the path." He wasn't happy but I think that reached him and he moved. What a bunch of confused people looking for a fight.

January 19, Tuesday

We are still waiting for word on a closing date for the lake house. It could be this week! The bank approved Noemi doing power of attorney. It's amazing how hard this is for the bank and lawyers, like they've never heard of a pandemic.

Tomorrow Biden is inaugurated. Until that moment I'm on edge for what crazy shit Trump or his supporters will pull before then, whether substantive or just to distract from the transfer of power. Will he pardon someone unforgivable, like the recent protesters, or himself? Will he try a legalistic coup? Will he bomb Iran? He seems so desperate and unhinged, with no "adults" around to keep him in check.

January 20, Wednesday

What a day! I woke all stressed, anticipating something crazy from Trump, as always, as I have for four years. Then I celebrated and cried all afternoon and night and now I feel great. A few moments from the day:

Noemi paraphrased something she read: at noon today it was like a car alarm had been going off for four years and someone finally turned it off. We've been suffering from bearing down in the face of it. We'll suffer PTSD until we adjust to its absence.

A client today said she hated who we had to be in response to the constant and vile lies, who it made us be as a people, and was looking forward to getting to call forth our better selves.

A text from a friend: "It's amazing how much better I feel now that Trump is out of office!"

Headlines all day in *The New York Times*: "Quotes Biden: Democracy has prevailed." A recognition and affirmation of how much was at stake.

Amanda Gorman, the remarkable poet, had me in tears, especially with "even as we grieved, we grew. "

When Lady Gaga broke the phrase "and our flag was still there" into three pause-laden beats, turning to the flags on to the Capitol building behind her, I burst into tears, reminded that the building and the institutions it represents, overtaken two weeks earlier by insurrectionists who have long since been banished, is indeed "still there."

I watched the inauguration on MSNBC streamed live on TV, with Akiva and Noemi; during lunch I watched the "virtual parade" online on my computer and during work; evening celebrations on TV and later repeated on YouTube while chatting with the supper club. It was an emotional time with lots of personal sharing. One note: Sam, who works for the NYC DOE, said barely 50% of kids are showing up to their remote classes each day.

Another time I lost it was when the Foo Fighters transformed their song "Times Like These" into an appreciation of school teachers and all they are doing during the pandemic. "It's times like these we learn to live again. It's times like these we learn to love again."

Tonight ended with Katy Perry on the Mall singing her song "Firework", over fireworks. A little on the nose but I was moved, and in awe, watching the shot of President and Dr. Biden from behind experiencing it all over the mall from their new home: the White House.

January 21, Thursday

Yesterday was the removal of Trump, the welcoming of Biden and Harris, a win for Black Lives Matter, a response to the January 6 insurrection, and the first public mourning for the pandemic, all rolled into one.

Today was memes of Bernie Sanders and mittens. Noemi, wanting to compete in a text thread with our friends seeking the best one, asked me to make one for her to share. It shows Bernie sitting on the dock of our soon-to-be lake house. The caption: "Where is the goddamn closing date?" Debby responded, "You win!"

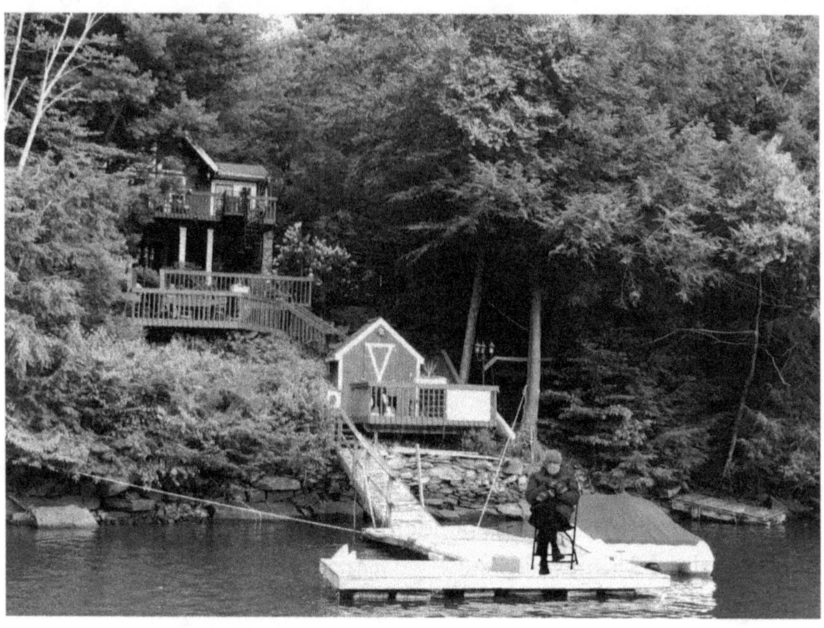

January 22, Friday

We bought a new dining room table.

We did not buy a new table, exactly. Last June Steven decided to stop leasing his office, as everyone is working from home. He generously offered us any furniture we wanted. We arranged for a moving company to pick up a table for us. This was June. No non-resident was allowed in our building at the time, but the company was willing to hold it until the pandemic improved. It did in July and they delivered it. It was broken, by their staff, in multiple places. Totally unusable. It had originally been purchased from DSW, and had been produced in a factory in Lithuania. The movers offered to pay for the replacement parts. Due to the pandemic they were not in production. We contacted the Lithuanian factory every month this fall. By December, no change. So I just asked the movers for the cash they had offered to spend on the replacement parts and with those funds Noemi picked out a new table. It came with three leaves and can stretch to sit 12. Today it arrived and we put it together.

Now comes the punchline.

Noemi said it is quite a feat of optimism during a pandemic to buy a table that seats a dozen.

January 23, Saturday

We all went up to the lake house today. We still don't have a closing date from the bank—we have no clue what the delays are about, and the mortgage broker contracted COVID a week ago—but the owner said we could meet there with potential contractors, and meet the housing manager we might hire. It was so beautiful being up there—on a frozen lake in the winter. And being in the house, emptied, for the first time, seeing it at its core as we'd hoped it might be, was so exciting. Even the kids got into re-designing, coming up with secret closet passageways and fireplace ladders.

I just want to go sit on the side of that lake. Heck, I can't wait to walk across it.

January 24, Sunday

Wow! They want to publish my book on digital design in museums. That's crazy. I spent a decade writing *Seltzertopia*, and three more years looking for a publisher. Last fall I spent a week or two looking for a publisher, for an idea I never considered until I was out of work, and found interest immediately. How cool. Could it be there's extra interest during a pandemic in digital engagement. Naw...

January 25, Monday

Steven got his Oculus!! We lost a few hours this morning trying it out together. He was just like me last October—amazed that we can finally do this, terrified it will make a world where it's all anyone does.

January 26, Tuesday

I finished digitizing my old family home movies—80 of them. One is the Marx Brothers musical I starred in as Harpo, my junior year of high school. It's amazing the careers of so many of my fellow classmates—two are Broadway stars. I realized it might be fun to get on Zoom with the cast—34 years later—and re-watch it together. It's still so funny! And as a result I reached out to the drama teacher who I adored but haven't connected with since graduation. I'm glad I finally did that, and thanked him for all he did for me.

January 27, Wednesday

I applied to some conferences today, to get myself out there and promote my new design book. The pipeline is weak now for my consulting business and it's making me nervous. Once my new website is up I'll start a harder press looking for new clients.

January 28, Thursday

We don't yet have a closing date… but it's close. We have to be ready. We don't want two friends and Noemi's mom to have to figure out how to get to the Catskills to sign all the paperwork, nor I since someone should stay with the kids. So we sent powers of attorney docs to all and today I drove into Manhattan to pick up the signed and notarized docs from Deb and then went over to New Rochelle to pick up one from Oma's. It was nice to travel around the city—felt refreshing—and to see them both. Steven and I did ours by a web-based notary, which is freaking out our lawyers (even though the Governor approved its use during COVID). I'll do the same with an online notary with Noemi across all four of the documents. Our lawyers are acting like we're babies. They literally argued with me, "These were put in place in case of an emergency. Is there an emergency?" Um, It's called a pandemic. I guess rural New York is responding very differently to COVID than New York City. Did I mention our mortgage broker told us last Friday he has been out the previous week sick from COVID?

January 29, Friday

Time. It's so weird, now.

Yesterday Miri asked, "Dad, when's Friday?" I said, "Friday is tomorrow." She replied, "So today's Thursday?"

Later, Miri was saying how weird it is that she can look back at the year and remember one thing distinguishing each month. I asked, "Why? Because there's just not much going on, so one thing can stand out?" She replied, in agreement and seeking confirmation, "Right?"

Email: Important update

From: COVID-19 Oral History Project
Subject: Important update
Date: January 29, 2021 at 3:36:09 PM EST
To: Barry Joseph

Dear Project Contributor,

To all of those who generously shared their stories with us for the COVID-19 Oral History, Narrative, and Memory Archive: thank you!

We began recording preliminary interviews for this project in March 2020, and over the next nine months we recorded 287 sessions with 176 narrators from all five boroughs. Over half of the narrators who filled out our demographic survey are people of color. About 20% were not born in the United States and about 20% made less than $50,000 last year.

We recorded the stories of

- midwives and people who gave birth
- doctors, nurses, and patients
- volunteers who fed their communities and people who were hungry
- people who stayed home and people who kept the city running (and people who kept the city running while staying home)

Our original plan was to record three sessions with each narrator within a year. We imagined that the final session would be a chance to look back at the pandemic and begin to reflect on its meaning. We now realize that, unfortunately, for most of us that distance will not be coming as soon as we had hoped. **In December we made a decision to postpone our third round of interviews for at least a year** for three reasons:

- so that we can raise additional funds to robustly support that work
- so that our final round of interviews can be further removed from the most intense phases of this time period
- So that we can focus on processing the interviews we have collected so far and begin to amplify some of the extraordinary stories you have shared

This means that you can expect to receive a copy of your transcript, audio, and video recordings from your interviews in the next few months. We will ask if you have any changes to make or any concerns about including the interview in the archive. **Once each narrator has had the chance to review their interviews, we will begin making the collection public** through our collaboration with the Oral History Archives at Columbia and through our own curatorial work. Artist and oral historian Nyssa Chow joined our team as a fifth co-director in July and she is leading the work of planning how to amplify your stories in public. We will be asking for your input on this work, and inviting you to participate.

Note that we will be continuing to collect chronicles so will not be sending out your chronicles for review yet, if you wrote any!

Please do not hesitate to reach out with any questions or concerns, either to us or to your interviewer.

And thank you once again for sharing your stories with us. It has been an incredible privilege to listen to you as we all go through this together, and we are excited to enter this next phase of work.

Sincerely,
COVID-19 Oral History Project

Daily Diary Entries

January 30, Saturday

Today we're celebrating Miri's 12th birthday. While her outdoor soccer practice was canceled since we're experiencing sub-freezing temperatures, we will still be meeting a few kids in the park downstairs to do socially-distanced woodworking. Seems crazy, but it's what she wants. We'll try to have hot drinks and not run it for too long. Frankly we're not sure how any of it will work.

January 31, Sunday

It worked! Holy cow—for two hours we sat outside in the park in 20° weather eating lemon squares, drinking hot cider, and hammering nails. Miri was so happy; she leads and we follow.

Our neighbors Ceecee and Joe walked by at one point and I waved to them. They came over, looked at the kids with hammers, and asked if we worked for the parks department. Turned out they were absolute strangers. Between winter hats and COVID masks, all I can see are people's eyes, and this happens all the time!

Carol told us yesterday that she received her first vaccine shot. I'm so happy for her but don't know how she got the appointment. After Oma's appointment this week was canceled, both she and Noemi called every day and nothing was available. Then yesterday a spot opened up and she felt so thankful, even though it is scheduled two months from now, right before Passover.

FEBRUARY 2021

In which a site is hacked… snow falls… a house is purchased… offices re-open… felines are denied… Clubhouse is a thing… lines are drawn (in chocolate)… contractors are welcomed… middle school re-opens… blursdays remain…

Daily Diary Entries

February 1, Monday

I woke up Saturday to an email notifying me that my about-to-launch business website[59] had been turned off by my host provider as it was compromised, sending visitors not to my new web site but instead to a fake virtual-currency phishing site. I'd never fully trusted my web developers but I'm still shocked it happened. I logged into the server and looked at the code to discover that hundreds of files had their URLs replaced to an assortment of phishing sites. I'm still working with my host provider to re-secure it, to revert to a backup, and locate the IP address of the culprit so I can confront them with the evidence. The gaslighting is the worst, as the web developers are still asking for site access. I wish they'd just admit, "you caught us!"

For one client I've been interviewing science teachers in Utah. One explained they are meeting in school in person but quarantining documents. A student turns something in, and then it sits for three days due to COVID, then the teacher reviews it, then it sits for three more days, then the student can get it back. This is escalating school efforts to get all the students 1:1 chrome books, as with Google's G Suite there's no need for a six day-cycle quarantine.

Yesterday the mortgage broker, who is still sick with COVID, emailed me to say that it looks like the bank wouldn't close on our lake home and we'd lose it. "My closing department is having a huge issue with digital powers of attorney… This whole thing is a problem... I'm not sure unless all of the powers of attorney are actually physically signed by them and a notary, that this closing is ever happening." 10 minutes later, a follow-up email: "I just saw some good news… They

[59] BarryJosephConsulting.com

are allowing us to use what we have." Good news indeed, but it's still galling. "Allowing"? The closing is this Friday at 9 AM. We're not supposed to complain that it requires Noemi to get up at 4:30 AM and drive five hours (there and back) to make it happen.

February 2, Tuesday

What a snow storm! 18 feet, I've heard. Miri got me out there at 4:30 this afternoon, on to the basketball court, and we built, one brick at a time, a 7-foot high snow fortress. It was epic. Every kid wanted to join in, an offer I had to refuse, in part because of COVID. But that just turned them into security guards, telling OTHER people they had to come back after it was complete. Kids!

Some days I feel excited building my new business, doing work I love with great people who appreciate what I can offer. Other days I am anxious and unsure about how I'll ever find new clients and like someone who is just out-of-work with no prospects on the horizon. Sometimes I feel both at the same time, but it's usually one or the other.

February 3, Wednesday

At supper club tonight folks traded tales of returning to their offices. The transportation. The security. New COVID protections in place. The quiet. The creepiness. I have no choice but to imagine what it would have been like for me as I'll never be returning to the office I left last March.

We also started talking about what practices we will keep up afterwards. The Temple has already decided to keep Zooming services. We talked about who will return to gyms and folks we know who love Zumba-at-home who will probably keep it up. I do our Scientific 7-minute Workout each day, plus *Supernatural*[60] for around 20 minutes 2 to 3 times a week. Can I keep that up? A year ago I did none of that—but also walked 12+ miles just in my regular weekly work commute. I have to assume a year from now kids are physically back in school, Noemi back in an office, and I just spend my days working from home, alone.

February 4, Thursday

Last night we celebrated the 14th birthday of cousin Max (who lives in Philly) through a family round of *Among Us*. If there was ever a game better themed for the pandemic—a game played remotely on personal devices about a bunch of crewmates trapped on a tiny spaceship with one or more imposters out to kill them—I have yet to find it. It's insane how popular this iOS knock-off of *Werewolf/Mafia* became this past year.

Tonight a client called to triple my hours with them. Yes!

[60] A VR workout on the Oculus Quest 2.

Tomorrow, at this time, we will own the lake house. It feels so crazy. Crazy, as it's a financial risk. Crazy, as we never imagined we could have such a thing in our lives. Crazy, given the complicated pandemic-driven path and bureaucratic obstacles encountered along the way. If all goes well, we will spend the weekend and wake up this Sunday at a lake so frozen we can drive a car across it.

I like to imagine what a collected version of these diary entries might be called. The latest: *Friday is Tomorrow.*

February 5, Friday

Let me jump to the end: we got the house! Mind blown.

Before Noemi arrived at the closing our lawyer called me—the bank had prepared the documents incorrectly. Could they correct them in time or will the closing be canceled? Will the bank refuse to change them and the sale will be off? 30 minutes later all was fixed—but, seriously?!!

There's more—driver's licenses (or images of them) were then requested from four of our people not in attendance. These had not been requested in advance, and we had provided those time and again to our lawyers. So of course we rallied the troops, turned them around in record time—but I'm not sure they even looked at them.

No matter. After first having the idea eight months ago, visiting the place seven months ago, having the offer accepted six months ago… the lake house is now ours.

February 6, Saturday

The man turned to me, as I stood alone amidst the crowd in the theater, and said, "You are a ray of light." I was dumbfounded. Awestruck.

Last night we watched Hulu's filmed version of that show, *In and Of Itself*, which I had seen twice in person off-Broadway. The film captures the experience well, how the magician used the mechanisms and rituals of theater to create a safe space for people to become their most vulnerable, to allow themselves to be seen, and allow him and all of us to meet that moment together.

Earlier I had entered the theater and chosen from the wall the card reading "I am a ray of light." Many cards had already been taken but others remained for those like me still deciding. I handed it to the usher, this self-selected marker of identity, as I entered the theater and my ticket was ripped. Towards the end of the show, the performer welcomed any to stand who wished. I did, from where I had been sitting in the front row. This final act of the night began with him telling me and all in the room what hours earlier I had chosen… then, to my sister, he shared what she had chosen, and then, to each and everyone else standing, the same. It's incredible to see, even more so to experience, extra so as the first to be identified as I never saw it coming.

As we watched the show on Hulu, I had no memory of what I had chosen three years earlier. After the film ended, Miri asked, in amazement of what we had just watched, what I had chosen. I couldn't recall. But then Akiva told us all, "you said 'a ray of light.'" Once again I was in awe. How did he remember that?

I told him, You are a ray of light.

He said, You too.

I said, Let's shine together.

February 7, Sunday

We spent the weekend—our first weekend as owners—at our second home, the lake house. I still can't wrap my head around it. As a raised upper middle class White man it shouldn't be such a surprise. But we never had a second home growing up and it's never something I ever expected for myself. It feels indulgent, and remarkable, and so driven by the pandemic.

The pandemic drove us out of New York City last summer to (re-)discover the Catskills, it afforded us the down payment by killing my dad (who would've loved the place, by the way), and it opened Noemi and I up to taking risks and trying new things. It's such a big responsibility, and Noemi is throwing herself into the renovating and decorating.

But there's no doubt—even though it's totally empty and we slept in our sleeping bags on the hard floor—it felt like such a treasure last night after dark, under the stars, to go outside in the freezing weather with Miri in our bathing suits and hop into the hot tub. And today, during the new snowstorm, Noemi, Akiva and I took a walk on our rural dead-end road. Afterwards, Akiva and I shovelled a path to the dock to look up close at and across the frozen lake.

I just wish my dad could be here to see it, and that while we're enjoying this luxury people across the country weren't under increased risk of eviction due to pandemic-driven job loss.

We realized with a slight shock we can stay an extra day—as none of us needs to actually go anywhere tomorrow—but I wish this abnormal freedom would please soon come to an end.

February 8, Monday

Well, that came out of nowhere. Today the mayor announced the middle schools would re-open February 25, in two weeks. When they closed, both middle and high schools, in early November, we figured that was it for the year. But they announced not only that they would re-open but 50% of them will get to go fully five days in person. Holy cow!

We have no idea if Miri's school will be one, when we will learn, or how it will be decided, but she hasn't gone to school every day in almost a year. That would be crazy, crazy awesome—to return her to that social normalcy, and crazy risky, given the explosion of the new virus variants and the lack of any vaccines for children. We pushed so hard last summer for both kids to return to school in September. Now that we might get the option for Miri to return, is there a possibility we might not let her?

February 9, Tuesday

There are all sorts of anniversaries. July 1 is our wedding anniversary, once a year, like clockwork. This year will be our 20th.

New Year's is easy; its date is in its name.

In the spring of 1992, I got in my car in Santa Monica, California after work to head back home to Brentwood, right on the hour, so as I turned on the car the radio played the top of the news report: "Not guilty. Not guilty. Not guilty. Not guilty. Not guilty." That night the L.A. riots began, after the police who beat Rodney King were acquitted. That has an anniversary.

9/11 comes with its own date. I missed the first plane, as I was still in the bathroom getting ready for work. Waiting for the bus, however, on E. 10th Street I heard what I thought with a truck inexplicably falling over onto its side. I observe that anniversary religiously.

But when did this pandemic start? Did I miss the anniversary? It was January last year that I first heard of COVID. As well as Wuhan. It turned out my graduate student intern attending Columbia University (yes, the same University that invited me to write these chronicles) told me she was from Wuhan, that her family was still there, and that they were living under quarantine. What did that even mean, back then, to be living under quarantine? I couldn't imagine. Was the anniversary in January? Did I somehow miss it?

Or should it be February, when the first COVID case in the U.S. was detected?

Or in March, when all 50 states had at least one case? Or the date March 11, my first day not going into the office, or the day before, my last day going into the Girl Scouts, or the Monday that followed, the 16th, when schools closed in New York?

Or April 22, when my dad died?

I occasionally imagine after a year of COVID I would collect these into one book and share it with the world. But I can't figure out when we transitioned from never having heard of Wuhan to accepting that all the world was Wuhan. And that there might be no going back.

February 10, Wednesday

I never thought Miri would return to school this year, that her weird six day schedule would stay in the past. Instead, we are moving to what they are calling a four day schedule: Group A on Monday and Tuesday, Miri's Group B goes in Wednesday and Thursday, while Group C will be disbanded—sorry kids—and be folded into the other two. And on Friday? Everyone remote. So why isn't that a five day schedule? In any case, it means she can now only go in two days in a row but, miraculously, they will be the same days every week. Fancy that! But 2 of 5 actually feels more comfortable right now, with the infection rates so high. I think it will do her a world of good. Let's just hope they don't get cases and close right back up again.

February 11, Thursday

My entry today got expanded into a new post on my blog. Here it is. I called it "I am… Not a Cat: a Meditation on Zoom and Identity."

I want to reflect on a man who found himself in a situation where he was distressed upon learning others saw him as a cat. But first…

Yesterday I went to the State of the Hive 2021 meeting. As one of its founding members in 2009, I've always taken comfort and found inspiration among this community. Hive describes itself as "a city-wide learning laboratory for educators, technologists, and mentors to design innovative connected educational experiences for youth." Which is to say, it's a space for after-school professionals across sectors (school-based, libraries, museums, community centers, etc.) to connect as one broad youth-serving community and advocate in one voice for youth (usually through digital media programming). They currently operate as a self-described anarchist collective, and are powerful; when NYC suddenly cancelled the Summer Youth Employment Program last spring (which serves 75,000 teens), they claimed partial credit in how the city brought it back.

I have not been to a Hive meeting in perhaps 8 years, but as part of my activities revisiting my professional past I wanted to reconnect. Many of my old friends were there, creatively tackling how to deliver youth programming during the pandemic. But what struck me the most was how this space—youth development—truly grounds itself in its commitment to those they serve. It opened with two students, taking time away from school to attend, reading poems they had written. Two young people of color held our attention, riveted, as they shared with us their struggles and their dreams. One opened with their preferred pronouns and focused on identifying as non-binary and their efforts to conceal how their body presents itself so they can be viewed as they truly see themselves.

Preferred pronouns. Non-binary. Terms like these, and other terms on the front-lines of genderqueer expression, were mostly new to me until a few years ago. But as is often the case, the youth are paving the way. In our New Year's Eve Zoom-based party a few months ago, I noted within the breakout room for the kids, most had preferred pronouns appended to their names, and not just the more common he, she, or they: pansexual, agender, "no pronouns", ace boi.

Last week my family and I watched the filmed production of *In and Of Itself*. The show "begins" when audience members arrive at the theater and are confronted by a board filled with tags that read "I am…" followed by a specific role. In a variety of ways, the show explores how people often try to define us, we often try to define ourselves, and how the show offers a crucible for us each to explore our struggles to claim our own multifaceted identities.

What does all this have to do with a man whose card would have read "I am... not a cat"? I had seen the video the day before, but with news coverage I returned to it after the Hive meeting.

When I first saw it I couldn't stop laughing, and I shared it with all I could. A man is on a Zoom hearing with a judge when accidentally he turns on a filter that transforms his talking head into an animated kitten. I will break this down into four beats so this hilarious bit of Zoom silliness can be used to reflect on what it might teach us about our current age of Zoom and identity fluidity.

Beat 1. The Judge says: "Mr. Ponton, I believe you have a filter turned on in the video settings."

Beat 2. Mr: Ponton: "Augggh,"

Beat 3. Mr: Ponton: "I'm here live. I'm not a cat."

Beat 4. The Judge: "I can see that."

In the first beat, Mr. Ponton learns that someone else is viewing him in a way he does not view himself. Zoom allows him to see it as well, as Zoom is a praxis for allowing us to view how others view us.

In the second beat, he shares how he feels about this, "Augggh." As one YouTube commenter wrote, he is a man who "sounds terrified about being trapped inside his new cat form." Now that Mr. Ponton is aware that he is being viewed as something he is not, he does not like it, nor know what he can do about it.

Then he realizes there is, in fact, something he can do. He can't change how he is being viewed (his assistant is working on it, he assures the Judge) but he CAN tell the Judge that he, himself, does not view himself the same way. That brings us to the third beat. What was originally funny, him desperately, absurdly declaring, "I am not a cat," I now see as shared trauma, like the young non-binary teen I heard earlier in the day describing efforts to flatten their chests to not present as female. Mr. Ponton was saying, in effect, "I am not who you see me as."

Then, the Judge, in the fourth beat. After a pause, he says to Mr. Ponton, "I can see that." Originally, this had me in stitches, highlighting the absurdity of Mr. Ponton declaring that he was not a cat.

But now, I heard it in a different way. I heard it as the Judge saying, "It's all right. I know you are aware that you are presenting as something you are not. But I want you to know, I am not confused. I see you as who you are. I affirm your self-identification."

And that isn't hilarious. That is touching and, like the end of *In and Of Itself*, opened my eyes to a wider reality.

February 12, Friday

Is Clubhouse still a thing? This call-in radio show/chat line on the mobile net exploded in the last few weeks—thank you Mr. Musk[61]—and I've been networking like crazy on it. I love jumping into new mediums. In a week I'm going to a new conference (for me) to network, all online of course. I talked the chair into my running Clubhouse cocktails of a sort as a daily recap/next day. There's nothing like getting to know a new community by jumping on the stage and breaking into song.

Valentine's Day is Sunday. And we wanted to get my sister something to thank her for all she did to help with the house. And yesterday Noemi discovered a 95-year-old chocolate shop 10 minutes away down Woodhaven Boulevard. So I went today to surprise Noemi on Sunday and surprise Debby with a care package we will drop off at her place tomorrow on our way up to the lake house for a week.

I walked in the store and it would've been so charming if we weren't avoiding each other like the plague we are in. Margie, the owner, and granddaughter of the founder, announced my newbie status to all in the store. "Give him a tour!" the other customers demanded, and they did, pointing out where the fire damaged the tin ceiling, and how the tiled floor needs to be cleaned.

[61] Elon Musk.

A customer came in and Margie hugged him, twice. I was shocked. She cried out for all to hear, "I believe in hugs. I believe in hugs," as her mask kept slipping off. I believe in not dying in a pandemic, I thought, but kept my mouth shut, accepted the free chocolate samples they kept feeding me, and left thinking about the decisions we each must make about where and why we draw our lines.

February 13, Saturday

Yesterday, Deb called me from the street in tears. Winter last year I was helping my dad think about getting her a piece of jewelry for her 50th birthday in November. She treasures the jewelry from Mommy and it would mean so much to her to have something from him for such a special event in her life. Then he died. I knew she wanted something to go with the diamond earrings she has from Mommy. Deb is sentimental like that. So last fall I told her about this original plan with Dad and suggested, as executor of his will, I could still do this for her. I had a few thousand we could spend on it, suggesting a lab-grown diamond, as they look the same and cost a fraction. She said she only wanted a real one, because that's what Mommy had. She priced out what she thought would match the earrings. It was crazy, like $30k or $40K. So that ended that.

Then in December, she realized she lost one of Mommy's earrings that she had worn into work. She was beside herself. She took in the one that remained, to see what it might cost to replace it, or turn into a necklace. Guess what? It wasn't real. So now a lab-grown diamond was more than acceptable. If it was good enough for Mommy...

So, to replace the missing earring, and get something for her from Dad for her 50th birthday, we worked together and she got a new one. Coming back from the jeweler (our friend Israel Bien), after walking down the eight stories to avoid the COVID-risky elevator, and escaping from the 47th Street Diamond District, she called me, so overwhelmed and touched by it all. I'm so happy this worked out and that, during a year like this, she still gets to have this.

Today Debby got something else from me: on our way to the lake house we dropped off the box of chocolates with her doorman, to thank her for all her help getting this place, then drove up. It's so beautiful here. Our new neighbors were shoveling snow. The guy seemed my age and his son around Akiva's. Turned out he now lives practically across the street in Long Island from where I grew up, and his kids go to the same Friends Academy school in Locust Valley that I went to. On one hand, pretty crazy. On the other hand, sometimes what feels like coincidence is just the mechanisms of privilege, the illusion that our lives aren't boosted by the tracks grooved by race, class, and ethnicity.

February 14, Sunday

Our first full day at the lake house is also Valentine's Day. I got Noemi socks with the date of our wedding nearly 20 years ago, chocolates for the whole family, and we watched a smart romantic comedy before bed. In the daytime we got in the car and set off for adventures. The first was the southern end of our lake. Watching ice fishers like dots out in the middle, we explored the edges, marveling at the 1 to 2 foot thick slabs of ice stranded on the exposed shores when a week earlier the power company lowered the lake by 10 to 20 feet. We ended up by a bald eagle blind on a river that was half running/half frozen. We had a blast breaking ice, tossing rocks, and listening to the unearthly sounds produced by both. Then we drove until I was lost, discovered ice cream, and found our way back to the house.

The New York Times had a great article on schools in New York City during COVID. One quote really struck me, from a mom: "We haven't been able to find a rhythm at all."[62] That really nails it. So yes, in a week, Miri returns back to school, and she will go in four of every ten school days. But how long can it last; 50% of New York City schools have closed at least once, due to COVID, for at least two weeks, since the beginning of January.

February 15, Monday

Being off for President's Day, we tried to enjoy the lake area before having to return to work tomorrow ("returning" to work means stay all week at the lake house as these days no one has need to see any of us in person for work or school). After some effort we found a place

[62] "Despite Bumps, New York's Move To Open Schools Pays Dividends". *The New York Times*, February 14, 2021, Page A1

to rent snowshoes, which directed us to a great lake (Frick) we could hike around. I have never done that before and thought it was really fun. Also, we were the only ones in the park! How indulgent during the pandemic to have so much outdoor space to ourselves.

This morning we found a bagel store established in 1967 and renovated in a playful steampunk style. The counter person asked me, "Do you live in the area?" I paused a moment then had to respond, "Why, yes I do." To get there we first had to prepare the car, as it was covered like a Christo in a thin sheet of ice. I haven't had a car I parked outside in almost 30 years and it feels funny to be re-learning it all.

February 16, Tuesday

It still feels weird, as it did last September on Lake Tennanah, for us to be out of New York City at a "vacation" home when the kids are off from school (winter break) but it's a "regular" workday for me. I have to keep making the decision, over and over, to keep working, as so much of the structure of my day is at my own whim. To counter that I decided to take a few minutes to walk outside, before work each day this week, even though it was in the middle of an ice storm, and our sloped driveway felt like an ice-skating rink turned on its side. At the top I slipped and started sliding down the hill. It was awesome.

February 17, Wednesday

This morning Noemi said, "Sometimes it feels overwhelming to think about everything." Amen to that. She said one way she's learning to deal with it is to make a list. Here's my list of today's everything:

Figured out how to get garbage to the top of the driveway for pick-up.

Did a lot of work today to make a living, including deciding which book publisher to go with.

Our place turned into Grand Central Station! The contractor, his electrician, and painter, to scope the coming work renovations. Lee, the new—what to call him?—business consultant on how to run the property as a rental. The chimney sweep, to clean the chimney. Then UPS, with the delivery of sheets for the beds. Afterwards I wanted to disinfect and fumigate!

During all that I took the kids and we joined the neighbors and their kids out on the lake to ice fish, sled, and generally walk all over the frozen lake, more than 5 feet thick, and for the first time stand on the opposite shore.

We ended the night with supper club. There are nine of us. Four are already or almost vaccinated. One is a healthcare worker. One works in the New York City education system, and when she got hers she inquired and before long her husband got one as well; they got their second shot last weekend. And another is a university professor; he couldn't get a date until March but then his daughter was at a friend's for dinner, the dad is a county health commissioner, there was a snow storm, appointments were canceled, and before long, due to this connection and the turn of events, he gets his shot next week.

Sometimes I wonder if that's what this diary is: my list to manage the everything.

February 18, Thursday

Why do I include the day of the week for each of my entries? I used to think it was because the context of the day made a difference. But now I think it is a way to assert that the day of the week SHOULD make a difference.

February 19, Friday

My college friends gathered last night for a Zoom call. One friend asked my sister and I, who had joined us, if it had been upsetting to hear the new revelations that the Governor undercut the death count last spring from nursing homes. It looks like half of the deaths from nursing home residents were attributed to hospitals, the place they died, rather than the nursing home, the place they contracted it. To me, in either case, Dad's death was counted, and the loss of life to the virus mattered, which I guess is all I care about.

Around one third of deaths nationally have been from senior living facilities, but that's not new news. We faced that horror last spring. And I'm not sure having a more accurate account at the time of where they contracted it would have made a difference—we all knew it was an extreme crisis, with responses severely limited by hospitals being overwhelmed. Looking back I still can't see how anyone—assisted living facilities, the hospitals, or us could have done anything much differently. But maybe that's part of it as well—if I open this closed case does that mean I have to revisit and re-interrograte my own complicity and pandemic-constrained actions (or inactions)?

Debby had a more straight-forward response: What's the use of getting angry at someone about it? It won't bring Dad back.

February 20, Saturday

Today we went shopping for carpet for the lake home, broke off 4-foot long icicles from the house and from the dock tried to toss them in the lake, ordered delivery from a place that made me a hamburger stuffed and topped with macaroni and cheese, we made a fire and watched a movie together. Throughout we worked on the house—revising plans, reviewing paperwork, taking the garbage to the dump, shoveling snow, and more. All in all, a lovely day.

February 21, Sunday

Deb asked me what we will do in April. Tomorrow will be two months out from the one-year anniversary of his death. Last year we had no doubt that by now we'd be planning to head out together to the cemetery, being there together for the first time, and joining some other family members at his grave site.

We couldn't have been more wrong.

I presume I will go, but on my own. She doesn't want to rent a car, has to keep distant from me and others, etc, I can presume. Next year. We will do it in 2022.

Until then we will be watching movies. Starting in March, every week or two, through June, I have scheduled home movie watching parties, over Zoom. I've invited family and friends to choose their priorities, and I curated the two hour sessions accordingly. From black and white 8 mm silent clips when he was a toddler in the 1930s, to his stint with the army stationed in Iran in the 1950s, to our B'nai Mitzvahs in the 1980s, family trips in the 1990s, and more. I'm excited to take all I digitized since last summer and leverage the isolation forced on us by the pandemic to bring us all together in remembrance and in honor of my dad, and to bring us all closer to one another.

February 22, Monday

What a strange dream I had last night! I was working in my office in Manhattan—in retrospect, I have no idea what the business was—and I left the building to go do an errand. Maybe go to the bank. When I returned to the security station to get back into my office there were a few dozen people waiting to get in the building. But rather than line up with their IDs out, getting head temperature checks, they were all sitting on the ground, forced to debate the pros and cons of Palestinian statehood. No one was socially distanced nor wore a mask, I noticed, then wondered why no one at the bank had said anything to me, as I was also without a mask. And how was I going to get back to my office? More importantly, clearly no one was getting past this guard, and her endless discussion group. I called out, "As this is a discussion, can I ask a question? Who has been here the longest?" A few people raised their hand. "How long have you been here?" I asked one, who tentatively replied, "One hour and 20 minutes." I said, "That's ridiculous," and headed for the elevator. The guard said, "And where do you think you're going?" And after a few failed responses I landed on the perfect one: "This is your own personal super spreader event and I'll play no part in it."

February 23, Tuesday

Noemi's birthday is today. I organized a Zoom party with 1/3 coming every :30 minutes over 1.5 hours, to keep it all not overwhelming and still focused on her throughout. I think she liked it. Wish I could've done more.

Earlier in the day she was on the phone with her mom. When I heard Noemi say, "Mommy, that's great news!" I knew at that moment, without a doubt, she found a new and closer vaccine appointment (tomorrow it turns out).

Yesterday we officially reached 500,000 US-COVID related deaths. It's unfathomable.

February 24, Wednesday

Miri got her braces off today. So exciting. While they were inside I caught up on her latest TikTok videos (set to private) which is my best way to learn what's on her mind these days, whether about school, fanfiction, memes, or dance moves. Tomorrow she returns to in-person sixth grade—now the same two days each week. So will this be their eighth day back in the building this school year? I can't even count anymore. Nor hardly care to. Our whole family has to mobilize for the transition.

February 25, Thursday

We mobilized. And Miri took the lead and got herselves to school and back again.[63] The moment they left the house I felt that mixture of excitement (a taste of normalcy—the old normal!) and dread (Will

[63] Akiva's high school remains closed.

they return carrying the virus? How long will the school remain open before they're forced to close once again).

Oma received her first shot today. Noemi had tried to get an earlier date for her mom, but her sister pulled it off and told us how. She created an account in her mom's name on Walgreens' website. She then said her mom's address was further north than she actually lives, to keep her away from New York City. For one hour every day she diligently reloaded that Web page. It would search for a local opening and then sign her up or return with a "no availability" response. After days of reloading, reloading, reloading, one of those clicks returned with success.

Tonight was Purim[64]. Noemi made *hamantaschen*[65] for dessert, with apricot and poppyseed and Nutella. We dressed up for the Zoom-based celebrations—Noemi had glasses and her blonde wig while I used Zoom to give myself green facial hair, a unicorn horn, and a festive background. I opened the reading of the *Megillah*[66] with my hand puppet and Noemi later chanted beautifully in Hebrew as we all swung groggers at every mention of Haman. The rabbi—who used a filter on Zoom to appear as such but insisted he was not a cat—reminded us that last year's Purim, in March 2020, was the last holiday we celebrated together in person at the Temple. I recalled that—knowing COVID was coming, but laughing in the face of fear that night, unaware of how soon everything would be grinding to a halt, and never imagining the U.S. pandemic would start in New Rochelle, blocks from Oma's house. Tonight began our second annual cycle of holidays under the pandemic. We then held our annual Purim food battle debate: matzah pizza versus Chinese food on Christmas. Matzah pizza never stood a chance. When we went to bed Noemi said how surprised she was how the festivities were the

[64] An historical Jewish holiday often celebrated in playful costumes and through comedic theater.

[65] A three-sided cookie in the shape of the hat worn by Haman, the holiday's Jew-hating villain.

[66] The official retelling of this historical event.

most relaxed moment of her day: all four of us after dinner, cuddling on the couch in front of the Zoom screen, doing and saying silly things together, with each other, with our friends and community. I had to admit I felt the same.

February 26, Friday

I just realized we are now the only household among the five families in our supper club who do not have at least one vaccinated adult in it. We're getting there, one person at a time. And today, Carol received her second vaccination.

I signed the book contract today for my design book with the American Association of Museums. I just love to write and I'm so proud of having their name and credentials behind the project.

Every day this week in conjunction with a remote conference, MuseumNext, I ran an hour-long conversation on ClubHouse with a new colleague from England. I learned a lot about this exciting new audio-based medium and made lots of new contacts.

Noemi and I got "accepted" to the Facebook group for home owners around Swinging Bridge Lake. I introduced myself with a few photos from last week and really felt welcomed by the warm responses. The anti-Democratic party, proto-racist posts, however, that I saw from last September raised some concerns.

I forced myself to walk outside today, just to circle the park. It was hard to see it closed for months last year, to feel the distance between how it once was and how it is now, and the tension that comes from holding one's breath until something difficult passes. It made me wonder if I was somehow waiting for the pandemic to pass before I could let myself fully mourn the loss of my dad.

February 27, Saturday

I woke up this morning to Akiva knocking on the bathroom door. "Mom, it's almost 8." She replied, "And? "And he said, "I need to… Oh, it's Saturday. Never mind. I thought I'd be late for school." Every day is blursday, even a year in.

February 28, Sunday

"Are we the only ones waiting our turn?" That's Noemi's response to a Facebook post of a friend announcing recently their first dose. We didn't think they were any more in need of the vaccine than us—not a senior citizen, nor a healthcare worker or teacher, nor at risk due to health challenges. How could we justify taking a shot from someone like her mother?

MARCH 2021

In which pipes don't freeze… home videos are viewed… schools are opened… slopes are skied… schools are closed… ice cream returns… an anniversary arrives… an end is in sight… a final challah is envisioned… spring is sprung… appointments are made… vaccines are received…

Daily Diary Entries

March 1, Monday

We decided late in the day yesterday, after a weekend at the lake house, to stay an extra night. Thankfully we did. In New York City hot water naturally flows through pipes in our apartment, keeping us warm, while elves flip switches when I turn on the faucet. Which is to say, living in the city, I don't have the foggiest notion about how it all works, and the cost is rolled into our monthly maintenance. At the lake house, however, we have a giant propane tank in back of the home, the kind that I only see in action movies that require a car crash to end in a grand explosion. In January, they filled it and told us they put an automatic meter on it; should it drop below 30% full they'd automatically come over and fill it back up. Easy peasy. This morning we woke up to a 50° house and no hot water. Noemi ran down to the fireplace to burn some wood and raise the heat. I called the gas supplier and was like, WTF? Turns out they just hadn't gotten around to adding that meter yet. They sent me outdoors to go look with my own eyes. It was like 14°. I got on my boots, shoveled a path in the snow to our personal bomb, and found what looked like a meter. I had no clue what it was trying to tell me. I took a photo and emailed it to the person on the phone. "You're out," She said. We'd somehow used it all in six weeks, even though we've only been there for 10 or so days. I don't get how this works. Four hours later the truck came, filled the tank, and we were back in heat. Of course, by the time the house had warmed up, it was time to head back to NYC. What would have happened had we not stayed the night? When the pipes are frozen in the house, do they burst?

March 2, Tuesday

After months digitizing all my VCR and super 8 home movies, tonight launched the first of 20 or so weekly viewing parties that I've scheduled through at least June. We started with an evening about my mom's parents so the gathering was my sister and cousins Abby and Liz. We started with some shorts when we were all kids in the early 1970s—poor lighting, shaky camera, and bad sound. Priceless. The feature was an hour long 1996 trip to Miami for Meme's 80th[67]. Liz and her family were there, my dad, with Carol the year before they were married, and Debby and I. We connected over Zoom, streamed it to our TVs to get the bigger picture, and we chatted by voice and text as I played the video on my computer and shared the screen to all. I loved having a reason to bring us all together and trade family stories. And I was reminded of my initial motivation: watch all this old video of my dad. Hearing his appreciation for each flower in a basket. His vivid description of a sky full of clouds. Stepping into the kitchen at the party to take a call from a patient ("That was the site of the hematoma?"). Totally worth all the work.

March 3, Wednesday

Here is how most mornings work now around here. Akiva up first climbs into the living room couch to play a video game and watch YouTube. Noemi and I get up around the same time and go to separate bathrooms. We three eat breakfast and Akiva gets ready for the day. We three do our 7 Minute Scientific Workout, then Noemi and I do a 10 minute meditation on *Headspace*. Then we all get down to work, Akiva on his couch, Noemi at her desk, and me in my bedroom "office". An hour later we might see Miri, whose remote class begins at 9:30, or maybe an hour later during a school break when she leaves her room for the first time to eat and get dressed.

---

[67] Meme is my mom's mother.

But not today.

While I was in the bathroom I heard a commotion on the other side of the wall, in the other bathroom. Had the sliding shower door come off again? Then I heard voices and then Noemi completing her shower too soon. Once dressed Noemi told me what Miri had been saying with the banging: "Mom, I need to go to school!" We both forgot today was their first Wednesday back in person in school in their new, regular Wed/Thur in-person schedule, their first Wednesday in-person since November. Or was it October. We were so thankful she remembered. We will learn… until we need to learn something else.

March 4, Thursday

By lunch today we received the email from Miri's school: yesterday they ran a test of the students and one turned up positive. Since one last week was already positive, two students means Miri's school is now closed in-person, at least for tomorrow. By the weekend we will learn if they are closed now for two weeks. As Noemi responded, Good to know they're being cautious.

March 5, Friday

Just got the email: Miri's school is closed for a week (not two, like in the fall). Oh, and a second email came from school yesterday, as Miri was one of the randomly tested students. She doesn't have COVID.

I spoke today with someone at the Museum[68]. Almost no one is back yet in person, mostly just Visitor Services. Last fall they reopened with a 25% visitor cap, but the person said they've yet to hit that

[68] The American Museum of Natural History, where I worked in the Education department for six years.

number. How could they, with no school groups, nor international tourists. Maybe this summer, they hope.

Noemi was putting on a mask to go get packages downstairs and stopped. Before you put on a mask you first need to blow your nose. She said it's like making sure you pee before going on a car trip. And at supper club Sam said that when we start going back to work it'll be like returning after maternity leave: "Oh damn, I have to start buttoning my pants again."

The weather is getting warmer. The sun is in the sky later. On Monday renovations will begin on the lake house. I've scheduled an hour a day to work on my design book, now that the contract is in hand, which makes me infinitely happy. And tonight we're skipping Shabbat dinner to go to the New York Hall of Science to the drive-in movie premiere of *Coming to America 2*. I think we can all use a good laugh.

March 6, Saturday

After Miri's soccer practice we headed up to the lake house. I walked down to the lake, climbed out onto the docks – now more of a seasonal obstacle course as they are slanted down towards the frozen, lowered lake – and just listened to the sci-fi crackling of the ice shifting.

Tonight we watched the new Disney animated movie *Raya and the Last Dragon*. It's about a world in devastation because a plague-like force has swept the world. In the end the conflict is resolved by all the competing nations working together, causing the return of the thousands who have been taken from them—moms, dads, children. It was a gorgeously animated film but, given the timing, felt too soon.

March 7, Sunday

Heading back to New York City we stopped on the other side of Monticello at Holiday Mountain. The kids had a ski lesson. It was the first time they would ever ski. My dad learned to ski in college and took it on as a lifelong habit. My mom, terrified of skiing, knew she would have to learn if she wanted to marry him. So she did. Starting at five I learned to ski and most years we went for a week out west, and later to Europe. In the late 1990s my dad felt it was too unsafe and he stopped skiing. I think it broke his heart, but he never regretted the decision. I stopped a few years later, unable to afford it and not trusting in my own abilities as I aged; that was about 20 years ago. Today both kids took the hour lesson and spent the next hour or so going on runs on their own. I couldn't have been more proud of each of them. I just wish I could have picked up the phone tonight, called my dad, and heard the delight and joy in his voice when I told him what his grandchildren had just done.

March 8, Monday

Yesterday renovations began at the lake house. Noemi is running that show, and it's blowing her mind. She's doing great. She reminded me we never do big things like this and that in part is why we did it, and if you wanted that particular wall, sorry too late, it's knocked down, and that's on her.

The DMV mailed me the new registration. I now unfathomably own a boat.

In the last few days I've spoken with three different people at the Museum—two for my book and one about a conference; they are each different, and so wonderful, and hearing how their world has been turned upside down breaks my heart.

We watched that new Fran Lebowitz show and she's complaining about cabs in New York City, and she's going through the turnstile to sit on the subway, and I'm thinking, "What an interesting, quirky city. I look forward to visiting there someday sometime," because next week it'll be one year since I've ridden the MTA. It certainly feels like it all happened in an alternate universe.

March 10, Wednesday

Let it here be recorded that yesterday, at 2:56 PM, the first appearance of the ice cream truck was heard arriving in the park downstairs. It's reached the low 60s and if I hadn't just had a snack I'd have run downstairs and had a vanilla cone without hesitation. We have survived pandemic winter, which we had so dreaded. It has passed and each day I welcome increased sunlight.

Later: He came back, I went down, and that strawberry milkshake was luscious.

Email: One Year Anniversary of Online Shabbat Services at RTFH

From: The Reform Temple of Forest Hills
Subject: One Year Anniversary of Online Shabbat Services at RTFH
Date: March 10, 2021 at 2:20:44 PM EST
To: Barry Joseph

Dear RTFH Family,

This Friday marks the one-year anniversary of The Reform Temple of Forest Hills moving to online Shabbat services due to the COVID-19 quarantine. We miss each other in person and are working towards moving slowly back into hybrid in-person/online services in the months ahead. This Friday we will also recognize our year anniversary with special prayers.

While we lost a lot during the year, we also gained many things. I wanted to reflect on a few of them.

- More people have been coming to services online, including family and friends from miles away.
- Families have been owning their own Judaism leading the candle blessing on Friday nights and baking their own challah.
- B'nai Mitzvah students have been leading the service without the Cantor or Rabbi right next to them and doing it with more authority as young adults.
- We've recognized how much we miss casual conversations, singing together, and Onegs[69]. They will all be appreciated much more when we are back together in-person.

[69] If you missed my earlier footnote, a social period after the religious service.

What stands out as something we've learned and gained in the past year?

Stay Safe,
L'shalom,
Rabbi Mark Kaiserman

Daily Diary Entries

March 11, Thursday

That one year COVID anniversary, the one I didn't know when it might arrive? It's now, it turns out, right now, for the country at least. And everyone's talking about it. A client today tells me she can't bring herself to look at the paper, the headlines all about looking back one year and she can't face it. A year ago today the World Health Organization declared the coronavirus a pandemic. A year ago today Trump issued his first set of domestic restrictions. Tomorrow is the date Noemi's office first closed, which means this past Wednesday was the first day we both started working from home and this Monday is the anniversary of when the school system shut down. This Friday is the anniversary of the first time our temple shifted from in-person to online services; the rabbi's email yesterday recognized how much we had lost but also reflected on the many things we had gained. He asked us to reply with things we have gained. I replied, "I learned how strong and resilient my children are, and how bold our family can be; I gained deeper connections with many of my previous weaker ties and dove deeper with my stronger ones." He replied, "While the world has been devastated, we will come out stronger from this past year." To that I responded, "Indeed. We better, or we've learned nothing."

On one hand it all feels more hopeful. Almost 20% of the country has received their second dose. In fact, more and more groups of people are vaccinated, and can get together in person. Sam in the supper club is planning her birthday in a few weeks, meeting with her parents, outside a restaurant in the city. That feels like such a terrifying fantasy for me right now, but for her it's all within reach as they are all vaccinated. I have little hopes for my upcoming second pandemic birthday, but she gets to celebrate, suggesting what's around the corner for me as well.

Still, I hold my breath. As I have since this began. Girding myself to withstand all that comes my way. Knowing I can't yet relax and let down my guard, and can't submit to the present as a new norm. So I hold on to things that remain unresolved from before the pandemic: an email of a video I am not yet ready to watch, tickets I need to toss for cancelled theater events, a DVD in my work bag that I brought home a year ago and don't feel ready to remove. What will need to happen before I feel I can breathe freely again? My family all vaccinated? The freedom to hug my sister? Will I see the moment approaching over the horizon or, will it sneak up on me, like today?

March 12, Friday

This date last year Broadway Theatre's closed and as of now have yet to open. Today I watched it live on Facebook as the community came out onto the street, mic'd- and masked-up, to sing and dance in Times Square, before digital billboards for Disney-streamed movies and messages like "We will be back," belting songs like "On Broadway" and "We've got magic to do." Oh, yes they do! It brought tears to my eyes. I now plan to see every show I can when that sign finally changes to "We ARE back!"

Email: Stephen A. Halsey JHS 157 Weekly Update

From: Stephen A. Halsey
Subject: Stephen A. Halsey JHS 157 Weekly Update
Date: March 12, 2021 at 10:16:15 AM EST
To: Barry Joseph

Lock Down 1 Year Anniversary

It's hard to believe that it has been a year since NY State locked down. Many of us have been through some really tough times. We have gone on an emotional roller coaster from fear, to pain, to sorrow and grief, to frustration and anger. The schools shut down for full remote learning last year. We came back into blended and kept getting shut down. We would be kidding ourselves if we think there will not be any more school closures. We have to be prepared for it. The disappointment became normal. Now we sit here with hope that the light at the end of the tunnel is starting to come into view. More people are getting vaccinated, there is early excitement and talk about a pill in trial stages that helps people who contract COVID-19. There is even talk that come September blended learning will be a thing of the past. The choice between remote and traditional learning could be the option.

None of us asked for this and none of us deserved it, especially our children. Yet, here we are, 1 year later with 3 months to go in this school year. Let's stay strong, stay optimistic for a better tomorrow and get through these last 3 months Halsey Strong.

Daily Diary Entries

March 13, Saturday

I think I know now how this comes to an end, for me at least. On Tuesday I held the second in my season long series of Home Movie Viewing Parties. This one was just for Debby and I, with esoteric family ephemera only we should care about. The feature was a 1992 trip to San Francisco, just the two of us and Dad. Across its 90 minutes we could see what a good time we were having together, navigating the steep streets of San Fran, recounting tales of Italian restaurants, exploring the Castro district with a tour guide and learning the details of the then-new NAMES Project AIDS Memorial Quilt (with quilts commemorating a different pandemic, in a different time). But my memories of that trip were so different, about how hard we were working to reconnect after Mommy's death a year earlier, to find a new shape for our family around such a prominent missing piece. It left me with a deep appreciation for how hard my father must have worked to rebuild his life after her death, and to include my sister and I in that process.

Last night was our now-typical Shabbat dinner. What once had been a raucous affair—Noemi's mom, my dad and Carol, Debby, sitting around our extended table over the traditional prayers then a hearty home-cooked meal—is now just the four of us, comfortably situated around a table with no need for extenders, and Debby for a few minutes over FaceTime. At 7:00 or so I call her on my phone, pass her around to the kids to say hi, or keep her for myself, and then it's time for the candles. I light a match, first one candle then the second. I hold the flame between my fingers in front of the camera for Debby to pretend to blow out (as I do it for real off-camera). I lower her sound as the delay from her prayer is so dissonant with our own, but not too low, as it's more important we sing it together, the same ones we did every Friday growing up with our parents in our kitchen. Then the prayer over a glass of wine (Kedem grape juice), then over the gorgeous home-made challahs Noemi has taken to baking during the pandemic (everyone else can have sourdough; we have challah!). After we each take a piece of challah the meal begins, I show Debby what's on the table, then we sign off with a kiss and an I Love You.

Afterwards, I realized that is how this will come to an end, once we can finally be back together without requiring such extraordinary effort—weeks of quarantine, a garbage bag worn as a suit of armor—and finally begin the hard work of realigning into the new shape of our family. Once our traditions can return—family traditions, religious traditions—and we can return together to find the new shape of our post-pandemic world, accounting for those still with us, mourning those we've lost along the way. And then just getting on with it.

That night won't be the end of the pandemic but it will be the first few moments of the new world we form out of it. The end itself instead will be when I know that moment is about to arrive for my family and I, when that Shabbat is right around the corner with Debby at our table.

It will end when I can say, at long last, confident for once in the future, that Friday is tomorrow.

March 14, Sunday

This morning I took the leftover challah, mixed some scrambled eggs, and made myself a yummy breakfast sandwich. Noemi saw and commented this might be the last one. For the past year Noemi's been working from home, so she has had time on Fridays to make three fresh challahs: one for the table and two for the freezer for subsequent weeks. Of course, her office is not scheduled to reopen until October—seven months from now—but at least Noemi is no longer adding notches on an infinite pandemic list, and is now starting to transition to the other side of hopelessness, counting down the weeks to the last challah.

At dinner tonight we told Miri that school is opening back up tomorrow. "Boy," she said, "they sure have lots of reverse *Uno* cards!" We're open. We're closed. We're open. We're closed. She called that right!

March 15, Monday

Driving Miri back from her first spring-time-ish soccer practice, she said she'd like to cut her hair again. She said: If it's too short it's a pandemic—so who is going to see anyway?—and if it's really bad she can hide it under her new fashion accessory: a beanie. But then she said maybe she'd wait to have it done not by Mom but by a professional. And get her ears pierced as well, as a Hanukkah present. And that was her timeline—she figured she'd be able to do that some time between September and December, when things get normal enough for her to go into a hair salon. "And Dad, I hear they're testing a juvenile vaccine now as well."

All eyes are slowly rising towards the future.

March 16, Tuesday

Miri returns to school today, a third time this calendar year.

Last night I had to attend another Zoom *shiva*. I'm amazed that a year into this we still haven't learned how to do this right.

The evening closed with my next home movie viewing party. So lovely! This collection was themed around my high school buddies—our graduation, a trip to LA. But my favorite is 14 minutes of comedy gold: three of us on the couch in my living room, camera on a tripod, capturing us debating whether to see *Pretty Woman*, *Ghost*, or *Flatliners* at the multiplex. We go around and around, landing on one as fast as we reject it, getting nowhere, just really wanting to be together, unsuspecting the only movie we will be seeing is one starring us, debating what movie to see, watched over three decades later as we hang around remotely in our 50s during a global pandemic.

March 17, Wednesday

Tonight at supper club the vaccinated shared their tales of where they got the shot—at a local community center, at a hospital, in the parking lot of the racetrack, at Stony Brook University with empty lines winding like Disney World after dark. We joked they could start meeting for dinner while the rest of us Skyped in. Nick said, at his office, they announced once you had your second shot, after showing documentation, you now have to start returning to the office. I noted we were about to have our year anniversary of the pivot from our monthly in person dinners to our weekly Zoom gatherings. Michael looked it up. Tonight was actually our first night of our second year. It feels special. Not like we all accomplished something—we never planned to be isolated for this long—but that we've held out for each other, continuously, re-committing to our friendships one week at a time, maintaining a thread of normalcy throughout the chaos.

March 18, Thursday

First, the expected: Miri's school has a new case of COVID. Not in her class. School will still be open Monday, but if one more occurs I think they close.

Now, the unexpected. Against all expectations Akiva school reopens this Monday. First time since mid-fall. He is scheduled to go in two days a week. But he doesn't want to go, due to COVID concerns and that it's all a pain. If he went in then five of his seven classes would be in person, with teachers he only saw a handful of times last October; the other two would be in the library, meeting remotely with his teachers. That means, however, when he's there in person he'd not be with five teachers that he has been seeing most days consistently for over four months. Why disrupt that, especially when he is excelling academically? The answers are obvious to Noemi and me: his social well-being, his mental health, and his physical health. But are we just dreaming that two days in school—with most socializing discouraged—would help him in these areas? For now, we're letting him decide—but if he stays home I understand that that's it, we're locked in, 100% remote for the rest of the year. So we agreed on one condition: he takes more ownership over his social, mental, and physical health and shoots for certain metrics to reach for each day and week. If he's going to stay home, we need more from him. He'll consider it.

March 19, Friday

One of the best things about my "job" is getting to choose whom I speak with. Today I got to connect with someone I love from an Israeli museum and someone I equally adore from Haida Gwaii. They both exemplify the mutual respect for a grounded human connection underneath any work; getting to live with that and include it in my work day is a privilege, as well as a challenge to do it more. And both reflected back to me how they see me, how they value what I can bring to the project – not just my skills and talent but my personality and approach to life—which has too long been missing in my "office jobs." No wonder striking out on my own has felt so liberating and reaffirming. Now I just need more paying clients…

March 20, Saturday

It is the first day of spring. I went into the park and experimented with my new 360° camera. It's quite satisfying to geek out on a new tech toy. But frankly I'm not confident that it worked. It doesn't matter. It was sunny and beautiful and I was out in it, just observing.

It was far from easy, but together we agreed to heed Akiva's request to stay home from school for the rest of the year if he'll work with us to counter some of the harder places for him during the pandemic. Meanwhile, an hour after putting Miri to bed we hear her yelling in her room, debating with her friends about sexism, racism, and homophobia; we said: That's great, go to bed, the struggle won't end overnight.

March 21, Sunday

Today we celebrated my birthday a few days early, the second under COVID. With the weather in the low 60s, I asked us all to go bike riding to Flushing Meadows Park, former site of the two Worlds Fairs, *Men in Black*, and numerous Marvel movies. It felt like Queens was out in celebration, not about the end of COVID—most wore masks and kept their distance—but that we survived a whole year, past the winter, and made it to the new spring. Families out picnicking, teaching their children to ride bikes. Skater kids, both boys and girls, dominating the skate park. Pakistanis, or perhaps Indians, preparing for cricket. Latino soccer players transforming the empty fountains into playing fields. A senior Asian couple dancing to older Chinese pop music while dancing what looked to my untrained eyes like the hustle. We lay underneath the Unisphere—that 12-story high spherical skeleton - watching the underbellies of planes pass by overhead as we gazed up into this awesome monument to global interdependence, observing the world from the inside out.

March 22, Monday

My head is spinning. Did this really just happen? The nice lady on the phone asked, "Before I do, are you sure you want to cancel your COVID vaccine appointment?"

Wait—first, I need to get the other things out of the way.

Akiva did not go into school today, the first day this year he didn't when he could have. Instead I submitted the form to the Department of Education to turn him from blended to 100% remote. No turning back now.

Debby met me downstairs in the park, bringing me my favorite Chinese dish from my old work neighborhood[70], a cupcake with a candle, and a birthday present, as she was off today and working Wednesday, the day of my actual birthday. It was so sweet of her, and I really appreciated it. But I can feel, both today and yesterday, that I've been unusually reluctant to fully embrace my birthday this year, to let down my guard and let in the love, because it feels like if I did I might crumble and be unable to put the armor back on.

Back home after lunch, doing work, the Governor tweeted breaking and unexpected news: all New Yorkers over 50 are vaccine eligible starting 8 AM tomorrow. Where'd that come from? I thought it was June 1. I started trying all the websites. For hours, nothing. Nothing. Nothing. All so complex, confusing, unnecessarily decentralized. All I could find were two vaccination locations in Staten Island an hour away, at 3:00 and 3:30 AM in the morning.

After dinner everything changed. Spots were opening up. I saw one in lower Westchester, north of the city, with 97 spots! Boom—I got it. 4pm tomorrow! Then Debby got one, and realized it was for city employees only. Then she heard if she was an NYU patient she could

70 Slow Simmered Fish with Chilis and Soft Tofu

get one at NYU. She was last fall, when I picked her up from the city! Using their app she got one, then canceled that first appointment. And Steven got one too, on Wednesday, in Middle Village, 15 minutes from here. How crazy! He gave me the information and five minutes later I had one there as well, same time as Steve.

That's why I told the nice lady on the phone, "Thank you, but yes, I'm sure I want to cancel. I have another appointment closer to me."

On my birthday, by the batting cage, the bread factory, and the wholesale sturgeon dealer, I'll meet Steven and together we will get vaccinated. We spent months trying to get our parents vaccinated and within hours it became so easy that we can now go together.

Noemi is so happy she now has one less reason to think I might suddenly die.

How do I feel? Like maybe I can almost maybe look forward to breathing easier, to a weight being lifted. Like there was an unannounced draft and I won in reverse. I will get my first shot in two days, Debby hers this Thursday, and if Noemi's age group opens in a few weeks… before long Debby and I won't have to sit apart downstairs in the park to see one another, with no hug hello nor goodbye, nor masks on when we're not eating, and instead she'll be coming up upstairs to break bread and share Shabbat with us, in person, surrounded by hugs.

March 23, Tuesday

Along with being my birthday tomorrow it is vaccination day! Debby, Paul, Steven, Claire, and I will all get our first shots[71], and Oma her second. This means all but two people in the supper club will have

[71] Paul found a place in Brooklyn and Claire (from the supper club) got a later appointment on the same day at my location in Middle Village.

had one shot. It also means among most all of my closest friends here locally, after tomorrow all will have had at least one shot. I can slowly feel some tension lift, like I've been walking in thick humidity and now it's starting to dissipate.

But not yet. New issues arise. Are we carriers to each other? That is, could someone vaccinated pass the virus to me and from me to Noemi? What about our kids? And what about new variations that I might not be susceptible to? Today Miri was speculating at Passover this weekend they can finally hug her grandmother, just not kiss her. Is that correct? How can we know? How will we decide?

After more than a year of putting up such strong protections around our family bubble, on one hand we are desperate to be free from it strictures, and yet, on the other hand, we don't want to naïvely or lazily do something stupid and waste all the effort we put into keeping all of us, and our loved ones, safe.

Email: Confirmed: Vaccination

From: Centers Urgent Care
Subject: Confirmed: Vaccination - Middle Village 3/24 - 3/29 with Centers Urgent Care on Wednesday, March 24, 2021
Date: March 22, 2021 at 9:35:19 PM EDT
To: Barry Joseph

Hi Barry Joseph,

Your Pfizer COVID-19 Vaccine with Centers Urgent Care at 03:30pm (Eastern Time - US & Canada) on Wednesday, March 24, 2021 is scheduled.

Location: 6122G Fresh Pond Road Middle Village, NY, 11379

Your Answers:

Do you qualify under the guidelines published by NYS for 3/23/2021 vaccine eligibility?
Yes

What category do you qualify under?
Over the age of 50

Will you be able to provide proof of eligibility? Note: Centers Urgent Care will not be able to provide vaccinations without proof of eligibility.
Yes

I agree that If presenting with a co-morbidity or underlying condition a signed letter from a primary care physician will be

required. Without such documentation Centers Urgent Care will not be able to provide a vaccination.
Agree

Please complete the NYS Vaccination form at vaccineform.health.ny.gov and please bring ID, proof of insurance, and proof of eligibility to your appointment.

Please confirm that you will be coming by replying to this message.

Daily Diary Entries

March 24, Wednesday

Today was an overwhelming confluence that I can only make sense of by focusing on the details that stand out from the others.

A Facebook message from Ralph, one of my dad's best friends, who never connected with me beyond bad "dad jokes" mixed with put down jabs, floored me with this message: "Dear Barry, I know how tough it is to celebrate your birthday without your father. I must tell you that I loved and miss your father. Paul was just the nicest, sweetest, considerate person that I ever met. Again, happy birthday."

Using bit torrent, Plex, Firefox, and the Oculus Quest 2 to watch the classic *In the Heat of the Night* for my first time, with Steven, for my birthday, instead of doing work.

Driving to the Middle Village strip mall urgent care center for my COVID test, sandwiched between classic Queen's cemeteries (as if I needed the reminder of why I was going).

Standing online to check in and seeing Steve outside pull up in his Uber from Manhattan. We talk most every day but we've only seen each other twice since the pandemic. Today, because the site only started vaccinating yesterday, we had an amazing two hours to hang out and chat with each other and a myriad of other vaccine recipients.

At check-in, the woman asked me, "What are your qualifications?" I said, "Over 50, and I really really want it." After she laughed I also pointed to my shirt: a defiant birthday cake asking "Wanna piece of me?"

Then Claire arrived! I had no idea our times would overlap! Now there with someone representing my childhood friends and someone representing the supper club. All I needed was a work acquaintance—then walked in someone from Facilities from the American Museum of Natural History whom I hadn't seen in years.

Fran, the modern Orthodox wife already vaccinated but there supporting her husband—the four of us (Steve and I)—in our own waiting room. "I'm here two hours but I need to be home preparing for Passover. God wanted to give me a break."

Steven and I get taken to a room so they could "take our vitals." The nurse was going to lose it after the eighth time the blood pressure band popped off our arms. They decided to stop taking blood pressure for everyone. The supervisor pulled the nurse aside and said, "I need you to please soften up."

The Pfizer shot was quick and painless.

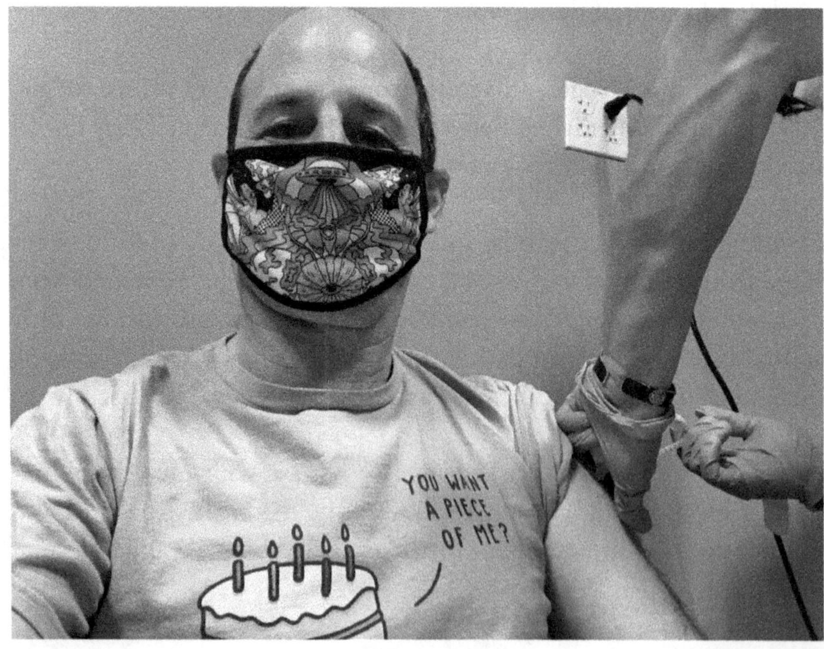

Steven and I photographed each other. We made appointments to return in three weeks for the second shot. Then, to wait our required 15 minutes, we stood outside and chatted, marveling at science, our good fortune, our hopes for the near future. His Uber arrived. Steve surprised me with "let me hug you." I immediately said, "No, but maybe in three weeks."

After that I hung out with Claire until her car came to take her home to Long Island.

Driving home in the pouring rain I passed two men who looked like day laborers, wearing nothing but hoodies and drenched. One man bent over, came up with a white umbrella covered in prints of colorful flowers, and proudly held it overhead.

After dinner Noemi served my favorite banana cream pie and surprised me by giving me a new white baseball hat with my company logo on it. I put it on and when I looked up all three of them were wearing the same. She told me as we four hugged, "We're your team."

One hour on Zoom with my old friends.

Another hour on Zoom with the supper club. Michael jokingly had cut out a scarlet "U" to wear on his shirt, for "unvaccinated", as only he and Noemi now remain. We talked about the possible importance of our vaccination cards, and what we might need them for moving forward beyond getting free donuts.

Debby sent me a selfie with the doctor who gave her her shot today.

Between my two Zoom parties, they were five of us who got our first shots today, while Oma received her second.

March 25, Thursday

Noemi told me that yesterday was a record day for New York State for vaccines given in one day: 202,000 people received a shot. There is an interesting symmetry here: my dad died almost a year ago riding the cresting wave of COVID deaths while his kids get vaccinated a year later riding the wave that we all hope will take us out of this nightmare.

March 26, Friday

I feel my energy returning. Not in a surge, but gradually. I was returning from the supermarket this afternoon after shopping for last-minute Passover ingredients for Noemi (almond flour, lemons, horseradish, Dr. Brown's Black Cherry) and I looked up at the sky and saw those full moons you sometimes see in the daylight. For some reason that made me think about that freakishly popular song these days about getting a driver's license and going past an ex-boyfriend and I imagined writing a parody about driving past Atria as if I was singing to my dad, the joke being he's no longer there, but the ironic stance crumbled and I just started crying—still in my imagination, the parody writer in my story crying—but then that made me cry for real. It's good, it's all good. As the energy's returning and as I start opening back up for business, the shit I had to hold in all year is going to start just bubbling on up to fill in the newly available space.

March 27, Saturday

Last year Passover fell in April, at the beginning of the lockdown. We managed to lead two creative Zoom-based seders, and marveled that we pulled it off. My dad had canceled in the hour before the second night—I held my worries at bay throughout and called him right after—and the next day was the day he first entered the hospital.

So although it's not yet April, in a way this is like a year since it first began, when we started to lose him.

His absence aside, this first night of Passover this year was just wonderful. We all managed to go up to New Rochelle to Oma's. In the mid-60s, it was sunny and warm most of the day. Debby Ubered up from the city. Becky and company drove in from Philly. And by now we have the routine down: four separate bubbles, one for each family unit, and Oma largely ran the kitchen. Noemi led her family Seder, and it was meaningful and participatory throughout. Before *dayenu*—as a song recognizing that each step toward our liberation from slavery would have, in and of itself, been enough—Noemi said this has been our *dayenu* year. We needed so much that we could not get, but we were so appreciative nonetheless of each step we achieved in the right direction: at least we could meet over Zoom, at least we could meet on the lawn wearing masks, at least we could celebrate a holiday at separate tables and share food. *Dayenu. Dayenu. Dayenu.*

On the Van Wyck Expressway on the way home the College Point AMC movie theater—which all year has served the same message promising the movies would be back—featured an ad for the new *Godzilla versus Kong*. The theater must have opened, at long last, a few days ago. I don't know what to make of the selection: the who-can-count-what-number-remake of two 60 to 90 year old franchises that each, in their own way, are about humanity being out-of-balance with nature and how, when it happens, it kicks our ass. But this time the title suggested they were going after each other. Good. It's about time. We need a break.

March 28, Sunday

Today I led the second seder—remote on Zoom—with 11 households participating. Boy, I hope I never have to do this again. Still it was great to bring so many people together and to use it to reflect on parallels between the Passover story and the journeys we've all been on through COVID this past year. I asked: How is this year's seder different from last year's seder?

People said:

- My hair is much longer this year...
- Still on Zoom, but much more hopeful
- Last year we didn't know what the future held. Now we believe we can see the beginning of the end.
- Last year we were scared of using technology to hold a seder. This year we are leveraging technology to hold THE BEST SEDER EVER!!!!!
- Last year it felt novel and heroic to have a Zoom Seder. This year it does not.
- We are on our way to being vaccinated.

I adapted what I did last year—one of our first Zoom events—but added more digital interactivity, music videos, and cartoons. I especially liked the ending with the now new classic song "Next year" from 2021's Saturday Night Seder (even if it was painful to see how we naïvely believed last year it'd all be over by now.)

I told Noemi: I thought more about what she said about *dayenu* yesterday. No one was standing at the Red Sea facing those waves, Egyptian army bearing down on them, shrugging their shoulders and saying, "Well, at least God took us this far." That person would've been an asshole. We can only say *dayenu* in a literal way once we are safe. Saying *dayenu* then is really more of an act of hindsight, something we can say about being in troubled times once the challenge has passed. Noemi naming this the *dayenu* year is an act of hope. It suggests safety is now in view.

March 29, Monday

Yes! Exactly a week to the moment I heard I could get vaccinated. Today at 1:25 PM Noemi texted me the new headline: "New York expands vaccine eligibility to those 30 and older on Tuesday." It's nearly 11 PM and registration has yet to open, so it's going slower than last week, but who cares. "So it'll be another week," she said. It doesn't matter. Her first vaccine shot, whenever it turns out to be, is just days away.

March 30, Tuesday

It's not like last week. There are no vaccine appointments to be found for Noemi. If one appears it's followed by two pages of personal questions, after which it returns "no appointment available." Insanely frustrating. It just doesn't make any sense.

This morning Noemi read the new CDC findings, that it looks like those who are vaccinated can't infect others. She almost teared up saying now she wants to go to her mom's this weekend and give her a hug. How do I respond to something like that, and caution patience?

Update: after hours of reloading webpages, clicking on links to appointments that always returned results stating it was no longer available, I came across a phone number, a last ditch effort before going to bed. An hour later we're all set—Noemi is scheduled, 7 AM, tomorrow at Citi Field. Yes! I can't put into words how relieved I feel, anxiety lifting in successive waves at the possibility that we are that much closer to the other side of constant terror of losing each other.

It's like birds on a wire. Hearing the news they startle and take flight. I'm the wire snapping back into place.

March 31, Wednesday

Noemi left this morning at 6:30 AM to go to Citi Field and by 7:20 she was all done. Simply amazing (like the Mets). When she checked in they asked if her eligibility was due to pre-existing conditions or if she was a city worker. When she said because she was over 30 the staff were shocked—everyone else so far has been there for one of the other two. Noemi was texting me photos, standing in front of the stadium, the moment she got her shot. One series are photos of paper screens in the observation area where you have to sit before you are allowed to leave—filled with all these emotional and heartfelt messages:

> Thank you to all the amazing immunizers and organizers! So thrilled to get stuck with two needles!
>
> Gracias. Muchas Gracias.
>
> Finally I got the shot! Thanks for all the hard work to help us get better.
>
> Next time shots on me.

What's even more amazing is I was wrong—I thought I had solved the puzzle of this appointment system, by making the phone call. But Michael did the same and after waiting for someone to answer, and going verbally through the same steps as the websites, they said there were no appointments available. I must've gotten Noemi's through dumb luck. Michael told me "It's like the craziest game of whack-a-mole ever." Tonight at supper club he was now the only one of us all without at least one shot of the vaccine.

APRIL 2021

In which a yahrzeit approaches… Blursday fades… a restaurant is patronized… shots are administered… a loss is observed… a lake house comes together… a new norm approaches…a bed is reclaimed…

Daily Diary Entries

April 1, Thursday

Last night at 11:09 PM Michael saw a dozen appointments open up on the website, at the City College of New York (one of my clients). He snagged one for today. Sounds like he was in and out in about 30 minutes this afternoon. So that's it—everyone in the supper club has at least one shot, and by the end of April we all will have had our second. Does that mean in May we could or even would return to having a monthly dinner together? If not then, then when?

Noemi realized we can consider going to the Forest Hills Stadium to see concerts this summer, at 25% capacity. Maybe we will. Akiva didn't like hearing that, concerned we can still be carriers. We told him the CDC said this week that it looks like the vaccinated aren't carriers. We're not making decisions for a while and will wait for more studies to confirm it. At least that's what we said.

April 2, Friday

I launched the website for my company this week. I even added a new page to promote my digital design book coming out next year. It's taken too long, but I'm proud of it. Next week I'll start using it to reach out to new leads. Monday I interviewed with a potential client—an after school program looking to hire a freelance micro-credentialing expert. I talked them into considering my company. We'll see. And Sunday night I will apply to a full-time job, the type I see about once a month which I only apply to if it looks amazing, and to keep me in practice. Today someone I know recommended me to them as well, and they reached out to me for an interview next week. It's a head of education position at this amazing museum, which would be a wonderful new adventure. But I'm not yet ready to give up BJC[72]. Not by a long shot.

The CDC walked back today their certainty that people with the vaccine can't pass it on to others. Grrrr. So confusing knowing what we can and can't do. Should Noemi get her haircut? Can we spend time in her mom's home? Who pays the price if we're wrong?

Working today I told Alexa to play some Pearl Jam. Their brilliantly titled "Elderly Woman Behind the Counter in a Small Town" came on. Eddie Vedder sang:

> I just want to scream hello
> My God it's been so long
> Never thought you'd return
> But now here you are and here I am

It's a song imagining what that tired looking woman serving Eddie coffee on some tour must be thinking, about the connections she's formed with her customers over the years. And yes, I've heard it a thousand times, but today I heard it in a totally new way. It made me think about all those people I used to see on a daily basis before the pandemic—the cashiers at my bagel place, the security guard at the office, my barber —and how I, too, want to scream out to them. But to survive emotionally this past year I've had to forget about them. Knowing that soon such relations will return to my life, and I will have to let them back in, caused me to burst into tears. I welcomed that release knowing tears melt these frozen places and are part of the path back.

April 3, Saturday

Today was a beautiful day. A bit chilly, but sunny and blue sky. The Hudson was gorgeous as we sat on the rocks in Croton, or walked

[72] Barry Joseph Consulting, remember?

the park. The Biens are in town, preparing their house for the sale in a few weeks[73]. They were one of the first, if not THE first, family we saw in person last year after the initial shut-down. It was in June, and Noemi found a park between us where we could picnic 20 feet apart and play games. Within weeks they had moved to Los Angeles. Tonight we sat around their fire pit—now only 6 feet apart—and ate takeout Thai food. When we left our car was full of items of theirs to give them a new home in the Catskills: a lobster pot, a pair of bongo drums, an old radio. Pandemic or not, I still miss them.

April 4, Sunday

Today's weather was even more beautiful than yesterday. We spent it on Oma's lawn in New Rochelle. The Philly nephews have been bouncing back between grandparents ever since Passover, so it was fun

[73] They had rented it out this past year.

to see them twice in two weekends. It was the last day of Passover[74] so we all started it together last week and ended it together over lunch today. Noemi chatted with Oma about lake house renovations. The kids sat in the driveway and played Duck Game on their Switches and made friendship bracelets. I fixed the patio heater for potential future use and sat in the grass leaning on the tree while reading the Sunday *New York Times*. Oma is now fully vaccinated and Noemi and I are on our way, but we still kept our distance and wore masks most of the time, as did all four of the kids.

April 5, Monday

"Spring break," is over so the kids went "back to school" today. Funny—looked just like last week. It's hard to believe this might be it, that in under three months this will be the end of this chaotic, stressful, discordant school year. And that this fall both kids should—might?—go back to school every day. What a shock to the system that will be to them. Or a relief? Maybe both. We'll see. Meanwhile the mayor announced they will stop closing schools with pandemic cases so often. They didn't say how, just that they will.

Good news is Becky and Scott unexpectedly got their first shots today. They were on a standby list and got called—first time I've heard of that working for someone. I'm so happy for them.

April 6, Tuesday

Today driving back from soccer practice, Miri said, "At first after four weeks we were like, I can't believe we've been in quarantine this long. Then at seven weeks we said it again. We were amazed. Then again in the summer, and we said it again in December. Now I'm saying it again, and it's been over a year." Miri said that when we no

[74] No leavened bread can be eaten during the Passover period.

longer have to wear masks she'll still flinch when someone touches her, that that's how she feels watching a TV show: when someone is in a crowd, she's yelling at the screen to keep their distance. So, Miri wanted to know when that would be, when we can all stop wearing masks. "By July 25?" she asked, the date sleepaway camp is set to begin. No, not that early, I said. By Thanksgiving or Hanukkah. But what the hell do I know. I sure hope by the B'Nai Mitzvah in February. Just to get to have that, without needing masks, would feel like a win. But I wasn't sugarcoating it. I said it all depends, on new variants, on people getting vaccinated. On one hand, she is so aware of it; on the other hand it forces her to understand herself situated in time in ways that challenge her cognition.

April 7, Wednesday

Tonight for the first time, everyone on the supper club, all nine of us, have had their first shot, with four of us still waiting for a second; next week only two of us will be waiting. I'm so excited for my second shot; Steven keeps texting me about it, in anticipation. Maybe we can walk over after our shot to the secret bread factory, if even just to smell it. Oh, and Claire's oldest, going to college next year, had her first shot today, now that yesterday the state opened to all 16-year-olds and over; she's the first of any of our children to get the vaccine.

Today I was volunteer live-tweeting from the MuseWeb conference (about museums and digital engagement). The keynote was from Lonnie Bunch of the Smithsonian. He was so inspiring. I loved so much of what he had to say:

> Cultural institutions are the glue that holds a nation together.
>
> The best institution used this time to re-imagine what our role should be and to rethink how we work with audiences.

> My goal was to use the Smithsonian to define reality and give hope.
>
> I created a New Normal group asking, How do we come out of this more nimble, changed, and accelerate the use of digital?
>
> The way forward is to help the public embrace ambiguity, to be comfortable with flexibility and nuance.
>
> I want to recognize by crossing racial lines they're able to challenge a country to live up to its stated ideals.

April 8, Thursday

The CDC now says the risk of infection through physical contact is minimal. Respiratory is the main factor. Good to know, now, but boy, all that time Noemi spent wiping down the groceries, and Amazon boxes, and door knobs…

I got an email from the cemetery. It's almost a year and he has no foot or head stone. I had presumed it would be automatic. Now I need to arrange that. Once I do, with his *yahrzeit*[75] approaching, I'll probably want to go out there anyway. Can we swing it for after Debby and I get our second shots? Could we actually go together? I also received paperwork yesterday I had never seen before, a copy of his death certificate. It's the first time I've read this formally declared: "immediate cause of death: respiratory failure. Due to or as a consequence of: COVID-19." Last night Debby, Todd, Noemi and I watched over Zoom our family home movies from the late 1990s of trips to the Chautauqua Institution. It made me so happy to see

[75] The observance of the anniversary of the death of a parent or close relative.

Dad at his favorite summer retreat, vibrant, joking around, dancing, doing things in his own idiosyncratic way, passionately sharing about the things that excite him. That's how I want to remember him.

April 9, Friday

I woke up today with an almost forgotten feeling. Anticipation? Excitement? It's a start of the end of the workweek. The weekend is about to begin. When did I last feel this way? Some time before the days all blended together, I guess. Can it be? Are Blursdays finally behind us?

April 10, Saturday

Miri had her first soccer game of the season. Like fall, all will be away games on Long Island. It was great to see them play (even if no one at the gas station was wearing a mask).

Then we drove up to the lake house. On the way we stopped at Panera for dinner. The weather was good and the open outdoor area was empty. That meant we could eat hot food at a restaurant, the first time I think since last summer.

We arrived at the house late, got the bags in and kids to bed, and marveled at the renovations. It looked gorgeous. We walked down to the dock, then out on the dock, in the insect-quiet of the night, marveling at the water, the trees, the house behind us, our good fortune. It all started to sink in. It felt like at last we'd arrived at our new home.

April 11, Sunday

I drove into town to bring back bagels for breakfast for all. Driving back and forth on our rural dead-end road I often pass neighbors of all backgrounds walking their dogs, or chatting with their own neighbors, and each and every one waves hello.

April 12, Monday

I texted Steven the daily update as I have since last week. Today's: T-minus 2 days! I can't believe I'm about to get my second dose. What will I stop doing first?

April 13, Tuesday

T-minus one day!

I'd like to leave it at that but...

Last night I dreamed the four of us were on a road trip. We parked the car and went into a restaurant. Upon entering a patron said someone had stolen our car ignition. How could he know? We went into the parking lot to find a plastic bag over our trunk and the entire car bent, smashed, totaled. A man gave me a magazine explaining that Donald Trump did it. Trump was filming a new reality show and jumped in a car and was driving recklessly. In fact this man took photos of it which were published in the magazine I was now holding. We looked at them—O.J. Simpson-style helicopter chase photos of the car doing crazy things, like driving perpendicular across a multi-lane highway. How are we going to manage the rest of the vacation? We went back inside to find the Russian mafia restaurant owners had roughed up a guy they said was involved in wrecking our car. They yelled at him to admit what he had done. Instead he sneezed on me, at which point I thought how rude, due to COVID. I went to the bathroom to wash my face and returned to conclude with Noemi that we really had no choice and the next day we would just have to take a taxi to Disney World.

So, yeah... T-minus one day!

April 14, Wednesday

T-minus zero!

I met Steven this afternoon at the urgent care center. We were both so excited. Last time we were there it was a disorganized madhouse. This time all was calm, orderly, and without drama. In fact, it felt eerie—where were all the other patients from two weeks earlier who should now be back getting their second dose as well?

Within 10 minutes we were in a room prepping for a shot. The blood pressure machine worked this time. A man entered, took my stats, and gave it to the doctor who typed it into a computer. Next thing I know he was jabbing my arm— never noticed when he'd taken over. He was nice about it and quite funny. When he saw I was taking a photo he hammed it up, asked for a copy, and for my permission to post it on his Instagram.

Claire arrived and Steven and I waited outside. I asked if he was ready to hug. Steven said, "That's what I asked last time", and I said, "Yeah, but we had just gotten the shot." It was our first time in over a year. It felt good. "What a year," Steven said. "What a year." Then my arm jabber came out and he told us his story.

He didn't work there! He was an EMT who was volunteering. He just wanted to help out. And he was so disgusted by how medical policy was politicized during the pandemic he decided to run for city council this year. Steven joked that's why he wanted to post the photo on Instagram, but warned him that I was publicly known as a Trump supporter. Slightly worried, he was relieved to see me shake my head. No, I said, Just a pedophile.[76]

Claire came out and we piled into my car, windows down, masks up, and we went to Eddie's Sweet Shop on Metropolitan Avenue to celebrate. We ordered inside and ate outside. I had my regular: orange sherbet with hot fudge. We all could barely get our heads around all the implications. Throughout I was sending photos to Noemi and Debby. Noemi texted, "So relieved that you are safe from this, I can't tell you." Steven got an Uber back to Manhattan, Claire one back to Long Island, and I drove back home.

[76] Not really!

Already Debby scheduled lunch with me for Monday, Steven promises one week after today's dose he'll be ready to have lunch together as well, and Andy said in three weeks there are new restaurants in Flushing Chinatown he's craving for us all to check out.

So much feels like it's returning back to normal. Yet the infection rate in New York City is going up every day. It's hard to make sense of the dissonance.

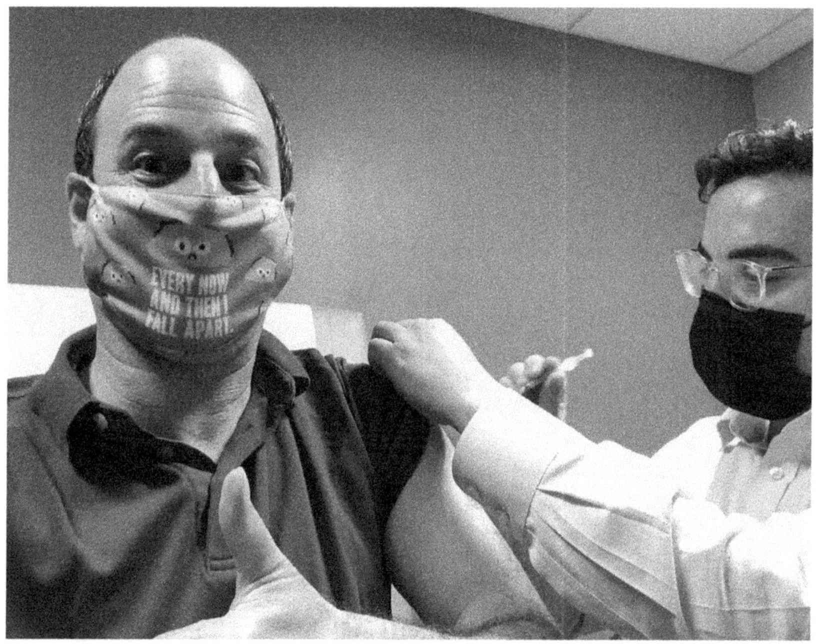

April 15, Thursday

Ugg. I feel like crap. I was okay enough this morning to do some work, but then I got foggy and achy and started watching the 2015 *Jurassic World* movie in 3D on my Oculus. I finished the recent *Kong versus Godzilla* film, then, for the first time, watched 1994's *Speed.* As my body battles the vaccine and builds antigens, I guess I just needed to watch things get mindlessly destroyed.

April 16, Friday

Debby will be fully vaccinated in two weeks. Noemi in three. That means it's coming soon: Debby, Oma, and Carol coming back to celebrate Shabbat with us.

A worker in our building, whom I've known for 13 years, was telling me last week he wasn't ready yet to trust getting a vaccine. I made the pitch, saying how great it feels to feel more normal and to know I'm not a threat to those around me. But I thought he might also have been saying something else. So I gave him an op-ed from *The New York Times* by a columnist who essentially said, as a black man, he had no reason to trust the American medical establishment given its history of racism—yet in spite of that he was still getting a shot. I ran into him a few days later; between that piece and his cousin, who is a doctor, he said he might now be convinced.

Debby and I are now working on the language for Dad's headstone. "When you gotta go, you gotta go," doesn't seem to cut it. This Thursday it will have been one year.

April 17, Saturday

Miri's soccer team won their first game of the season! That was exciting. On the way back from the game we passed a church; its sign read "Thou shall not COVID thy neighbor."

I've started compiling these diary entries into a possible book. I don't know if they'll provide any value or meaning to anyone else, but it feels useful just in the doing of the task. And in the reading, it gives me perspective, like last night re-reading for the first time the notes I made when Dad was in the hospital. How much was I fooling myself when I thought there was anything going on BUT COVID? And how hard must that have been when the situation turned so fast and there was no longer a path to recovery?

We're up at the lake house now. Tonight I read the diary entry about Paul first putting the idea in our heads to buy a second home (August 1) and our first visit to this place just a few weeks later. What a journey to get to this point! With Noemi's designs starting to come together—a carpet here, a chair there—it's really quite beautiful.

April 18, Sunday

It was so lovely over the course of the day to observe the changing textures of the surface of the lake. Miri spent her time at the house in her room all weekend. After packing the car to leave she went out and sat at the end of the dock, staring at the placid lake, and returned to say, "I'm going to spend more time there."

Debby's coming to lunch with me tomorrow, in the park. Will we hug? I bet we hug (with masks donned, but for how much longer?)

April 19, Monday

No hug. Debby said we should wait until Noemi is fully inoculated. Two weeks from Wednesday seems fine to me. That meant we could start the planning.

We decided what we will do: I pick Debby up then we drive to Long Island (windows open?). We then go to Dad's grave (Debby still hasn't been). Then she'll come back and stay for Shabbat, the first time since February 2020. It'll be something.

We also finished working on Dad's foot stone, four lines to match Mommy's:

> Devoted brother, husband, father, grandfather
> Quick to prescribe a bad joke
> Raring to ski, tennis, or play ball

Always loved a damn good peach

Debby said she's not weepy at all talking about Dad like she still is with Mommy. I suggested in part that was because she was so young when we lost her and it left a bigger hole. And that we're still in the pandemic. Be patient, I counseled. It will come.

April 20, Tuesday

Guilty, on all three accounts. Justice for George Floyd, perhaps? What a relief. What a year. How to build on that momentum? We must stop devaluing Black and brown bodies. At a gas station on Long Island during a recent soccer game I saw an anti-Black Lives Matter bumper sticker on the car in front of me. It said something like, "When you call for them after you defund them how will you feel?" It took me a few hours, to be honest, but then it struck me, the white privilege that imagines people of color have control over when and how they get to interact with the police. Like a contemporary "let them eat cake."

Tomorrow Noemi gets her second shot. Yes! Steven is going out for coffee, wearing only one cloth mask. Someone contacted me to promote my seltzer talk via Zoom to upwards of 400 temples. Things are shifting.

April 21, Wednesday

I woke up to this alert on my phone in my COVID Alert NY app: "The app has detected that on April 13, 2021 someone who tested positive for COVID-19 was within 6 feet of you for over 10 minutes." Well, I don't know how that's possible, as I wasn't around anyone for even half that time that day—I worked at home and picked up Miri from soccer. Hard to know how to process. And by then I was days away from my second COVID vaccine shot.

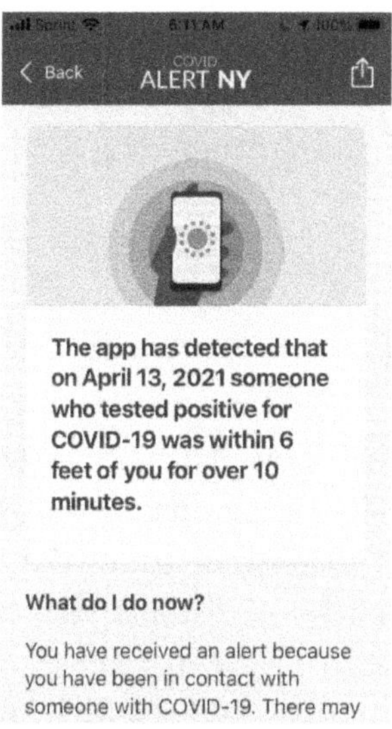

Noemi had no problem returning to Citi Field to get her second shot today. I asked her to send me photos but afterwards, sans photos, she texted, "It's done. I guess I was emotional because I forgot to send a selfie."

At supper club tonight Sam asked Noemi if she has any plans now for what she'll do in two weeks. She said, "Get my haircut." She already has the appointment. "And drive to New Rochelle and give my mom a hug."

April 22, Thursday

I can't believe it's been a year. Truly. I started the day posting on Facebook to thank all my peeps there for all the support last year. I shared the mock up of Dad's footstone, and that I was thinking of compiling all this into a book. Others said something similar, that they can't believe it's been a year. It's like Pandemic Time exists, in part, in its own bubble, and everything feels on pause during it. Then when it ends, time will resume. Everyone was so supportive. An old friend from high school said I was one of seven friends who lost a parent to COVID last year. She wrote, "Your story, reading poems to your dad, your unassuming and uplifting humor, was such an inspiration to me that I have shared it with clients on grief work this past year. Please, write the book." If I can help people like her clients maybe that's reason enough.

Tonight Debby Zoomed in and, with Noemi, we watched videos of our last international trip with Dad, to Israel in 2000. It was wonderful to see him so vibrant, relaxed, and jovial. He got excited by the slightest marvels: salt deposited at the Dead Sea, historical tidbits he was eager to share. It felt so wonderful being with him again. Deb and I now set the date—May 9—to travel together to his and Mommy's grave sites, then, finally, at long last, welcome her back into our home to celebrate Shabbat together.

April 23, Friday

Tonight attending Shabbat services, even over Zoom, was so nice. It reminded me of how much it can be a weekly communal meditation, to slow down and connect. I went to say the Mourner's Kaddish for my dad. It felt meaningful to mark the year in that way, within that community. The Rabbi said his name and it meant something real to hear it out loud, in that context, knowing it was heard and recognized by the community. Ilyse and Michael were there from the supper club and Noemi was by my side. I put on a button down shirt.

Steven took a subway today, and sent me photos. First time! Then he met Debby in Bryant Park and they hugged.

April 25, Sunday

It was a lovely weekend at the lake house. Most of the time I spent there getting it ready —laying rugs, building beds, marking the wall for art—there was also lots of time for staring at the lake, swinging in the chair hammocks, and playing old arcade games on the new machine that arrived. It's all coming together. We ended this trip eating out at Lake Kauneonga, as we did so often last summer, then getting ice cream from James at Sticky Fingers across the street, which just opened for the season. He said it's been a lonely winter, but he survived, and we were glad for it. When last we saw him we were tourists. Now we are members of the community. And any community with James in it—who is so generous, colorful, and full of dreams—is one for me.

April 26, Monday

I used to listen to podcasts on my commute to work. Now I just listen while doing the dishes. Tonight I started the series from the COVID oral history project at Queens College, with whom I shared some of my stories. The first episode was about April 2020, everyone staying home, the roads abandoned by all sans city buses and ambulances. Now, that all feels so far into the past. Noemi and I are considering seeing a movie (without the kids in the theater, in June). Debby and I have our cemetery/Shabbat dinner date in a few weeks. This Wednesday I'll be fully vaccinated. It feels like we're approaching the other side of the pandemic time bubble. But then I read the paper and see the infection and mortality rates and have to ask myself how both can be real, how my lived experience can be so hopeful in the context of figures that show a pandemic that is still raging.

April 27, Tuesday

Biden said today, "As long as you are vaccinated and outdoors, you can do it without wearing a mask." Wow. I don't know if I can. Noemi said she can't yet as she still needs to maintain the expectation for those not yet vaccinated.

I told this to Steve, who joked I had to do what the president said. Last Friday Steve got me to buy some cyber currency. He just wants to share his new interest with me. It's up 20% since I bought it on Friday. After work today he tried to teach me to appreciate liquidity pools. Makes my brain melt. I told him, "Tomorrow is the day." He asked, "What happens tomorrow?" I said, "We're fully vaccinated." He texted back, "No no no. That was a week ago. Pfizer=1 week." Looks like I've been overcautious then and missed observing the moment. Better late than never, so here we go:

Hip Hip Hurray!

April 28, Wednesday

Supper club was lovely tonight. Chris finally brought up the white elephant: if we don't need masks, if we are vaccinated and outdoors, and as they have a backyard, is it time? Opinion was unanimous: Hell yeah! Noemi will be fully vaxed by next Tuesday and Michael in two Saturdays. So next week we'll start looking for a date. After 14 months of meeting weekly, well… that'll be something.

Nick gave us his regular update on the subways (faster, still empty) and on Manhattan (suits returning, more crowded). He said he even saw the street vendors selling bootlegged products, to which Michael quipped, "New York is back when the fake Gucci's have returned."

April 29, Thursday

I had a nice chat with Denise from Columbia today. This time I was the one scheduling the meeting, on my terms; she joked I turned the tables on her. I told her about my plans for a book based in part on our interviews. She loved the idea and couldn't have been more supportive. She said I can include her parts and our interviews—they are already in the archives anyway—and I should feel free to edit. That was really generous of her. While this project inspired me to start journaling—after a break of many decades—she shared for her it was the opposite. When this project started for her she stopped journaling, she stopped writing about all of this. She described it for her as a "year of listening." And, in fact, she said today was "the hinge." The college semester ended. Graduation was held. She turned in her grades last night. Now she has no more excuses and can shift her focus. Now she and her grad students could start coding the entries like mine and could devote herself to the research. I can't wait to learn what she finds.

April 30, Friday

Today, as usual, Debby FaceTimed in to join us for saying the Shabbat prayers over the candles, wine and challah. As usual. When did that become usual? And will this truly be the last time we four welcome the Shabbat at our table with no guests? Next week will we finally get back to the way it was—our house full of people? I sure hope so. But even if so, my dad's absence will be felt every time, especially when I put away the challah, noticing the portion that went uneaten.

In April of last year Miri watched a new video posted on the Girl Scouts at Home website that I produced just a few weeks earlier. It was about picking a spot in your home and making it special to be in. Miri chose the corner of her room, surrounded by pillows and stuffed animals. She started sleeping there occasionally, then every night. Not on top of anything, just on the floor. With no explanation, tonight, she climbed into that unused bed, said "I love you", and "good night."

MAY 2021

In which a rainbow shines… normalcy intoxicates… and Friday, at last, arrives.

Daily Diary Entries

May 1, Saturday

Last night at sundown Noemi called for me to come out on the balcony. There was a double rainbow, she said. All day the weather has been crazy, with blue skies, then storms, then back again, as if the world couldn't make up its mind. By the time I got onto the balcony, in the same place we gathered a year earlier to give 7 PM thanks to frontline workers, only one remained. But it was glorious. Below in the park the teams playing basketball, the children in the playground, all the life that had returned marveled up at it. It reminded me of another rainbow. This fall it will be 20 years. We lived in Manhattan at the time, in the East Village. After the planes hit, the sky no longer looked safe. As air traffic across the country was halted, the absence of planes just reinforced their foreboding. For a time the sky was only crossed by military jets. Not much better. By November regular air travel had returned but by then I had stopped looking up. Until that one day, that is, after a heavy rain, heading east on 14th street. I looked up into that boulevard-wide sky to see a striking rainbow. It brought tears to my eyes with its promise, like to Noah, that the worst was over and now we'd be all right. That the sky was ours again. That it was safe to look back up. Last night, watching the rainbow fade over the park, with Noemi by my side as the sun rapidly set, I heard a young child cry to their caregiver, "Look, a rainbow! It's a rainbow!"

May 2, Sunday

This weekend we went up to the lake house. We went right to dinner, by Lake Kauneonga, at a place where we ate last August. I'd written about it here at the time, the place closed for dining but when we ordered take-out they said we could eat it outside; when they ended up serving it to us, Miri had to say, "I'm confused. Are we doing take-out or eating in?" I was confused too and explored how stressful but rewarding it was to set boundaries with the restaurant. This time, what a change! On one hand, the area is at 75% dining capacity. They were packed indoors (it seemed to be adults only). When I went inside this time they immediately told me just what to do: order here and they will service us outside. It was comforting to see that while inside things were returning to normal (even featuring a jazz musician) outside they still supported our transition from this liminal space and could do so with minimal stress for all. In the end, the food wasn't great, but it didn't have to be. The taste of normalcy was intoxicating.

May 3, Monday

Today I received a bill for Dad's stay in the hospital thirteen months ago. That was unexpected. $72,071.57 or maybe double that, as it's listed twice. Anyway, it's not actually a bill. It literally says on every page "This is not a bill." But it's a record of what was submitted to the health insurance company, $72,071.57 (or $144,143.14), how much the plan paid, $11,412.78 (or $22,825.56), and "your share," which, in either account, says $0 dollars. I'm so thankful he had such good health insurance, but still angry at how messed up health care coverage is for so many. What if he had little or no insurance? What would we do if this WAS the bill? I can't begin to fathom the health care costs being paid by families around the country in the face of the pandemic given the extreme fiscal inequality our society is willing to tolerate.

May 4, Tuesday

She finished it: right before the pandemic started I picked up this crafting activity for Miri, a type of paper folding that was new to me called quilling. She started it during the pandemic, then proudly showed it to us yesterday, all done.

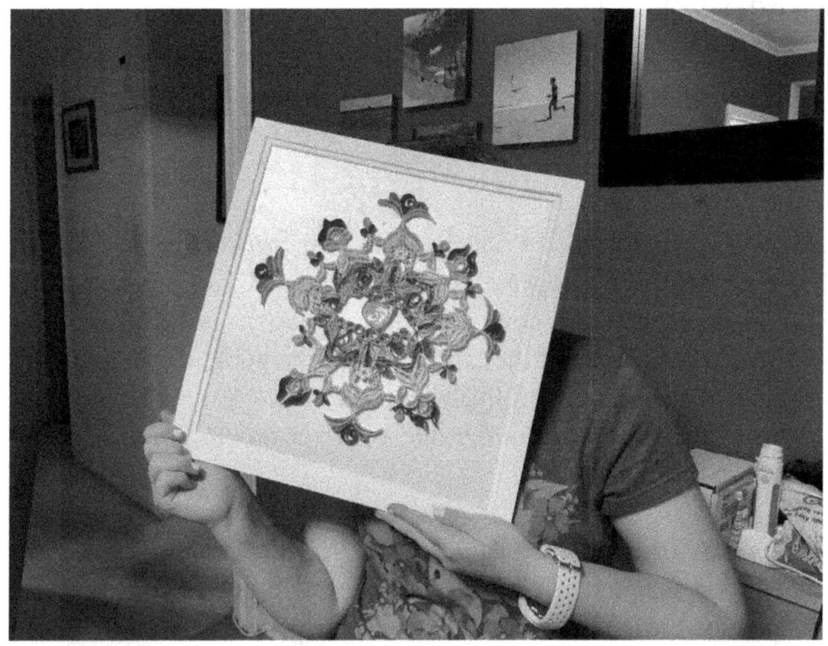

Tomorrow is Akiva's 15th birthday. We will celebrate at home over a dinner of fondue—cheese then chocolate—and watch his favorite TV shows. Then on Friday, it's Oma, and Carol, and Debby coming to celebrate, both his birthday and Shabbat, together in our house and our home. It's finally happening. And earlier that Friday I'll pick Debby up and we will go visit our parents' burial sites. At last.

Today I was interviewed for a new podcast themed on grief. They heard of my story. They wanted to see what I might share over an hour that they could edit into 10 minutes. In advance they asked me to bring an object as a grieving stick. I didn't know what they were talking about, and I didn't want to be inauthentic. But I pulled down the Billy Collins' book of poems that I haven't looked at since I read them to my dad. When it felt right I read the opening of the first poem to them, to hear how it sounded. I think now I was just trying to warm myself up. I'd been looking back with them on my grieving process, and what it was like the day when he went into the hospital, when we thought he'd recover, then losing him, during

COVID, and needing to re-design what it meant to mourn during a pandemic, and then what it's been like ever since to go through the stages: anger at COVID for taking my dad and keeping those he left away from each other, disbelief that this was happening, acceptance that he was gone.

It's now very cathartic to tell the story, not from the perspective of each moment as it happened, but now wrapped into hindsight, as a discreet thing that can now be behind me. So yes, when they asked if I would read some of the last poems in the book, the last words I read to my dad as he most likely had just died, I was fighting to read it through the tears, and it felt like a perfect way to honor him and put a cap on this period.

That's part of what I explained to them, that I'm putting all this together as a book, that part of my grieving process was to write daily, to be in the moment, and part of my process recently has been to compile it all into one package, looking back at it from a point past it, from within a moment of transition. And thus the two titles.

Friday is Tomorrow comes from that brief conversation with Miri. "Dad, when's Friday?" That feeling of being lost in time. "Friday is tomorrow," I said, which led them to ask in response, "So, today's Thursday?" as if we were stuck in an endless Blursday where the days of the week no longer fit together. That title is about speaking from each moment in time, without the shield or assurance of hindsight. And of course we can't ignore Little Orphan Annie singing, "The sun will come out tomorrow," itself a desperate act as she knows—being eternally a day away—hope's promise can never arrive.

The second title is the opposite: *The Dayenu Year*. I told the interviewer that during Passover, through story and ritual, we re-enact the exodus from Egypt. And after each step we say "*dayenu*", it would have been enough, if God had done just that and no more. But of course that's not true. At each step without the next they would have perished. *Dayenu* is a looking back, an appreciation of those key moments from a position of safety. It lives only through hindsight. The act of putting this book together, in shaping it where I could into a narrative, is a type of *dayenu*, a ritualized marking of the key moments now behind us, to appreciate each challenge we overcame, and giving thanks to all that allowed us now to say *dayenu*, as we can finally say "if that was all it would've been enough" since we know in advance that when we arrive at the end of our story we will have survived long enough to finally tell it.

May 5, Wednesday

Friday is shabbat.

May 6, Thursday

Friday is tomorrow.

May 7, Friday

Today is Friday.

Dayenu.

May 7, Fri:
Today is Fri.day,

Dayenu.

For Debby, in memory of our dad.

Friday is Tomorrow, or The *Dayenu* Year: Chronicles from the NYC Covid-19 Oral History, Narrative and Memory Archive

Authored by Barry Joseph
Editorial assistance by Michele Connelly
Line-edited by Maggie Jaris
Support and advice from Carolyn Starman Hessel

Published by Barry Joseph Consulting
For all general information, contact Friday@BarryJoseph.com

Identifiers: 979-8-9851898-0-3 (ebook) | 979-8-9851898-1-0 (hardcover b/w) | 979-8-9851898-2-7 (hardcover color) | 979-8-9851898-3-4 (paperback b/w) | 979-8-9851898-4-1 (paperback color)

Visit us on the Internet at www.FridayisTomorrow.com

ACKNOWLEDGEMENTS

This book is written in deep appreciation of everyone who allowed me to include them within these pages, the medical professionals who had no choice but whose heroics should serve as a guidepost for future generations, Denise Milstein and all at the NYC COVID-19 Oral History, Narrative and Memory Archive who inspired me to capture this period of time, and the readers who helped me to clarify and tighten (Abby Mason, Julie Wiener), Carolyn Starman Hessel for the tuna melts and challah french toast, and for my family without whom none of this would have been worthwhile.

www.ingramcontent.com/pod-product-compliance
Lightning Source LLC
Chambersburg PA
CBHW062145080426
42734CB00010B/1569

* 9 7 9 8 9 8 5 1 8 9 8 3 4 *